ECONOMIC DEVELOPMENT,
SOCIAL ORDER, AND
WORLD POLITICS

ECONOMIC DEVELOPMENT, SOCIAL ORDER, AND WORLD POLITICS

with special emphasis on

War, Freedom, the Rise and Decline of the West, and the Future of East Asia

ERICH WEEDE

LYNNE
RIENNER
PUBLISHERS

BOULDER
LONDON

Published in the United States of America in 1996 by
Lynne Rienner Publishers, Inc.
1800 30th Street, Boulder, Colorado 80301

and in the United Kingdom by
Lynne Rienner Publishers, Inc.
3 Henrietta Street, Covent Garden, London WC2E 8LU

Library of Congress Cataloging-in-Publication Data
Weede, Erich.
    Economic development, social order, and world politics / by Erich
Weede.
      p. cm.
    Includes bibliographical references (p.).
    ISBN 1-55587-620-X (alk. paper)
    1. Economic development. 2. Economic policy. 3. Social policy.
4. International economic relations. 5. World politics—1989–
I. Title.
HD75.W444 1995
338.9—dc20   95-33086
                                                        CIP

British Cataloguing in Publication Data
A Cataloguing in Publication record for this book
is available from the British Library.

Printed and bound in the United States of America

5 4 3 2 1

CONTENTS

PREFACE:
AN AUTOBIOGRAPHICAL NOTE

The roots of this book are to be found in the intellectual history of its author. Even before I had finished school and entered university (in the late 1950s) I had a keen interest in world politics—from the vantage point of an adolescent in a vanquished and divided nation, living less than a hundred miles west of the Iron Curtain. At that time I was skeptical of Adenauer's policy of cooperation with the Western powers, of the possibility of maintaining peace and gaining reunification through this policy. My mood was nationalist; my views could be called Realist—of course, at the modest level of theoretical sophistication to be expected from a teenager. In those days I regarded German North Atlantic Treaty Organization (NATO) membership as a mistake, nuclear deterrence as an invitation to failure, and German reunification made impossible as much because of Adenauer and the West as because of the Soviet Union.

Given these interests, it would have been natural for me to study political science with a focus on international politics. I decided not to do so because I felt some suspicion about the methodology of German political science in the 1960s. It was largely historical and descriptive or normative. In place of systematic theory there existed a gap that was only partly covered by some teaching of the history of ideas. But almost none of the political scientists in West Germany in those days were interested in testable and general theory. Even nowadays I regard the core of the discipline in Germany, i.e., testable theory, as neglected and largely empty.

This statement should not be misunderstood. In my view, testable theory is not necessarily characterized by the use of mathematical formulae, and tests do not only refer to statistical analysis. For example, I think that Jones's contributions (1981; 1988) to economic history, or Hayek's studies (1960; 1973–1976–1979; 1988) of a free society and polity, or Waltz's structural Realism (1979) are much more important steps on the road to testable theory, although they avoid mathematics and statistics, than almost all formal models or equation-fitting exercises, including my own contributions to the latter type of work.

A feeling of suspicion prevented me from beginning my scientific education on the wrong track: German political science. Instead I studied experimental and quantitative psychology under Peter R. Hofstätter in Hamburg, i.e., in one of the two German universities where such study was possible in the early 1960s. I got three things from this experience. I learned that testable and general theorizing is possible in the humanities and social sciences. Moreover, I learned that one needs statistical methods in order to test propositions. Finally, I learned too much about the substance of psychology to ever feel fully at home with the economic type of theorizing that I discovered much later. This legacy of latent suspicion grounded in knowledge was not important, however, for decades.

After earning my diploma (master's degree) in psychology, I began to study political science and sociology. In Rudolf Wildenmann I found a mentor who actually encouraged the application of statistical methods to political science problems. In Hans Albert I found somebody whose Popperian philosophy of science made sense: It could accommodate the search for general theory and for rigorous testing. Now I learned to argue—rather than merely to feel—why the social sciences should model themselves on the image of the natural sciences rather than fight one lost battle of retreat after another for the sake of Geisteswissenschaft. Thus, my first firm views and my first applicable skills in political science were methodological. I began to look for falsifiable propositions and possibilities to test them.

In the late 1960s this approach was underdeveloped even in the United States. In world politics it was an infant even at the most advanced universities. Fortunately, I got a chance to study with Harold Guetzkow at one of those institutions, Northwestern University. Although originally attracted by internation simulation, I soon found the work of Rudolph Rummel and David Singer more appealing. My dissertation was a path analysis linking war involvement to national characteristics. Seen from my current perspective, it was a mere calculation exercise, like much other early work in quantitative international politics. But calculation exercises may prove to be useful stepping stones.

In Germany, a Ph.D. is not enough even to apply for a professorship. You have to write a second thesis, a Habilitation, in order to get a so-called Venia Legendi, a permission to teach. Under the distant influence of Rummel—I have seen him only once or, at most, twice in my life, but he still sends me reprints of his work—I changed my unit of analysis from the nation-state to the dyad but retained the focus on causes of war from my earlier work. In my Habilitation work (Weede, 1975) I made a discovery that I still believe in, that I was able to support in later work (Weede, 1983c; 1989b; 1994; Chapter 7, Section 2 in this volume), and that changed my political views: Deterrence, or "peace by fear," does work. Before the mid-1970s I regarded NATO and West German membership in it as an obstacle to German reunification without significantly reducing the risk of war. After the mid-1970s I regarded NATO as a means to underwrite the avoidance of war by extended deterrence. Before this intellectual turning point I was emotionally opposed to making West Germany part of the Western community of nations. Thereafter, I regarded my own former views, and neutralist or pacifist views in general, as a threat to peace. From a political perspective, my views changed from parochial and nationalistic to more universalistic. From a theoretical perspective, it was a conversion within the Realist paradigm.

In the late 1970s in West Germany, knowledge of quantitative data analysis was not an asset but was nearly a disqualifying attribute for applicants for a professorship in political science (outside the narrow fields of survey research and voting). However, West German sociology was not as consistently biased against quantitative methods as West German political science. Thus, I became professor of sociology in 1978. Development studies was an obvious bridge from international politics to sociology. In those days, dependency and world systems theories offered an explanation of development failure in the South. Some of this work offered quantitative and cross-national evidence in order to support its claims. I looked into the matter, reanalyzed a lot of relationships, and found the claims of dependency and world system theories misleading (Weede, 1986d; Chapter 5, Section 1 in this book).

Much of what goes for theory in West German sociology looks to me like a declaration of war against common sense as well as against sound method. (Even some Americans are bewitched by this kind of "theorizing.") Thus, I looked for something better and found it in some pieces of economic theory: first, in public choice, especially in the works of Olson (1965; 1982) and Tullock (1974; 1980; 1983; 1993), thereafter in the writings of Hayek (1960; 1973–1976–1979; 1988). The theory of the rent-seeking society (Buchanan, Tollison, and Tullock, 1980; Tullock, 1993) and Olson's (1982) work, *The Rise and Decline of Nations,* made me understand how special-interest groups capture the state in order to undermine more encompassing interests. In a series of cross-national studies I claim to have found evidence to support the view that democratic politics tends to reduce growth rates and to reinforce income inequality at the same time; that the welfare state is part of the problem rather than part of the solution (Weede, 1986b; 1986c; 1990c; 1990d; 1991; 1992a). These findings made me receptive to Hayek's view, to his emphasis on liberty and responsibility.

Being (paid as) a sociologist, I felt compelled to study some classical sociologist seriously. I picked Max Weber for his interest in the rise of Western civilization in comparative perspective. On my own, or with the intellectual assistance only of German-speaking students of Weber, I would probably never have got much out of him, but Anglo-American writers (Andreski, 1968a; 1984; Collins, 1980; 1986; Jones, 1981; 1988; North, 1981; Rosenberg and Birdzell, 1986) who investigated problems similar to those studied by Weber, who were more interested in valid answers to the problem than in Weberian orthodoxy, made me appreciate both Weber and more recent writings in economic history and comparative sociology. My own interpretation of the rise of the West is most directly influenced by Jones (1981) and Hayek (1960). It has previously been published in English (Weede, 1990b) and has been amplified, revised, and updated to become Chapter 4, Section 1 of this book. Together Chapters 4 to 6 attempt to provide at least a loosely integrated theory of the development of capitalism and prosperity in the West, of stagnation in most developing countries, and of the likely decline of the West and the rise of East Asia.

The public choice school of thought has existed for more than a quarter century and comes close to being established. By contrast, the related (and largely overlapping) rational choice approach in sociology is more recent. The advantage of a nascent rather than established school of thought is a comparatively greater readiness to focus on basic problems rather than peripheral detail. My almost forgotten background in psychology—I earned my diploma in 1966—may also have been useful in reminding me of the shakiness of the behavioral assumptions underlying rational choice and public choice theorizing. Many writers who share my interest in macro issues such as economic development or war seem unworried about a lack of realism in their assumptions about human behavior. As long as the deductions work, they feel good. Since false assumptions, however, guarantee nothing, not even empirically false deduced statements, comparative success in explaining macro events does not convince me if the explanation is built on micro assumptions that are sometimes directly testable and known to be false. Chapters 2 and 3 attempt to outline the limits and consequences of a rational choice approach to economic development as well as to (the avoidance of) war. Although placed at the beginning of the book for systematic reasons, these are the most recent fruits of my thinking.

In the late 1980s, under the impact of public choice writings and my own quantitative research, I became ever more skeptical about the economic consequences of democratic welfare states. Simultaneously, a steady and growing stream of quantitative studies, beginning with Rummel's 1983 paper, accumulated and demonstrated that democracies almost never (or never) fight each other. Placing myself in the Realist and deterrence camp of international politics, I was skeptical at first and not easily persuaded. But ultimately, the weight of the evidence and some research of my own (Weede, 1992b; also discussed in Chapter 7, Section 2 of this book) convinced me. Now, my own theoretical position in international politics is something of a halfway house between Realism and what is often called liberalism: Systemic characteristics, the security dilemma, and the balance of power still define the rules of the game, but some state characteristics matter. Some domestic reforms, i.e., democratization, may facilitate peace. This suggestion raises another issue: how to promote democracy and how to keep it compatible with efficiency and economic development. Currently I am engaged in investigating the compatibility of a libertarian brand of public choice and a half-Realist, half-liberal approach to international politics. Chapter 8 contains some preliminary evidence of this endeavor.

Why did I sketch my intellectual autobiography? I want to convey the message that an interest in politics per se is a good starting point. If you adopt a methodology that allows for the elimination of errors, then the substance, or even narrow-mindedness, of one's early political concerns doesn't matter too much. For methodological reasons, i.e., because of the evidence, I had to change my political as well as my theoretical views a couple of times: from an intuitive hostility to the Western alliance to an appreciation of its role in the avoidance of war; from a disbelief in nuclear deterrence to its endorsement; from full albeit implicit acceptance of Realism to an explicit but quite far-reaching modification; from a denial of the usefulness of the economic model of man to its (severely) qualified acceptance; from an implicit emotional hostility toward capitalism to an appreciation of the close link between capitalism and freedom, even between free trade and peace. Of course, there is no guarantee that my current views capture the truth. Almost certainly a lack of future changes of mind would not reflect how close to the truth I already am. Instead, it might testify to some loss of intellectual alacrity.

$-E. W.$

1

INTRODUCTION: A SYSTEMATIC AGENDA

The purpose of this book is to analyze the interdependence of economic development, social order, and interstate conflict. Instead of describing my agenda in a series of detailed questions, I want to make some bold assertions that summarize my conclusions: Without political organization and order there can be neither economic development nor interstate conflict as we know it. Without interstate conflict, the domestication of authority could never have happened. Without the domestication of authority, capitalism would never have overcome mass poverty. Since capitalism is a prerequisite of prosperity, it is also a prerequisite of democracy. Democracy, however, tends to undermine capitalism and, thereby, itself. Democracy greatly reduces the risk of war in the democratic zone of peace, but certainly not beyond. In relationships between democracies and authoritarian regimes, democracies seem to be at some disadvantage.

At a more abstract level of analysis, many of these issues and propositions can be understood as specific instances of the more general issue of institution- and organization-building. While individual choice may approach rational decisionmaking, at least under appropriate circumstances, groups or collectives are rarely capable of pursuing the common interests of their members. The more encompassing a collective, the less likely it is to be organized for collective action. Among such organized groups or collectives, some members or subgroups or special interests are likely to capture positions of leadership and to distort policies for their own benefit. Therefore, domestic as well as foreign policies often hurt the interests of those in whose name they are executed. Unfortunately, understanding and explaining policy failures often give us no more power to correct them than understanding stellar movements allows us to put stars into a different orbit.

Where human beings get it wrong, there is a reason. Policy recommendations and optimism often rest on an implicit or explicit decision not to face those reasons. Economic policies, as well as international security policies, often rest on a solid consensus among politicians to reinforce popular misunderstandings and to exploit them rather than to make a serious intellectu-

1

al effort to understand the issues first and campaign for political support thereafter. While many economists find it difficult to understand why politicians so frequently reject good professional advice, a background in public choice makes one wonder why collective decisionmaking doesn't generate an even worse mess than it does, and it makes one look for the rare circumstances under which collective decisionmaking produces satisfying results.

*   *   *

Although most of the content of Chapters 4 through 8 was conceived years, and occasionally decades, before the first three chapters, I do think that the more abstract and basic chapters belong at the beginning. I do not claim that my theory is deductive, although I would like it to be. This is a distant aspiration. A fully deductive theory would have to be a formal or mathematical theory. Unfortunately, most of the formal theorizing[1] that I have seen either concerns specific problems or rests on assumptions that strike me as somewhere between merely unbelievable and outrageously wrong. Not traveling the formal modeling route in itself almost guarantees that coherence and consistency within and between chapters leave a lot to be desired. Science depends on criticism, not least the helping hand of one's intellectual adversaries. It is always easier to spot a minor weakness in one's fellows than a major deficiency in oneself. In order to speed the process of mutual correction and criticism, I believe exaggeration to be a lesser evil than tautology-generating caution.

In Chapter 2, I discuss the economic model of human behavior, summarize some of the most powerful criticism of it, endorse it nevertheless as a basis for macrosociology and political science, and then proceed to outline the marvel of the market. In the market we observe cooperation in spite of selfishness. The market is an imperfect and partial substitute for altruism—but a substitute it is. By contrast, group decisions are likely to be deeply flawed. Government is a Faustian bargain.

Chapter 3 analyzes how the nonexcludability characteristic of public goods encourages freeriding and why groups of people find it so difficult to cooperate in the procurement of collective goods. But cooperation is not equally difficult for all groups. Some are destined to succeed, others are destined to fail. By and large, small and privileged groups stand a much better chance of overcoming freeriding and prevailing against less organized groups than do large groups of resource-poor actors. Often government becomes a tool of special-interest groups instead of being an impartial guardian of property rights and a bulwark against rent-seeking, i.e., against the quest for special privileges and safety from competition.

After the relatively abstract theorizing in Chapters 2 and 3, Chapter 4 turns to history and to the issue of why the West was able to outperform the great Asian civilizations. At the beginning of the millennium, Sung China was undoubtedly a more advanced civilization than Western Europe, and it was still uncertain whether Western Christendom could outperform the lands of Islam. I argue that Western failure to overcome the security dilemma and political fragmentation generated a set of constraints on rulers that made feasible the evolution of the prerequisites of prosperity—i.e., law and liberty. Nobody planned to establish law and liberty to overcome mass poverty, but it happened. The third section of Chapter 4 analyzes China and its comparative stagnation in some detail; it also contains some comments on India and Islam.

Since overcoming mass poverty happened in the West, one may ask why many poor countries of the contemporary world do not emulate the West. Part of the reason is that many national decisionmakers in the Third World did not face the kind of constraints that Western elites did until recently. Moreover, some Western intellectuals systematically disseminate false advice, which is why Chapter 5 contains some criticism of dependency and world-system theories as well as an application of rent-seeking analysis to the Third World.

Chapter 6 compares the contemporary West and contemporary East Asia. Admittedly, catch-up opportunities may have contributed to the Japanese miracle, the even more miraculous performance of the four Asian small tigers or dragons, and the rise of China since Deng turned to creeping capitalism under the stewardship of the Communist Party of China. But the power of special-interest groups in Western societies, the competition between politicians in serving them rather than the national interest, and the divorce between decisionmaking and accountability in Western welfare states are also part of the story of Western decline. It does not seem to be a mere coincidence that Mainland China introduced some elements of a capitalist order under the label "responsibility system." East Asia still holds people responsible for the consequences of their actions and thrives; the West no longer dares to do so and slowly declines.

Chapter 7 discusses why and how interstate relations are predictable, even if rational action by *unitary actors* is ruled out. Until the twentieth century, there was but a single way to overcome the endemic risk of war between political units: successful conquest to the limits of civilization and imperial rule. During the twentieth century nuclear deterrence and democratic peace have provided additional routes to peace.

The concluding chapter ties together what has been said about distributional coalitions, rent-seeking, and economic development on the one hand and world politics and war avoidance on the other hand.[2] I argue that global peace depends on all major powers becoming democracies, that democracy requires prosperity, and that prosperity requires free trade. Unfortunately, distributional coalitions in rich Western welfare states have turned against the competitive and open order that was the secret behind the rise of the West. Distributional coalitions that merely fight for a bigger share may simultaneously undermine prosperity and a peaceful future for all of us.

Certainly some readers will find my arguments insufficiently coherent and occasionally contradictory. Some of this incoherence is certainly unnoticed by myself and therefore unintended, but some of it actually is intended. This book is a stock-taking exercise. In my view, the problems of economic development and prosperity, social order and liberty, and international relations and war are more closely interdependent than the compartmentalization of the social sciences and the tendency of many economists, macrosociologists, economic historians, comparative political scientists, and international relations specialists to ignore each other's work suggest. Any attempt to relate these diverse traditions of inquiry to each other and to integrate some of their findings must leave a lot to be desired. Since I regard the reunification of the social sciences, or the overcoming of arbitrary albeit institutionalized distinctions among them, as an important goal, even partial success might justify the effort.

There is an even deeper reason for some incoherence. According to Kuhn (1962) and Lakatos (1968–1969), all theories suffer from anomalies, i.e., from evidence that calls them into question. In facing this predicament there are two options: One can sweep the anomalies under the rug, deny them, or overlook their existence and thereby gain in consistency and even elegance. I definitely do not want to use this option. Second, one can discuss anomalies and evidence pointing incoherently in different directions in order to underline the need to improve our theories. Knowing that all theorizing is provisional and debatable, yet another peril still has to be avoided, i.e., theorizing that escapes falsification and inconsistency by saying ever less about the observable world. In order to avoid this peril, I build some strong—and therefore falsifiable—assertions on an often shaky empirical basis. Although this strategy will look inconsistent or incoherent to some, my reading of Popper's (1959) methodology necessitates it.

Notes

1. For some recent discussion and criticism of formal theorizing in economics, see Mayer (1993).

2. A modified version of Section 2 of Chapter 8 (Weede, 1995) has previously been published by the *European Journal of International Relations*. I appreciate permission to publish this material here.

2

RATIONAL CHOICES AND RESPONSIBLE DECISIONMAKING

1. Rational Action by Individuals

According to the rational choice or economic approach to human behavior, individuals perceive some set of options, evaluate the beneficial or harmful consequences of realizing these options, form expectations about the probability distribution of gains and losses attached to various courses of action, and then choose the expected utility-maximizing course of action (for example, see Coleman, 1978; 1990; Lindenberg, 1985; 1990; McKenzie and Tullock, 1978a; 1978b; Nicholson, 1992; Opp, 1979; 1991; Tullock, 1974). In this perspective, rationality is an undemanding concept. As McKenzie and Tullock (1978a, p. 9) interpret it, the utility-maximization or rationality assumption comes quite close to the assertion that human beings are inherently greedy: "The individual will always choose more of what he or she wants rather than less. It also means that he or she will choose less of what he or she does not want rather than more." In this perspective, rationality implies neither education nor refinement nor common sense nor reasonableness. McKenzie and Tullock (1978a, p. 56) therefore do not hesitate to attribute rationality even to rats or to "seriously disturbed and/or very stupid people with no education and who had been institutionalized for long periods of time."

Rationality need not imply a conscious comparison of the expected utilities to be derived from various courses of action. The economic approach explains behavior, not mental processes. We may retreat to the assertion that individuals behave *as if* they were rational, as if they attempted to maximize utility. The theory does not prohibit the notion that our efforts may fail. We may not perceive the full set of possible courses of action; we may misjudge utilities and probabilities.

Unfortunately, the theory runs into some problems. In experiments we may place subjects in a situation where they face a limited number of options, give them excellent information about the monetary consequences of their actions, and provide them with full information about probability

5

distributions. Still, there are systematic deviations from serious attempts at utility maximization. As far as gains are concerned, most people are too cautious. As far as losses are concerned, most people are too reckless in their attempts to avoid them. Most people put an unreasonable value on their possessions merely because they are theirs. Moreover, the frame in which a problem is presented affects choices. The less transparent the situation, the less likely people are to choose the optimal action. These and other anomalies of behavior have been well established by Kahneman and Tversky, (1979; 1984; Tversky and Kahneman, 1986; Tversky, Slovic, and Kahneman, 1990) and others. We do know that the microfoundation of the rational choice approach, whether in economics, sociology, or political science, is shaky and in need of improvement. But we also observe that almost all macroapplications of explicit decisionmaking models start from the simple, classical, and somewhat discredited model of rational economic man.[1]

Ultimately, the defense for such a model seems to be that it is too difficult to base economics, macrosociology, or political science on a more complicated model of human behavior. There seems to be no model of man that is as simple as the classical economic model and that suffers as little from anomalies at the macro level (Plott, 1990). Moreover, in certain spheres of life there are competitive pressures that punish deviations from rationality and thereby either induce learning and improvements or weed out "irrational" (i.e., not utility-maximizing) actors, as the market may do with incompetently run businesses (Alchian, 1950; Frey and Eichenberger, 1991).[2]

Most applications of the rational choice model are nonexperimental. Usually we want to explain observed actions in cases where the observer or social scientist lacks reliable information about the preferences of individuals, about the options and probability distributions that they perceive. Often—this seems to be true for almost all macroapplications, which I find interesting—there is no alternative but to substitute assumptions for unavailable or too expensive or too late information. In such a case, our "auxiliary" assumptions about available options, utilities, and probabilities must carry much of the burden of explanation—and these assumptions deserve much of the credit if we should be successful (Brennan, 1990; Simon, 1985).[3] In practice, some assumptions are so popular that they have almost become a part of the rational choice or economic research program.

First, we usually postulate that people care only about the consequences of their actions *for themselves* and disregard the beneficial or harmful consequences of their actions for others. In my view, this assumption is less realistic in family affairs than in the market or in international politics. Second, we usually postulate decreasing marginal utilities. For example, the first thousand dollars of monthly income provides more utility than the second thousand dollars, which still provides more utility than the third thousand dollars. Again, there might be exceptions, as in the case of addicts.

Third, we usually focus on only some preferences and corresponding incentives, for example, profit maximization in business, national survival under international anarchy, or office-holding in domestic politics. In my view, this practice is justified when we succeed in identifying the most relevant preferences and incentives. Such identification is much more likely in high-cost decisionmaking than in low-cost decisionmaking.[4] Wherever the beneficial or harmful consequences of all available courses of action are quite close to each other, the opportunity cost of missing the best alternative is low. Then information and decision costs and soft incentives, such as social approval or consonance between self-image and action, might count for much. Since it is much more difficult to reliably assess small differences in net benefits concerning a large number of preference dimensions than huge differences in benefits related to a small number of preference dimensions (ideally a single overriding preference, such as one for more rather than less profit), the standard economic approach is likely to be in deep trouble if applied to low-cost decisionmaking because the applicability of the standard approach so often depends on substituting assumptions for unavailable or too expensive information.

To clarify this point, consider the issue of voting. We have to explain why people vote at all, i.e., why they walk or drive to the polling booth and fill out a slip of paper. It is quite difficult to explain, from a rational action perspective and in a nontautological manner, why so many people do so. This is a low-cost decision, but casting an intelligent vote is costly. It requires investing time and other resources in the acquisition of information. Given the likely lack of impact of an intelligent vote on policies and on oneself in any mass democracy, one should not waste one's time in becoming an intelligent voter. An economic or rational choice approach has little difficulty in explaining the rational ignorance that can so often be observed because intelligent voting is a high-cost action. Given my skeptical attitude toward the applicability of rational choice to low-cost decisionmaking, I shall not even try to explain the low-cost act of voting, but I shall make rational ignorance a bedrock of some arguments later in this book.

While I reject the contention that a refusal to apply rational choice to low-cost situations and actions is an "arbitrary domain restriction" (Green and Shapiro, 1994, p. 58) and therefore illegitimate, I must admit that occasionally voters in less developed countries (LDCs) have had to waste hours in polling lines and to face threats of violence, i.e., to face high costs. Nevertheless, hundreds of thousands voted under these circumstances. From a rational choice perspective, this action is an anomaly that can be "explained" away in a tautological manner only by ad hoc invocation of special incentives to fit the case. So, Green and Shapiro's (1994, p. 69) indictment of rational choice has to be accepted: "The phenomenon of voter turnout may, in the end, say more about rational choice theory than the reverse." My defense for sticking with a rational choice approach in spite of the anomalies pointed out by Kahneman and Tversky or Green and Shapiro is based on the philosophy of science of Kuhn (1962) or Lakatos (1968–1969), according to whom all theories are born refuted but may nevertheless be retained until there is a better theory. For purposes of macrotheorizing about economy, state, and society, I simply don't see a better alternative.

Some of the most interesting applications of the idea of rationality presume that people are free, i.e., that they face a wide set of choices rather than being threatened or coerced to make a choice imposed on them by someone else. As Hayek (1960, chapter 5) or Murray (1984, p. 146) have emphatically pointed out, freedom and responsibility belong together. Liberty provides rational actors with the opportunity to do their own thing, to attempt to improve their circumstances in life. Responsibility means that one is held responsible for the consequences of one's actions. If one invests one's time and other resources wisely, one is likely to be rewarded—if unwisely, punished. From a rational action perspective, responsibility, or suffering the consequences of one's actions, constitutes a learning environment. If rewards and punishments, or profits and losses, were randomly assigned to actors, then it would be impossible to learn to do a better job next time.[5] Therefore, being held responsible is a prerequisite for serious attempts at rational choice. Being absolved of responsibility must make rationality less likely. Since the free market is the setting where responsibility prevails, the market is my next topic.

2. The Marvel of the Market and Social Capital

According to Buchanan (1988), there are two basic approaches to economics: one that focuses on gains from trade and one that is concerned with efficient resource allocation. Of course, this distinction is not watertight but is a matter of emphasis. After all, the division of labor and mutually beneficial exchanges are themselves means of promoting the efficiency of resource allocation. With Buchanan, I find it useful to start with a focus on gains from trade and the market. Like command, the market serves as a mechanism to coordinate human behavior. In contrast to command, the market needs little backup by coercion (Friedman, 1962). Given agreement on what belongs to whom, i.e., agreement on the assignment of property rights, actors in the market may exchange goods and services at any freely negotiated price. The residual backup by coercion that market exchange requires is limited to a guarantee of property rights and the enforcement of freely agreed-upon contracts. Such a residual backup by coercion serves to reduce transaction costs and thereby promotes market exchange.

Pushing coercion into the background is but one of the advantages of the market. Another is the minimization of the need for consent. According to Hayek (1973-1976-1979, vol. 2, pp. 109–110), "the order of the market rests not on common purposes but on reciprocity; that is, on the reconciliation of different purposes for the mutual benefit of the participants." If two actors want to exchange goods or services on the market, and if there are no significant external effects, then bystanders are not asked, should not be asked, even must not be asked for consent. The requirement of consent has to be strictly limited to those who participate in market transactions. Otherwise, bystanders who might wish to acquire some good or service themselves—probably for less than the price negotiated between the two participants in the transaction—could veto market exchanges that are perceived as benefiting the participants concerned. Thus, a market order not only requires pushing command and coercion into the background and confining it to a strictly limited role, it also requires a minimization of the requirement of consent.

For simplicity's sake it is assumed that there are no external ramifications to this transaction. If two persons who want to trade goods or services with each other were forced to consult with bystanders or even to acquire their consent before the exchange could take place, then transaction costs would steeply increase. Worse still, bystanders would have power without responsibility. They would not suffer the consequences of their actions, of their denial of consent, so the door would be wide open for irresponsible decisionmaking: Some people would participate in decisionmaking but not in enjoying or suffering the consequences of their decisions. In my view, unnecessary requirements for consent are an evil that a free society must avoid. Otherwise there are high transaction costs, irresponsibility, a poor learning environment, and—to be discussed next—strong barriers to innovation.

The incompatibility between exaggerated requirements for consent and innovation has been well argued by Rosenberg and Birdzell (1986, p. 310): "A society which delayed innovations by the amount of time required to reach a political consensus would fall further and further behind a society which did not. . . . It implies the substantive criterion that the benefits of the innovation are sufficiently understood and predictable that they can be persuasively verbalized in advance of its adoption—that is, that everything is too clear to need the test of experiment."

In principle, one may distinguish two types of market failure. The first one is described by Buchanan (1988, p. 5) in these terms: "Market failure, by definition, means that there exist unexploited gains from trade, and the economist diagnoses such failure by identifying the barriers that prevent the potential gains from being exploited by the persons whose interest would be served by their removal." This type of market failure results from restrictions on individual liberty. The more efficient social and political institutions are, the less they tolerate such restrictions. The second type results from an abuse of liberty, i.e., where two persons or groups or enterprises make an agreement at the expense of a third party. Voluntary agreements in restraint of trade, or cartels, are typical examples. Often the abuse of liberty by some generates restrictions on the liberty of others. Thus, the two types of market failure are intimately related.

Exchange on the market for mutual welfare enhancement depends on the division of labor. The more different things we produce, the greater the potential gains from trade. As Adam Smith (1776/1976) pointed out long ago, the division of labor and market size are interdependent. A larger market permits an ever more refined division of labor and thus higher productivity. More division of labor permits more exchanges and thus mutual welfare improvements. Production for free markets forces even egoistic producers to act as if they were interested in the welfare of their fellows. If one produces what nobody wants, one finds no partner for trade. If one produces what few others can produce but many others would like to get, then one easily finds partners for exchange and is likely to get things in return that one desires but others can produce more easily or in better quality. Thus, disregarding the interests of others simply does not pay. Pure self-interest suffices to generate a keen interest in serving other people's needs; that is, a free market is a partial substitute for altruism. It generates incentives to specialize according to comparative advantage to serve others—ultimately in order to serve oneself. A market economy where everyone is self-employed solves the incentive problem.[6]

As Hayek (1960) has pointed out, the market solves another problem too: the application of knowledge. Some people know how to plow a field, others how to fix a broken car, still others how to heal a patient or to earn a good return on financial investments. Some knowledge is practical; other knowledge is highly theoretical. No person even comes close to mastering the body of human knowledge. Moreover, it is impossible to centralize this knowledge in a single head, or even in a single authority that at least knows who commands what knowledge. If knowledge, including knowledge about who knows what, cannot be centralized, then centralized decisionmaking by itself guarantees that much knowledge will never be applied in spite of being applicable. Thus, we need a knowledge-revealing mechanism, i.e., the market.

By and large, individuals know what they themselves know fairly well. A free-market order provides the necessary incentive to apply one's knowledge and abilities in such a way as to produce goods and services in strong demand at a good price rather than to squander one's abilities, knowledge, and talent in socially useless ways. Moreover, since knowledge (or human capital) makes people more productive, a free-market order provides incentives to acquire knowledge, to innovate, to produce new goods and services, or to reduce the costs of production of traditional goods and services.

The positive functions of the market depend on scarcity pricing. If there are numerous independent producers and consumers in a market, then scarcity pricing is almost inevitable. Those who offer goods and services in excess supply suffer from low and declining prices. Those who offer goods and services in excess demand benefit from high and rising prices. Wherever demand exceeds supply, there is a scarcity premium. Therefore, every market participant faces incentives to shift production from goods in little demand to those in excessive demand. Only scarcity prices that respond to changes in demand and supply provide incentives for a welfare-enhancing division of labor and a corresponding pattern of production.

Market exchange and the division of labor depend on finding partners for exchange, on agreeing with them on the terms of trade, and on enforcing the terms of the agreement. The lower the sum of these costs, the lower the transaction costs. Some of these costs are reduced by a growing size and density of population (Smith, 1776/1976; Durkheim, 1895/1930).[7] According to North and Thomas (1973, p. 38), "an increase in local population density widened the market, lowering transaction costs and initially encouraging the establishment of such industries as handicrafts and various services." This is not a one-sided causal relationship, however. Higher population densities, larger societies, and better means of transportation increase the size of the market, enlarge the scope for the division of labor, and thereby increase productivity. Increased productivity then permits the survival of a larger population within the same land area, providing another stimulus to more division of labor, and so on. Where productivity growth outpaces population growth, life in a more crowded society may even become a better life—as it obviously can be if one compares the crowded Netherlands or Japan with sparsely populated Russia.

Thus, self-interested attempts at utility maximization may have beneficial consequences in a market setting. Producers may allocate resources according to comparative advantage and demand. Incentives to work hard, to apply one's knowledge and skills, and to innovate are strong in a market setting. People behave responsibly because they are held responsible for their actions (Hayek, 1960, chapter 5); i.e., they benefit from or suffer the consequences of their actions depending on the usefulness to their fellows of their products and services. Market exchange, however, presupposes some clarification of property rights and the prohibition or (at least) limitation of the use of coercion. One would hardly exchange one's own product for another person's product if the prospective partner in trade is combating others who claim that the product is or should be theirs. Moreover, markets work best if nobody can prevent others from entering the market and offering better products or services at lower prices. Agreement about property rights, the prohibition of the use of force, and free entry into markets (or the absence of restrictive practices) do not themselves arise through market coordination by self-interested actors. Instead they result—if they actually do—from collective action, which is to be discussed in the next chapter.

While a market order promotes freedom and prosperity, it also requires factor mobility, including labor mobility. Workers must move from poorly paid to better-paid positions if the wealth-generating potential of markets is to be realized. Most workers are likely to respond to incentives most of the time, but by their doing so, the moral foundation of capitalism may be undermined.[8] This undermining has been a long-standing worry for scholars (for example, see Schumpeter, 1942; Hirsch, 1976). From a rational choice perspective, the problem has been analyzed by Coleman (1987; 1988; 1990). He argues that productivity depends on social norms, institutions, or laws that may generate either incentives or disincentives for production, which may either increase or decrease transaction costs. Since norms, institutions, and laws produce effects on productivity similar to the effect of physical capital, Coleman (1987; 1990, p. 302) has proposed the term *social capital:*

> Social capital is defined by its function. It is not a single entity, but a variety of different entities having two characteristics in common: They all consist of some aspect of social structure, and they facilitate certain actions of individuals who are within the structure. Like other forms of capital, social capital is productive, making possible the achievement of certain ends that would not be attainable in its absence. Like physical capital and human capital, social capital is not completely fungible, but is fungible with respect to specific activities. A given form of social capital that is valuable in facilitating certain actions may be useless or even harmful for others. Unlike other forms of capital, social capital inheres in the structure of relations between persons and among persons. It is lodged neither in individuals nor in physical implements of production.

Examples of social capital endowment are trust, social norms, and authority. If members of some social groups tend to trust one another, cooperation among these people is much easier. If one can rely on or trust in most people's conforming with social norms, then the cost of coordinating human actions is much reduced. So it is if members of some group can readily agree on who should give orders and who should obey. Of course, authority relations also presuppose some trust. Those who freely accept the authority of others must trust in the competence of those others as well as trusting in their benevolence, in their firm subjection to social norms, or in the efficacy of some control mechanism.

According to Coleman, (1988, pp. 107–108) social capital is best preserved where individual mobility is limited.

Closure of the social structure is important not only for the existence of effective norms but also for another form of social capital: the trustworthiness of social structures that allows the proliferation of obligations and expectations. Defection from an obligation is a form of imposing a negative externality on another. Yet, in a structure without closure, it can be effectively sanctioned, if at all, only by the person to whom the obligation is owed. Reputation cannot arise in an open structure, and collective sanctions that would ensure trustworthiness cannot be applied. Thus, we may say that closure creates trustworthiness in a social structure.

If closed social structures promote social capital–building and, as importantly, the reproduction of human capital in the next generation, as Coleman (1988) argues, then some limitations of mobility rather than its promotion and expansion might provide societies with a competitive edge.

While I have argued that freedom itself constitutes social capital and promotes growth, freedom is not the only kind of social capital. It is inherently difficult to say how much freedom and mobility societies should trade for other types of social capital that reduce transaction costs. Obviously, the United States stresses freedom and mobility, whereas Japanese society is characterized by more closure. Western Europe seems to be somewhere in between. Strong social control in Japan does reduce crime rates (Hechter and Kanazawa, 1993) and may even promote economic growth. After all, committing crimes is a very effective route to unemployability, as can be observed in urban America.

3. Group Decisions and Government

Human beings do not live in isolation from each other, meeting each other for market exchange only. Most aspects of social interaction, of family and group life, are simply beyond the scope of this book. But some characteristics of group decisionmaking and team production need to be discussed in preparation for the analyses linking economic development, political order, and world politics.

As Buchanan and Tullock (1962) pointed out, group decisionmaking imposes two different types of costs. If the group decides to do something and you dislike it, you suffer an external cost. The only safe way to prevent this from happening is by obtaining a veto. The external costs of group decisionmaking become zero if everyone's consent is required. Unfortunately, the unanimity solution would raise the other type of costs, the decision costs. In very large groups decision costs under unanimity approach infinity. What groups should do is minimize the sum of external and decision costs, i.e., interdependence costs. It is not obvious how to minimize interdependence costs, and the idea that the widely used simple majority rule provides the answer to the interdependence cost minimization problem is quite dubious. For important problems (where external costs really matter), rational individuals should insist on a more inclusive criterion than simple majority (say three-fourths or two-thirds). Alternatively, rational individuals may prefer to delegate truly trivial problems to a single individual—who might even be chosen by lot—in order to avoid being bothered with time-consuming participation in such decisionmaking.

Repressing doubts about the wisdom behind the wide use of simple majority decisionmaking does not provide an end to our troubles because there is no assurance of the transitivity of group preferences established by simple majority voting. If you prefer A to B and B to C, you should prefer A to C; otherwise rational decisionmaking is impossible. As theorists have repeatedly demonstrated (e.g., Arrow, 1951; Frohlich and Oppenheimer, 1978), the transitivity of all individual preference orders does not guarantee that there is a collective preference order that is both transitive and not imposed by some dictator or minority group. Decisionmaking by majority vote may be compatible with transitive social preference and therefore with rational decisionmaking under certain circumstances,[9] but it is not necessarily so.

Further doubts about the usefulness of majority decisionmaking may also be introduced. The majority rule is least likely to provide satisfactory results where distributional decisions have to be made. Usher (1981) has made this point with a beautiful mental experiment. Imagine a group consisting of fifteen adult members. The group faces only a single problem: It has to divide an income of $300,000—assumed to have fallen from heaven—among its members. Obviously, they could divide this sum by 15 and assign $20,000 to each group member. Rational egoists, however, will recognize that the majority rule, if properly exploited, offers a better deal to some members. A majority of eight members may "expropriate" the others and assign $37,500 to each of the eight. This result is neither ethically appealing nor likely to be stable.[10] The seven losers might approach one of the eight winners, offer him or her more than $37,500—say $90,000; one could not turn down this offer—and thereby create a new majority. Of course, there is no reason why the distributional struggle should be settled at this particular point.

As it is usually practiced, majority rule suffers from another deficiency. It neglects the intensity of preferences. If you go to a market in order to buy something, you express the intensity of your preference for some good by your highest bid. At elections (as practiced in the West) the weight of your vote is the same whether you care a lot about the outcome or whether you would happily exchange your vote for a dime. It is quite conceivable that a majority of 51 percent of the voters makes a decision it is lukewarm about against the intensely felt desires of 49 percent of the voters. The selling of votes might improve matters, but it tends to be illegal under almost any circumstances in the West.

So far I have assumed single-tier decisionmaking. Matters may worsen in two-tier decisionmaking, where group members first elect representatives, who thereafter make the decisions. Under winner-takes-all voting systems, though not under systems of proportional representation, it will happen that the minority view within each voting district is not represented by a decisionmaker at the second level. So it may happen that 51 percent majorities within each district in 51 percent of the districts—say about 26 percent of the voters—make the decisions that everybody has to live with.

To recapitulate: It is not obvious why rational individuals should wish to submit to group decisionmaking by the simple majority rule. If they do, it may or may not result in a transitive preference order. If it doesn't, there is no hope for rational decisionmaking. The majority rule is least likely to provide stable results where distributional decisions have to be made. The majority rule, as practiced, doesn't consider intensities of preferences. In two-tier decisionmaking with single-member representation, the majority rule may result in the neglect of the preferences of even overwhelming majorities (up to 74 percent).

When individuals make decisions, when they enjoy or suffer the consequences of their decisions, they face incentives to do their best and to learn over time. It is quite difficult to put decisionmaking groups into such a rationality-enhancing situation. This difficulty is obvious when a dictator makes a group's decisions. Under the standard assumption of selfishness, the dictator is likely to make decisions under which most of the benefits fall on him and most of the burdens fall on the other group members, that is, his subjects. By definition, a dictator (as long as he[11] is one) cannot be held responsible for the consequences of his decisions. He faces few incentives to make more efficient or wiser decisions. After all, it is other persons than himself who suffer from his unwise actions. The situation improves little if there is a ruling minority or oligarchy rather than a single dictator. In such a case, the oligarchy is still likely to make decisions that concentrate benefits on its members and burdens on the majority of subjects or commoners. There is still little connection between the commission of errors and the suffering of consequences. Unfortunately, not even majority rule establishes such a link. In contrast to a competitive market in which everyone is a price-taker and everyone enjoys or suffers the consequences of his or her actions, majority rule is still a political decisionmaking mechanism under which some make decisions and others suffer the consequences. Therefore, I posit that all widely used political decisionmaking mechanisms—dictatorship, oligarchy, majority rule—provide settings that do not encourage even serious attempts at utility maximization. Instead, some costs imposed by political decisionmaking are unlikely even to enter the decisionmaker's calculations. Thus, sensitivity to costs will be attenuated in political decisionmaking, compared with individual decisionmaking.

In large groups or societies, majority rule suffers from additional shortcomings on top of the temptation for majorities to exploit minorities. Indeed, majority rule in large groups has disadvantages that even dictatorship may avoid: rational ignorance and casual decisionmaking. Imagine a group or society consisting of millions of members and decisionmakers (say, by referendum). For each person, one vote applies, and every decisionmaker knows that the group decision is almost unaffected by his or her individual decision. If the issue to be decided is inherently complex, if the gathering and processing of information is costly in time and effort rather than entertaining, then a rational or utility-maximizing individual will not invest the necessary effort in order to make an informed decision. The typical individual will feel only the costs of informed decisionmaking and will recognize that the decision itself results from what millions of others do. So he or she remains rationally ignorant. Since this reasoning affects millions rather than a single person, majority rule in undifferentiated large groups should result in a lot of poor decisions. After all, majority rule is a decisionmaking mechanism in which the link between decisionmaking and enjoying or suffering the consequences of one's actions is necessarily weak in a large group. All primarily suffer the consequences of the decisions made by equally poorly informed others.[12]

Collective decisionmaking has other undesirable characteristics in addition to either prohibitive time costs or a tendency to revert to coercion (e.g., of minorities). For example, it suffers from a systematic tendency to rely too much on consent. Social psychologists (as summarized by Hofstätter, 1957; also Weede, 1992a) have performed many experiments in which people had the task of finding the right solution to some problem but ended up consenting to some (often false) solution. In some experiments there was no obvious incentive to arrive at a common solution. The mere fact that people got together and discussed the problem sufficed to generate the spontaneous desire to agree on some solution. People seem inclined to take consent as a substitute for or indicator of truth. From the history of science we know that consent is sometimes a poor test and an unreliable guide to truth. From Janis's (1972) study of foreign policy decisionmaking we know that politicians and their advisers are also inclined to maintain consensus at almost any price. Unfortunately, general agreement generates the aura of certainty and the illusion of possessing the truth.

Collective rather than individual decisionmaking is the root cause of much prejudice. People tend to make distinctions between in-groups and out-groups. By and large, desirable attributes are ascribed to those groups to which we belong, and less desirable attributes are ascribed to other groups. Such stereotyping results in discrimination, i.e., in the victimization of others. By and large, shared prejudices do much more harm than individual prejudices: It is much worse to be the target of the prejudice of many rather than the target of the prejudice of an isolated individual. Moreover, similarly prejudiced people reinforce each other, whereas isolated prejudices do not benefit from such props. Finally, prejudiced groups tend to succeed in making their targets suffer the consequences of the prejudices. By contrast, individuals with idiosyncratic prejudices often pay the price of their own views.

Take for example a prejudiced employer who desires a specific kind of skin color in his employees. If almost all employers in a given society share this taste and prejudice, the discriminated-against groups suffer. If, however, one's prejudice is unique, it is likely to interfere with one's recruitment of the best available labor at the lowest price, whereas one's competitors will not suffer from such a self-imposed handicap. In such a case the prejudiced employer pays some price for his views. Where such a price is high enough (because the prejudice might be incompatible with the facts), the prejudiced individual faces incentives to improve his views. Unless he does, his command over resources is likely to decline. Thereby the social weight of his prejudice is likely to decrease.

Comparing individual decisionmaking in markets and democratic politics, Seldon (1990, pp. 317 and 320) arrives at the following conclusion:

> The market process characteristically induces individual action at its best; the political process generally induces individual action at its worst. The market impels responsible spending decisions informed by knowledge of costs of alternatives to themselves and of the opportunity costs of resources as a whole. Political motivation incites irresponsible decisions: in the polling booth irresponsibility is fomented by ignorance of the costs (or benefits) of the policies to be supported by votes. . . . The political process . . . transforms the scrupulously conscientious individual as a shopper in the market into a cynical dilettante in the polling booth.

In practice, large groups or societies have to rely on two-tier rather than single-tier decisionmaking; that is, they have to appoint or elect representatives, politicians, or administrators who then make the decisions for the group or society. This system generates an agency problem because politicians or administrators are agents of some collective or voting body. Unfortunately, there is no guarantee that the preference order of each agent is identical with the "collective" preference order. Even if these orders were miraculously the same, it may be too personally costly for an agent to execute a decision of which he fully approves. Representatives or lawmakers, like policemen on the beat or university professors in class, may prefer to have a good time rather than to serve their constituents, their public, or their audience. In short, conflicts of interest between groups or collectives should be expected to be ubiquitous. When agents are not under close supervision, we should expect them not to serve groups, collectives, or societies faithfully. A specific agency problem is analyzed in Michels's (1910/1970) iron law of oligarchy.[13] According to Michels, organization necessitates leadership, and leaders invariably develop interests of their own, for example, remaining leaders even if others could lead more effectively.

When a small group of people is empowered to make authoritative decisions for a much larger group of subjected people, the result has often been "death by government" (Rummel 1994a; 1994b). This result is true not only for the barbarian past of humanity but well into the twentieth century. According to Rummel (1994a, p. 2), "this century's *megamurderers*—those states killing in cold blood, aside from warfare, 1,000,000 or more men, women and children—have murdered over 151,000,000 people, nearly four times the almost 38,500,000 battle-dead for all this century's international and civil wars up to 1987." Although communist and Nazi dictatorships lead Rummel's (1994a, p. 3) list of abysmal government murderers, democracies are not entirely absent because the United Kingdom makes it to number 18 on this list. The delegation of authoritative decisionmaking by the many to the few, or the invention of government, has largely been a Faustian bargain.[14]

By and large, there are significant differences between autocratic and democratic regimes. Autocratic regimes have killed their own subjects[15] by the millions, whereas democracies have killed their victims in much smaller numbers, preferably killing foreigners rather than their own citizens, and killing in secrecy. In summarizing his monumental research on lethal politics, genocide, and mass murder, Rummel (1994a, p. 8) arrives at this conclusion: "The more power a regime has, the more it can act arbitrarily according to the whims and desires of the elite. The more freely a political elite can control the power of the state apparatus, the more thoroughly it can repress and murder its subjects and the more insistently it can declare war on domestic and foreign enemies."

My treatment of the market and of government has not been evenhanded. In the previous section of this chapter I focused on the strengths of the market; in this section I focused on the near inevitability of government failure. Similar views have recently been expressed in *The Economist* (1994b, p. 11):

> In a sense market failure is pervasive. Competition is "imperfect", production and exchange involve externalities, the future is uncertain; for all these reasons, markets fail to allocate resources precisely as they would in the textbook world of basic economics. . . . But this century's most important economic lesson is that, except in textbooks, government failure is broader, more damaging in economic terms and much more threatening to individual liberty than market failure.

Although bankruptcy, unemployment, and other personal disasters do not necessarily testify to market failure—if waves of bankruptcy shatter an

economy or tens of millions are unemployed, then the apparent market failure may still be a symptom of underlying government failure—they certainly reduce the legitimacy of the market.[16] Undoubtedly, competitive markets
cannot avoid generating losers. Why should losers accept the rules under
which they lost?[17] After all, their self-interest should be as much taken for
granted as the self-interest of successful market participants. It is equally
legitimate. Dahl (1993, p. 78) has elaborated this dilemma clearly:
"Ironically, the assumption that society will benefit if everyone acts from
motives of rational self-interest . . . stands in sharp contradiction to the
requirement that the victims of competitive markets must somehow be prevented from acting selfishly in order for the optimal state of affairs to be
reached." Adherents of the marvel of the market may regard protection of
the market against its losers and their sympathizers as a task of government.
As Dahl (1993, p. 81) points out, this requirement may easily degenerate
into a call for authoritarian politics: "If a free-market economy can only be
maintained by a nondemocratic political system, then the vision of nineteenth century liberalism lies in utter ruins." Irrespective of the efficiency of
the market, it is compatible with a politically free society only if it is widely and spontaneously accepted.

Losers may either accept the market for sentimental reasons and thereby make its existence compatible with democracy or they may demand compensation. The first argument amounts to a suspension of the rational action
assumption. In my view, Lipset (1993, p. 123; 1994) endorses such an intellectual strategy when discussing democracy and arguing: "A crucial condition for a stable democracy is the presence of major parties with large and
virtually permanent bases of support among the voters. That support should
be so uncritical as to survive clear-cut policy failures and scandals." If what
I call a sentimental attachment to parties can strengthen democracy, then a
sentimental attachment to the market may similarly save capitalism.
Unfortunately, this argument would be ad hoc at best—if you start from my
assumptions about human behavior—and not a very plausible one at that.
Alternatively, a capitalist order may buy the support or acquiescence of
losers. For this the number of losers must be limited or losers must be compensated in order to avoid both rebellion and the need for repression.
Compensation, of course, opens the door wide for subsidies, protectionism,
and the welfare state. These instruments and policies carry their own dangers, to be discussed in the first section of Chapter 6 and in Chapter 8.

Notes

1. Homans's (1961) work *would be* an exception if it were a true macroappli-
cation of learning-theory assumptions about human behavior. Lindenberg (1989)

provides an interesting approach to a macrophenomenon, i.e., social revolutions, that does not rest on the classical assumptions about rational behavior. Simon's (1982) ideas of bounded rationality and satisficing constitute another alternative that has been influential in administration science and transaction cost economics (Williamson, 1981; 1987).

2. Of course, there are other spheres of life in which irrational behavior may persist for very long periods of time. As far as collective decisionmaking is concerned, some of these circumstances will be discussed below.

3. Simon (1985) has made this point in the context of comparing the maximizing and the satisficing assumptions. In my view, the distinction between maximizing and satisficing carries little importance unless we refer to mathematical formulations of these theories. See also Coleman (1990, p. 18).

4. Interesting but somewhat different recent treatments of this topic are Elster (1990); Homann and Suchanek (1992); and Kirchgässner (1992).

5. Although random assignment does not happen in observable societies, the assignment of money, prestige, and other rewards on the basis of traditional or other ascriptive criteria does happen frequently. Such assignments of rewards do not promote utility maximization or rationality.

6. Of course, such a pure market economy doesn't and probably never did exist. Some people have been or still are coerced to work for others, such as slaves, serfs, or prison-camp laborers. Other people voluntarily work for others because they expect to get a better deal by working for others than by working for themselves. Cooperation within hierarchical organizations may reduce transaction costs and therefore be preferable to universal self-employment and market exchange (see Coase, 1937; Alchian and Demsetz, 1972; Williamson, 1981). These topics are largely beyond the scope of this book. Here it suffices to outline the contribution made by self-employment and market exchange to improving incentives to do one's best to satisfy the wants of others.

7. Although Durkheim and Smith differ in their image of human beings and society, they do agree on the effects of size and density of population.

8. I have repeatedly been advised to avoid the word *capitalism* and to replace it by *market economy* or some reference to competition. According to Berger's (1986, p. 19) definition, capitalism is "production for a market by enterprising individuals or combines with the purpose of making a profit," i.e., capitalism is a synonym for the market economy. In my view, private property rights (in the means of production) and competitive markets constitute a package. The more private property rights are reduced and the less competitive markets become, the less capitalism there still is and the less its residues should be expected to work.

9. Similarity of preferences may help. Obviously, if everyone had the same preferences, aggregation would pose no difficulties.

10. Not even killing the losers would provide stability. Thereafter, a majority of the survivors would have an incentive to form a new majority among the survivors, and so on.

11. In my view, "he" is not sexist language because historically almost all dictators have been men. I see no reason women would wish to share the blame for their deeds.

12. The idea of rational ignorance has recently been criticized by Green and Shapiro (1994, pp. 94–96). In their view, human ignorance can frequently be observed where individuals could capture all or most of the benefits of better knowledge and choices themselves. Thus, ignorance about collective goods such as policies or policy outcomes is not as special as suggested by the rational ignorance

proposition. I do not want to discuss the fruitfulness of the rational ignorance proposition at the microlevel of analysis that is the focus of Green and Shapiro's work. It may be that microresearchers did not elaborate clearly enough what conceivable events would make them refute the rational ignorance proposition. At the macro level, however, the rational ignorance of the electorate is an absolutely essential ingredient of an explanation of why politicians pander to special interests, why they distort prices and reduce growth rates, or why even democracies engage in *regressive* income distribution (see Chapter 6, Section 1 for some *falsifiable* propositions that rest on the postulate of rational ignorance).

13. Wippler (1982) has argued that the degree of validity of this "law" depends on group size, heterogeneity of members, and interaction density. Oligarchies are most likely to arise in large groups with poorly connected members who are very differently endowed with resources.

14. In a German drama, Faust sells his soul to the devil in exchange for power and knowledge.

15. Given the lack of rights to which people under these regimes are entitled, I think the term *citizen* would be a misnomer; under a Hitler, Mao, or Stalin one is a subject rather than a citizen.

16. Frey (1986) and Frey, Pommerehne, and Gygi (1993) provide some evidence of the lack of popularity of the price system on which free trade rests compared to queuing or administrative decisionmaking.

17. Lipset (1993, p. 129) makes the same point: "Even in purely economic terms, the free market offers no cure-all and promises no utopia. At best, it holds out the promise of an unrigged lottery, but as in all such contests, the jackpots go to a minority of players. Hence there must be many who are (at least in a relative sense) 'losers'; some of these will be receptive to reformist or anticapitalist movements."

3

COLLECTIVE ACTION, GOVERNMENT, AND PROPERTY RIGHTS

1. Collective Action, Public Goods, and Positional Goods

The pursuit of common or group interests is most difficult when people want public, or collective, goods.[1] Olson (1965, p. 14) defines these goods by their nonexcludability. If any one group member gets them, they cannot feasibly or easily be withheld from other members. This characteristic of public goods instigates a freeriding tendency, thus impeding their procurement. Collectives may agree perfectly on the desirability of some public goods, as well as on their relative importance, but rational members might still choose not to contribute to their procurement unless coerced (Olson, 1965). In a large group, the beneficial impact *on oneself* of one's own investment is often insufficient to induce voluntary contributions, even when the beneficial impact of each and all contributions on all members is significantly greater than the cost incurred. So collectives may desire such goods, even unanimously, without being able to effectively act to obtain them.

According to Olson (1965), the probability of procurement or the degree of suboptimality in the provision of public goods depends on group size. The larger the group, the less important each individual's contribution to the provision of the public good and the stronger the incentive to attempt freeriding. Moreover, in larger groups or in groups of transient composition, moral pressure and the vicarious enjoyment of the well-being of one's fellows are less likely to work as selective incentives to contribute to common endeavors than they are in smaller groups.[2] Unequal interest in the public good or unequal power of group members may help, however. A strongly interested and powerful actor might rationally provide a collective good, even if he had to pay for it alone, permitting others to freeride or to pay less than their share.

In Olson's (1965) account, selective incentives and coercion are essential to procure collective goods, at least in large groups. One may raise three

23

types of objection against Olson's theorizing. First, one may perform experiments on public-goods procurement and find out whether the obstacles against the provision of public goods are really as strong as suggested and whether freeriding is as attractive to experimental subjects as the theory implies. Unfortunately, the evidence is ambiguous at best (Green and Shapiro, 1994, pp. 88–93). Sometimes (e.g., Kim and Walker, 1984) the theory does fairly well. According to Marwell and Ames (1979; 1980), however, the freeriding tendency is much weaker than it should be, although it seems to go up with increasing returns available for successful players in the experiments. As far as I can see, the following results, reported by Isaac, Walker, and Thomas (1984), illustrate the type of findings produced by experimental studies: Only 19 percent of their subjects aimed at the optimal provision of public goods, and 30 percent of their subjects did freeride whenever they could. The first number illustrates Olson's notion of a tendency toward a suboptimal provision of the public good. The second number illustrates that people in general do not freeride as consistently or frequently as they should according to Olson's logic of collective action. While this weakness of the logic of collective action should be noticed, I shall nevertheless continue to rely on it for the following reason: Almost all experimental studies put their subjects into low-cost situations. Rational or utility-maximizing behavior is not greatly rewarded because no experimenter can pay successful players, say, thousands of dollars. Similarly, irrational behavior is not significantly punished. Experimental losers do not have to pay thousands of dollars. They are not caned or tortured or killed. As I suggested in Chapter 2, in low-cost situations the rational action approach is least likely to be successfully applied.

Second, one may doubt Olson's (1965) relationship between group size and collective goods procurement for purely theoretical reasons. This has been done by Oliver and Marwell (1988). In my view, their arguments point to the need to qualify Olson's argument, which is likely to hold up under some circumstances but to be false and misleading under others. Oliver and Marwell (1988, p. 3) observe, "If the cost of a nonexcludable good increases proportionately (or more) with the number who enjoy it, larger groups are much less likely to be provided with the good than smaller groups. . . . There really is a dilemma of collective action for public goods, but the dilemma adheres to the high cost of providing them, not to the number who share in them." Sometimes, however, costs do not escalate with increases in the number of people who share the benefits. A lighthouse does not become more expensive to build or to operate because it improves the safety of many rather than of a few ships and their crews. Therefore, we should not expect that lighthouses with few beneficiaries are built, whereas lighthouses with many potential users are never built. This example also points to the necessity of considering jointness of supply or rivalry in consumption. Unless sea lanes around a lighthouse are crowded, there is almost perfect jointness of supply and almost no rivalry in consumption. Benefits to one ship and its crew do not reduce benefits to another ship and its crew. Therefore, Olson's proposition about group size is most realistic either where there is some rivalry in consumption, because other beneficiaries reduce one's own benefits, or where the cost of procurement rises steeply with the number of beneficiaries of the good.

Oliver and Marwell (1988) underline Olson's point about heterogeneity and public-good procurement: The more heterogeneous the group, the more likely it is that some individual or some subgroup of members does procure the good. Moreover, Oliver and Marwell argue that group size should be correlated with heterogeneity, and heterogeneous large groups should stand a much better chance of public-goods procurement than would be expected on the basis of group size alone.

Third, one may argue that Olson's insistence on selective incentives and coercion is question-begging. Elster (1989, pp. 40–41) launches such an attack:

> The provision of selective incentives cannot be the general solution to the collective action problem. To assume that there is a central authority offering incentives often requires another collective action problem to have been solved already. . . . To assume that the incentives are offered in a decentralized way, by mutual monitoring, gives rise to a second-order free-rider problem. . . . Punishment is almost invariably costly to the punisher, while the benefits from punishment are diffusely distributed over all members. It is, in fact, a collective good. To provide it, one would need second-order selective incentives, which would, however, run into a third-order free-rider problem.

Now, it looks as if Olson can explain public consumption goods procurement only by assuming the existence of a public production good, such as leadership or another mechanism to apply selective incentives and coercion.

This point is where Hechter's (1987) two-stage theory of the procurement of collective goods provides a solution.[3] In the first or initial stage, collective goods cannot be produced at all. But there are some excludable goods that can be produced more efficiently, or even only, by a team of people who pool their resources rather than by isolated individuals. Utility-maximizing actors will adopt resource pooling whenever it pays. Since those who do not contribute can be excluded from the benefits, freeriding is no problem. But somebody has to administer the pool of resources and to coordinate the actions of the coproducers. Somebody has to become the leader or entrepreneur. A resourceful person probably takes the initiative in resource pooling. Possibly the leader even pays the members of his team for their input and becomes the residual claimant on anything that is produced.

Then he or she would face an incentive to observe and punish shirking, and he or she might reward the most active and efficient members of the team.

Once an administrator, coordinator, or agenda-setter, an entrepreneur or leader, exists, we have one answer to Elster's (1989) question about who applies selective incentives or punishment: the group leader. He or she does so because resourcefulness makes retaliation by those who suffer punishment less likely and because resourcefulness permits him or her to reward others. Benefiting more than others from group activities—after all, he or she coordinates the group's agenda and thereby gains special influence—he or she faces incentives to apply rewards and punishments, or selective incentives and coercion.

The core idea of Hechter's (1987) theory is that you first have to pool resources in order to produce excludable goods. This pooling is done in the first stage, and a side product emerges: a rudimentary social structure, or at least someone who is capable of and interested in administering selective incentives and coercion. Thereafter, in a second stage the group or its leader may switch the group's purposes to the production of truly collective or nonexcludable goods. The more dependent the team members are on the goods provided by the group and distributed by the leader or some governing mechanism, the more burdens the leader or the governing body of the group may impose on its members. The fewer the exit opportunities for group members, the more severe the punishments that may be imposed.

There is a subtle difference in emphasis between Hechter's original account and my use of it. Hechter (1987, p. 121) focuses on overcoming the freerider problem without necessarily invoking an incipient hierarchical division of labor between leaders and followers, between order givers and order takers; the flavor of his theorizing can be appreciated in the following quotation, in which he explains the establishment of mutual insurance groups: "Since they are formed for the provision of joint *private* goods, there is no initial free rider problem. To obtain their insurance, members are led to adopt formal controls that protect the common fund. Once the fund is intact, it can be used in a variety of ways. There is no inherent reason why the members of an insurance group cannot convert their assets into a strike fund and reconstitute themselves as a trade union." Of course, trade unions are in the business of public-goods procurement: They want to increase the pay and to improve the working conditions of their members.

I have no difficulty in accepting all of these ideas. But I want to add the point that somebody has to take the initiative even before the first phase. Actors differ in resourcefulness. Therefore, initial differences between persons become magnified by social cooperation. Leadership and privileged positions necessarily get established. Actually, the hope of becoming a leader or, more generally, of occupying a privileged position is the most important selective incentive to elicit organizing efforts in the first place.

The effort to pool resources and to act collectively necessarily starts a process of social stratification. Human beings cannot obtain collective goods without generating positional goods.[4]

A large homogeneous group of people interested in attaining a collective good would probably never even try to get it if positional goods, such as leadership, did not exist. Without using the term *positional good,* Michels (1910/1970); Frohlich, Oppenheimer, and Young (1971); and Blau (1964) provide some evidence on this point. While leadership implies the burden of responsibility for the provision of public goods, it simultaneously implies the privilege of strongly influencing the definition of which public goods a group or society wants and what the priority of various public goods is or should be. The existence of privileged or commanding positions within groups or societies provides a selective incentive for those who would like to occupy such positions to invest their time and resources in collecting a multitude of individual contributions to the provision of the public good. In other words, in organizing for the provision of a collective good a group necessarily becomes more unequal. Ordinary members exchange their subordination to leadership and their other contributions for the provision of private and public goods. The extraordinary input of the leaders, or of activists and staff in general—whether in time, talent, or other resources—is solicited by offering the subordination of the many to the few who contribute more than an equal share of input for the provision of public goods (compare Frank, 1985).[5]

2. Government and Property Rights

A competitive market order may be regarded as a public good. Competitive markets are desirable. They provide room for a division of labor and for productivity. They provide incentives to work hard, to innovate, and to satisfy the wants of others. They provide an opportunity to exploit the knowledge that is scattered among thousands or millions of humans beings. Scarcity prices provide signals showing where effort is most likely to be rewarded. But even the most superficial look at economic history or the contemporary world reveals that the benefits of competitive markets do not suffice to bring them into existence every time and everywhere. Thus, the question is: How can we get them? In principle, there are at least two ways to approach this problem. In this section, I shall start with a mental experiment suggested by Tullock (1974) and Olson (1993) to highlight the obstacles to the establishment of a productive competitive market order. In Chapter 4 I present and discuss how the West could overcome the ordinary condition of humans, i.e., mass poverty, by establishing property rights and competitive markets.

Imagine a society without generally acknowledged property rights.[6] It would provide no incentives to invest resources for productive purposes. In such a society, if a family grows food in a field or garden it cannot expect to enjoy the fruits of its labor because someone else may come along and take the produce. Although the concept of theft would be absent in a society without property rights, the act of taking what has been produced by others would be frequent. After all, such takings are very effective labor-saving devices. The individually rational pursuit of self-interest, however, implies a collectively disastrous result: Incentives to do productive work would be extremely low.

Even in the propertyless society of our imagination, productivity could not be zero. The less is produced, the more difficult it will be to find something worth taking. But those who recognize the unproductivity of preying on others and the fruits of their labor, who therefore prefer to work—say, in a field to grow food—cannot avoid a conflict of interest with those who still want to prey. Therefore, the would-be producers have to invest resources into making predation more difficult and less worthwhile. They might build fences and guard their barns in order to increase their chances of keeping what they have produced. Such sheltering devices on the part of the producers may be necessary to reinforce incentives for productive work, but they tend to elicit countermeasures on the part of the predators, who are likely to gang up, to arm themselves, and to guard the hideaways of their loot.

Since the efforts of producers and predators in a propertyless society partially neutralize each other, simultaneously increasing the costs of production and of predation, it seems to be in everyone's interest that such costs should be avoided by the imposition of property rights, for example, by somehow guaranteeing that everybody has a right to the fruits of his or her labor. After the creation of such rights, some former predators might respond to the improved incentives for productive work. Even those who continue to prey on others are likely to profit from the increase of prosperity resulting from more productive work and less predation. The fewer predators remain in business, the less rational it is for hardworking people to waste resources in protecting their property and products. Since the costs of predation are thereby reduced, even the remaining predators have an interest in seeing the number of predators decline.

This argument illustrates that property rights constitute a collective good. They eliminate or, if less than perfectly enforced, at least reduce conflict behavior through which some (maybe most) resources are invested merely to counterbalance investments by other actors. From a social perspective such mutual cancellation of efforts is obviously wasteful. Unfortunately, the establishment of property rights is not easy because they constitute a public good. Where a society is a large group, it is extremely unlikely that property rights can be established without coercion and selective incentives, including those provided by the creation of hierarchies.

In principle, one can imagine that the state, law, and property rights come into existence as the result of voluntary cooperation among would-be producers who recognize each other's right to keep whatever has been produced, or to exchange it for something else, or to give it away for whatever purpose satisfies the giver. But which person out of thousands or more has an incentive to propose a specific set of property rights, to talk to a lot of other people, to invite them for a meeting, to chair it, and to find administrative personnel after some social contract has been agreed upon? Whoever starts working for a social contract defining property rights faces uncertainty of success, benefits diluted by the large number of other beneficiaries (in case of success),[7] and significant opportunity costs. Whoever works for a social contract and the mutual recognition of property rights cannot, at the same time, either do directly productive work or prey on others.

Instead of would-be producers getting together, one can imagine some clever predators becoming upset by competing predators and the harm they do. Obviously, a monopoly in the predation business could help. Thus, some predators might combine with each other and start selling protection to producers against competing predators. The cost of anarchical predation would thereby go up, and monopolized predation might be called taxation. Since the resource-wasting conflict between producers and anarchical predators would be suppressed, even the theft monopoly would constitute a public good. Since a small group of predators enjoys much stronger selective incentives—that is, the possibility of becoming a repressive and exploitative ruling class, or "kleptocracy," as Andreski (1968b) would call it—than those motivating a larger group of producers to establish a statelike organization, the less desirable course of action looks much more likely than the more desirable one. Coercion, however, is but one essential ingredient in establishing social order and property rights, whether coercion is applied by the producers against the predators or, as is more likely, the other way round. Whoever wants to establish property rights, or "law and order," still faces the dilemma that the order aspired to constitutes a collective good for the would-be organizers of society. Again, selective incentives may overcome the otherwise existing tendency to take a free ride. Those who enforce order do so not only to enjoy the public good of "law and order" but also to obtain privileges such as being or becoming the ruling class. If there were no positional goods such as membership and rank in a ruling class, law and order could not be provided in a large group or society. Society purchases public goods by accepting, or even generating, positional goods. Privileged places in hierarchies may constitute the most powerful selective incentives among humans (Frank, 1985; Hirsch, 1976).

The argument I have just made suffers from two related weaknesses. First, the possibility of uncoerced cooperation among producers—of spontaneous mutual acknowledgment of each person's right to the fruits of their own labor—might exist, at least among small groups of people in which everyone knows everyone else, people repeatedly interact with each other, communication networks are sufficiently dense that most acts of defection will become common knowledge, and defectors can be ostracized (see the literature on iterative games, including Axelrod [1984], as well as field studies on common resources management such as Ostrom [1990]). In small groups or societies kleptocracy is not inevitable. Conceivably, cooperative states even historically precede exploitative states (as argued by Mann, 1986).

The second shortcoming in my analysis concerns the applicability and actual application of selective incentives and coercion in a large group or society. It is hard to imagine a single person rewarding some and threatening others and thus achieving societywide cooperation or respect for property rights. So some group ready to reward some people and to punish others, or some kernel of coordinated action and cooperation, has to exist already. Large-scale application of both selective incentives and coercion already presumes the existence of what might be called a collective production good, i.e., an organized capability for collective action. As I argued earlier, selective incentives and coercion merely transform the collective-goods problem. The existence of one type of collective good has to be assumed in order to explain the procurement of other collective goods. Kernels of cooperative relationships may arise in small groups. Once they exist, these solidaristic groups may wish to become ruling classes over wealthier groups (Ibn Khaldun, ca. 1377/1958; Mann, 1986; McNeill, 1963; 1982; Ruestow, 1950–1957; Tilly, 1985) and may thereby extend the size of society. Historically, this kind of extension has happened often, for example when mountain, steppe, or desert tribes have overrun richer and more civilized peoples dwelling on the plains. Alternatively, cooperative groups initially dedicated to the procurement of private goods—which, of course, include personal salvation—may also be used for the procurement of collective goods. Although this redefinition of a group's aims doesn't immediately or necessarily increase group size, one would expect the size of a society to be correlated to rule by a predatory class.[8]

If this sketch gets the pattern of the incentives needed to create an exploitative or a cooperative state approximately right, then we can make the following observation based on human history: Once societies become large—say, horticultural or agrarian societies with thousands or even millions of members—then exploitative states should massively outnumber states whose exploitative character is disputable. This observation seems to be true (Hall, 1985; Lenski, 1966; Lenski and Lenski, 1982; Mann, 1986; McNeill, 1963, 1982; Ruestow, 1950–1957; Tilly, 1985). Of course, conquest is the main mechanism for establishing exploitative orders. There are numerous examples of nomadic or seminomadic tribes that have conquered, plundered, enslaved, and ruled more civilized and more productive peoples than themselves. The Mongol hordes that overran Kiev and Baghdad and Beijing in the thirteenth century provide the most spectacular example.

If suffering from predatory rule is the ordinary state of affairs for human beings, then the question is how such rule could ever be overcome, or at least become very much mitigated, as it has been and still is in the West. Or, to put the question somewhat differently: Self-appointed "guardians" impose property rights in order to maximize revenue. Thereby, they do provide some degree of service to their subjects. After all, monopolists are lazier than competitive actors, and monopolized predation implies less predation than anarchy. But who guards the guardians? Of course, they might realize that promising their subjects a greater share of their produce, i.e., a lower tax burden, might make them more productive. Assume that a ruling class or dictator makes such a promise to their or his subjects. If the subjects believe it once—say, at the beginning of the sowing or ploughing season—but the rulers change their minds once the crop is in and confiscate a larger amount than previously proposed, what can the disarmed subjects do? They may rebel and be crushed; they may occasionally even rebel and win. More important for my current purposes, they can retaliate in another way: Next time the subjects can be as unproductive as they would have been if they had known their excessive burden in the first place. In such a situation, both ruler or ruling class and subjects could be better off if the rulers could bind themselves to keeping their promises.

Elster (1994, p. 29) has made the issue crystal clear in the following sentence: "A dictator may well announce a constitution with strong and unamendable guarantees for property, but nobody will believe him if there is no mechanism outside his control that can be counted on to sanction his violations." In principle, I can imagine two kinds of sanctions: either successful mass rebellion, which I regard as extremely unlikely,[9] or the threat of exit. If exploited subjects can run away and find shelter and protection someplace else, whether in virgin lands not yet really penetrated by administrative authority or behind medieval town walls or under the protection of some foreign prince, then it may be in a dictator's interest to honor his promises.

If the odds for successful rebellion from below are very poor, or if the organizers of mass rebellion should turn themselves into another exploitative ruling class, thereby merely starting a new cycle of repressive government, then the hopes for establishing property rights respected even by their guardians must rest on competition between ruling classes, princes, effectively autonomous political units, or states.

3. Escaping from Competition and Rent-Seeking

A competitive market order relies on scarcity prices, though of course all producers would like to do better than that. Deviations from scarcity prices presuppose either monopoly, cartelization, or government intervention. In general, monopolists tend to reduce the quantity of supply and to increase prices. This course of action implies three effects (Buchanan, Tollison, and Tullock, 1980; Tullock, 1993). First, there is some transfer that is usually regressive. For example, poorer consumers pay more, for the benefit of a richer monopolist who earns a rent.[10] Second, there is a true social loss, technically a deadweight loss. Those consumers who once were ready to pay the competitive price for some good but who are no longer willing or able to pay the monopolist's price become worse off. Not even the monopolist can exploit those who have stopped buying his products, so this reduction in the well-being of some is not balanced by an improvement for others. Third, monopolies and other restrictive practices are contagious. Successful monopolists provide a model for others to emulate. If you perceive that others do exceptionally well by eliminating or escaping from competition, you try to do so too. Since regressive redistribution[11] and pure social losses are undesirable from a societal point of view, the incentive for further efforts at monopolization must be bad. Still, even unsuccessful attempts to become a monopolist consume resources that are then no longer available for productive purposes. The fiercer the fight among monopoly contenders, the more resources are wasted for the sole purpose of neutralizing the efforts of other contenders.[12]

Some producers do not succeed in escaping from competition on their own, in eliminating all other producers of some good or service. Instead they score a partial success in reducing competition by erecting barriers to entry. This reduction in competition increases the scarcity premium for the affected goods or services. Moreover, barriers to entry and a smaller number of competitors simplify collusion and may permit the establishment of a distributional coalition or cartel. If members of some producer group could agree on limits to production, orderly market-sharing arrangements, and (high) prices, then they might act as if the group were a monopolist. The results are transfers, pure social losses, and further models to teach still others the benefits of escaping from competitive pressures.

Compared to a monopoly, however, a cartel or distributional coalition suffers from two shortcomings. First, sharing implies some dilution of benefits. Second, and worse still, it is difficult for members of a latent distributional coalition to get organized, to eliminate or greatly reduce competition between themselves, and to become a manifest and active distributional coalition. After all, cartels or distributional coalitions aim at the procurement of public goods for their membership. Restrictive practices and reduced competition provide benefits for all *producers*. From Olson's (1965) logic of collective action we know that nonexcludability results in freeriding tendencies and that large groups are less likely to succeed in overcoming them than small groups. Since the sum of all market participants, including consumers and buyers of intermediate products, who benefit from competitive markets, is always larger than any particular producer or supplier group that benefits from restrictive practices, upholding competition should remain a difficult agenda. Although competition is a public good for society, its avoidance is also a public good for parts of it.

Trade unions are a special type of distributional coalition or cartel. Since workers belong to large groups, there are strong freeriding tendencies. Therefore, workers need skillful political entrepreneurs (Frohlich, Oppenheimer, and Young, 1971) to guide them[13] and to manage the application of selective incentives and coercion. Moreover, it takes time to organize a union (Olson, 1965; 1982). But explaining how trade unions come into existence is not the purpose of this section. Here the concern is to understand their effects.

Trade unions try to increase the wages or salaries of their members. Since workers are usually poorer than their employers, a transfer of income from employers to workers is progressive. In this respect, unions seem to be better than most cartels, but in other respects they are not. If workers succeed in obtaining higher wages than they could in a competitive situation, then employers are likely to offer fewer jobs. Would-be employees in the unionized sector of the economy are thereby driven into the informal sector or even into involuntary unemployment (Hayek, 1960; McKenzie and Tullock, 1978b, p. 256; Olson, 1982, p. 201). In order to obtain wages that are inflated by the inclusion of a rental component, workers need to invest resources, i.e., to organize themselves, prepare for strikes, and prevent their employers from maintaining production with the assistance of nonunionized and possibly previously unemployed labor. Since employers dislike excessive wages and a profit squeeze, they are likely to invest some resources in canceling out the effects of the workers' efforts. Whoever wins this struggle, some resources will simply be wasted.

Rent-seeking requires government acquiescence or, better still, support. Most monopolies or cartels are organized at the national level, not on a global scale. Therefore, national governments could easily restore competition by abolishing all tariffs and nontariff barriers to international trade. Foreign producers could and would sell below monopoly or cartel prices, causing these prices to collapse and corresponding rents to disappear. Similarly, borders wide open to foreign labor would contribute to undermining union power. Although governments can decrease rent-seeking, they often contribute to it by granting monopolies, organizing cartels, helping trade unions, subsidizing some activities and applying discriminatory taxation against others, and interfering with international trade and migration. Tullock (1980b, p. 211) deplores these practices: "One of the major activities of modern governments is the granting of special privileges to various groups of politically influential people." Similarly, Buchanan (1980, p. 9) claims: "Rent-seeking activity is directly related to the scope and range of governmental activity in the economy, to the relative size of the public sector."

Rent-seeking is not only wasteful, it is also contagious. Imagine that there is a monopoly or cartel in some sector of the economy that produces goods, such as steel, that serve as important inputs to the production of other goods, say cars or trucks. Expensive inputs tend to make domestic industries uncompetitive compared with foreign rivals. If the government has condoned a monopoly or cartel of steel producers, it is likely to come under pressure from steel-consuming industries to protect domestic markets and/or to subsidize exports. In granting protection the government makes it easier or more worthwhile for the industries concerned to become cartelized as well. So the evil spreads.

The fundamental problem in rent-seeking societies is that economic actors and groups invest too many resources in capturing rents and too little in productive activities. While rent-seeking is obviously harmful to growth and prosperity, there is no reason to expect it to contribute to equity or equality. Small, elitist, privileged groups enjoy a head start in the game. The strong are likely to win distributional struggles and the poor are likely to lose them. Olson (1982, p. 175) puts this proposition into these words: "There is greater inequality . . . in the opportunity to create distributional coalitions"—whose purpose is rent-seeking—"than there is in the inherent productive abilities of people."[14]

Conspiracy is likely between rulers and producers interested in barriers to entry into their markets. Producers may pay the rulers to erect barriers to entry. Such a deal provides the ruler with revenue and the protected producers with rents. Of course, this deal is made at the expense of consumers. But inefficient arrangements benefiting powerful actors are to be expected. According to Scully (1992, p. 27), "political control of the economy leads to rent-seeking behavior. In the extreme, rent-seeking may take the form of endemic corruption. Inefficiency and low growth result. Limits on economic freedom are a form of taxation that lowers the rate of private capital formation, discourages innovation, and interferes with the gains from exchange." The question is: How can this sad state of affairs be overcome? The answer is that inefficiency within organized societies is most likely to be overcome by rivalry between societies, to be discussed in Chapter 4 of this book.

Before turning to that issue, I want to tie up the problem identified at the end of Chapter 2, Section 3 with what has just been said about rent-seeking. In Chapter 2 I analyzed the need to maintain popular acceptance of the market and the income distribution it generates. I have admitted that compensation payments, subsidies, or protection for likely losers might become unavoidable in a free society. If a polity ever sets this precedent, then it will reinforce rent-seeking because political interference with the economy and redistribution have been legitimized in principle, and the door will be wide open for creeping socialism. In my view, Talavera (1993, p. 106) is right on target when he identifies the meaning of socialism as follows: "At the heart of socialism . . . lies the belief that the economy ought to answer to the will of the people expressed through political channels." The trouble is that unequal opportunities to organize for collective action as well as the rational ignorance of voters and consumers provide ample room for rent-seeking and economic decline. It may be that free societies are damned if they do it—i.e., buy consent by compensating losers and opening the door to rent-seeking—and damned if they don't do it—i.e., lose popular acceptance of the market and thereby make capitalism and democracy incompatible in the first step and capitalism unviable in the next one. Once democracy is sacrificed, the will of *some* people expressed through political channels is likely to prevail over the market sooner or later. After all, there is no reason why a dictator or ruling class should freely accept the limitation of power that a market allocation of resources implies—unless there are hostile ruling classes, princes, or dictators in the neighborhood.

Notes

1. Although some writers make a distinction between collective and public goods, I use the terms interchangeably.
2. Frohlich, Oppenheimer, and Young (1971, pp. 148–149) criticize Olson for his inconsistent approach to interacting utilities. On the one hand, Olson (1965) employs the notion of self-interest, which is incompatible with interacting utilities. On the other hand, his proposition that small groups stand a better chance of supplying themselves with collective goods seems to rest on at least an implicit assumption of interacting utilities. While Frohlich, Oppenheimer, and Young advocate a rigorous reliance on self-interest, I am inclined to argue that interacting utilities or the vicarious enjoyment of other people's well-being is a variable that is itself dependent on interaction density, closeness, and group size. See Homans (1950) on the relationship between interaction and mutual sympathy.
3. I shall not use Hechter's (1987) terminology, which I find confusing, but I think that I faithfully reproduce his main idea. Even if Hechter should disown what I call the two-stage theory of procurement of collective goods, I would nonetheless endorse it myself.
4. The term *positional good* is borrowed from Hirsch (1976). Positional goods are defined by rivalry in consumption.
5. As Chapter 2, Section 3 has clarified, I do not contend that the impact of government tends to be positive. Within small groups or ruling classes, leaders have to offer some benefits to followers in order to obtain legitimacy. In large societies, leaders assisted by some privileged staff (including officials, military, secret police, etc.) may overcome this constraint.
6. I keep the term *society* for convenience's sake. Most sociologists would not call such an aggregation of people a society.

7. Here, I do not intend to suggest rivalry in consumption. Instead I want to underline the fact that only a small fraction of the benefits produced by one's actions accrue to each producer. Assuming selfishness, as I do, incentives must be poor.

8. Assume that a peaceable group builds a large and prosperous state because it defines property rights clearly and tolerates competitive markets. Surely it will attract outside predators.

9. According to my calculations (Weede, 1992a, chapter 21) most rebellions are elite rather than mass rebellions. Most mass rebellions do not succeed, and most of those that do succeed in replacing the old ruling class produce few other benefits. "Successful" revolutions even result in the type of megamurders discussed at the end of Chapter 2.

10. Tollison (1982, p. 577) defines rent as "a payment to a resource owner above the amount his resources could command in their next best alternative use," where the alternative use refers to a competitive market.

11. As readers of this book will see, I have my doubts about the capability of government to achieve (rather than merely promise) progressive redistribution. Certainly my views on redistribution will be controversial. So far I have found nobody who has argued in favor of regressive redistribution, though of course the practice is quite popular.

12. With Schumpeter (1942) one may argue that this treatment of monopolies rests on oversimplification. Monopolies may produce positive rather than negative effects because they permit economies of scale or provide incentives for innovation. The hope of achieving a temporary monopoly may provide one of the most important incentives to innovate. Therefore, innovators deserve and receive legal protection, although such protection limits competition. While I admit the validity of these arguments, I contend that on balance the negative effects of monopolies that are described in the main text dominate. Whether competition among would-be monopolists is harmful or not depends on how they compete. Price and quality competition may be desirable. Competition for political influence and legal protection of monopoly rights is almost always undesirable. Unfortunately, monopolists must aim at such protection or monopoly profits will be limited by the fear that fat profits may attract challengers and renew competition.

13. While workers need political entrepreneurs and leadership, leaders are likely to exact a price that Michels (1910/1970) has described in his discussion of the "iron law of oligarchy."

14. For a related evaluation, see Pampel and Williamson (1989, p. 110). Huntington and Nelson (1976) similarly suggest that political processes may enhance rather than reduce inequality among developing countries, although they postulate conditional rather than general relationships depending on the level of economic development and the degree of political participation.

4

DISUNITY, LAW, AND LIBERTY: THE RISE OF THE WEST COMPARED WITH STAGNATION IN THE GREAT ASIAN CIVILIZATIONS INTO THE NINETEENTH CENTURY

1. The European Miracle, or the Rise of the West

Western civilization and political culture rest on three basic political experiences and the corresponding ideas: first, on the limitation of governmental authority, i.e., the rule of law; second, on some separation of the economy and of science from government and religion, which ultimately led to an escape from mass poverty; third, on popular participation in government, i.e., democracy. In my view, there is a ranking order of these items. Historically, the limitation of governmental authority came first; the emancipation of the economy and of science from rulers and priests developed thereafter; popular participation in choosing rulers arrived last. Moreover, I subscribe to the theory that without property rights respected from above and without limited government, capitalism cannot exist, and that without capitalism, meaningful popular participation cannot exist. But this is not to say that there are no contradictions among these Western core ideas. While we still enjoy limited government in the West, this achievement remains precarious and may vanish (Brunner, 1978; Hayek, 1960; 1973-1976-1979; Jasay, 1985; Radnitzky, 1987a).

Half a millenium ago there was little reason to expect that Western Europe might outpace Islamic civilization and India and China in economic productivity, technology, and science. But by the nineteenth century, Europe had left all of the great Asian civilizations far behind. Mann's (1993, p. 14) crude estimates provide a feel for the size of the Western achievement: "In 1750, Europe and North America contributed perhaps 25 percent of world industrial production and, by 1913, 90 percent." How could the European, or Western, miracle ever happen? My answer to this question is based on the writings of Max Weber (1920/1972; 1921/1978; 1922/1964; 1923/1981) and Eric Jones (1981; 1988) but is also influenced by Albert (1986), Andreski (1968a; 1984), Chirot (1986), Collins (1980; 1986), Ekelund and Tollison (1981), Hall (1985), Kuznets (1966), Mann (1986; 1993), North (1981; 1990), North and Thomas (1973), Rosenberg and Birdzell (1986), and Wesson (1978). Moreover, I perceive economic history from a perspective very much influenced by Hayek (1960; 1973-1976-1979; 1988).[1]

According to Jones (1988, p. 1), economic growth is incompatible with too much rent-seeking: "Economic history may be thought of as a struggle between a propensity for growth and one for rent-seeking, that is, for someone improving his or her position, or a group bettering its position, at the expense of the general welfare. . . . When conditions permitted, that is, when rent-seeking was somehow curbed, growth manifested itself." Restrictions to rent-seeking depend on political circumstances. Jones (1988, p. 177) identifies the conditions that have reduced rent-seeking in the West as follows: "Competition for subjects and power among the states and kings and nobles seems in the end to be the answer. It abridged the worst behavior—not much, and only on average, but more than in other great societies of the world." Since rent-seeking is an attempt to evade competition in order to obtain returns above opportunity cost, one may say that competition in markets is best preserved when it is backed up by competition between rulers.

The great Asian civilizations—especially China, which was economically and technologically the most advanced society during the European Middle Ages—were burdened with political unity, whereas Western Europe was characterized by cultural unity and political fragmentation.[2] Interstate conflict in Europe led to many European wars, but conflict among relatively small European states and autonomous principalities[3] (at most the size of Chinese provinces) also effectively limited governmental power over subjects, whether producers or traders. Conflict among political units within a single civilization provides an opportunity for subjects to vote with their feet against outrages of oppression.[4]

In huge empires there is no such check on arbitrary rulers and their kleptocratic inclinations. The combination of rivalry among comparatively small political units and trade in mass-consumption goods contributed to European traders being conceded relatively safer property rights than their Asian counterparts. If some European prince tended to rob merchants crossing his territory, they could simply avoid it. If another European prince promised safe conduct for some modest protection fee, merchants would prefer routes through his territory to alternative routes. By their protection fees, they would strengthen the less kleptocratic prince vis-à-vis his more kleptocratic rivals.[5] Where shortsighted rulers suffer the fate of maladapted species, relatively safe property rights spread. The safety of property rights is perhaps the most important background condition for economic development and prosperity.

By contrast, "the competition among European monarchs for mobile capital in order to strengthen their defense was relatively unknown in China" (Chan, 1993, p. 17). Property rights were safer in Western Europe than throughout Asia, and these rights contributed to reduced transaction costs, thereby increasing the volume of trade and reinforcing the regional division of labor. Specialization according to comparative advantage and gains from trade also contributed to European economic development.

Interstate conflict in European history contributed not only to the spread of relatively safe property rights of merchants but also to comparatively decent treatment of peasants. If badly treated, peasants could run away to other territories or to towns where they became free after about a year. By its very existence an interstate system tends to limit the powers of ruling classes and governments, compared to continent-sized unitary empires. Wesson (1978, p. 41) summarizes the effects of political fragmentation by the following assertion: "The division of power in the world involves internal limitation of power and a looser kind of society, which has more place for private undertakings of all kinds, private ownership, commerce, and individualism."

Feudal Europe differed from the great Asian civilizations in another respect as well. In European feudalism there was some reciprocity between vassal and lord: Both had some rights and some obligations. The very ideas of mutual obligations and reciprocity imply some limitation on arbitrary and whimsical rule. Of course, the lords did not concede rights to vassals out of magnanimity. They had to do so because of competition and feuds among lords and because of the fact that vassals and self-equipped warriors could turn against their lords if they felt mistreated.

In the Middle Ages some European trading cities became independent from territorial rulers. Because these urban entities could defend themselves and withstand sieges behind their walls, their autonomy had to be respected by territorial lords. Merchants and artisans obtained political power within cities. In Europe pockets of citizen rule limited the arbitrary power of territorial rulers. Even peasants could and did escape from their lords and take refuge behind city walls.

Half a millennium ago European aristocrats were constrained by competition and hostility among neighboring rulers, by feudalism, and by autonomous cities that were dominated by market-oriented merchants and artisans. The fragmentation of political power in Europe generated relatively secure property rights, which provided essential incentives for hard and productive work. Moreover, in *politically fragmented* but *culturally united* Europe the idea could arise and spread that not only kings and their officials but also the lower aristocracy, merchants, artisans, and even peasants should enjoy some rights that ought to be universally respected. In late medieval Europe the limitation of the power of ruling princes led to the generation of representative councils and parliaments, thereby planting the seeds for what was to become political participation.

Without limitation of whimsical governmental power there are no safe property rights for the producing strata of society. Without property rights for producers and merchants there are few incentives to produce, to specialize according to comparative advantage, and to trade. Moreover, private property rights generate an opportunity for the exploitation of knowledge and for innovation. By its nature knowledge is scattered in millions of heads. Not all of it can be documented. Much of it is tacit, such as peasants' knowledge about what to grow where, or the knowledge of artisans about their craft. Only decentralized decisionmaking permits a society to mobilize the skills of its people. Without relatively secure property rights, economic stagnation becomes inevitable, as has been the fate of the great Asian civilizations.

Political disunity in Europe also limited the scope of governmental decisions. In fifteenth-century China the Ming court could outlaw overseas trade and the building of vessels fit for the high seas. The court succeeded in making this ruling effective—and in ending the Chinese era of exploration, thus leaving the oceans to the Europeans. European rulers could prevent their own bit of Europe from participating in the exploration of the globe and in exploiting the opportunities of overseas trade, but nobody in Europe had the power to overrule European curiosity and adventurousness on a continental scale. Jones (1981, p. 67) evaluates the contrast between China and the West in these terms:

> The record of Chinese exploration which was halted in 1430 and prevented by fiat from resumption in 1480 shows what could happen in a centralised empire that could not happen, or be enforced, in a decentralised system of states like Europe. Progress might be sluggish and frustrating but it was less likely to be permanently baulked; to pursue the example, Columbus did eventually find a sponsor. The other large societies of Eurasia that might potentially have developed as Europe did develop, tended to suffer from various disabilities including political centralism and whimsicality. Their earlier and perhaps greater intellectual promise was always stultified.

In the early modern age, many minor lords were subdued by major lords, and many cities lost their autonomy, although some retained it to varying degrees even into the nineteenth century. Some European principalities or kingdoms grew and became similar in size to the later European states. Large-scale state-building, the reduction in the number of effectively independent political units,[6] the weakening of many cities, and the replacement of feudalism by absolutism threatened the limitation of government in Europe. But one critical fact still constrained European kings in ways unknown to Chinese, Indian, or Ottoman rulers. In the European state system there was always an abundance of other states of roughly equal economic, technological, and military capabilities. People and capital could still evade their rulers because they were often welcomed elsewhere in Europe.

At the transition from the Middle Ages to the modern age, Europe experienced another fragmenting event: the Reformation and the rise of Protestantism. In the Middle Ages the rivalry between the pope and the emperor (ruling Germany, the Alps, and Italy) contributed to the limitation of power and to the evolution of Western law (Berman, 1983). After the Reformation, political power and churches were often closely allied. But the religious divisions between Catholicism and Protestantism and within Protestantism, as well as the fact that within some territories no church could prevail, contributed to fragmentation. Out of religious fragmentation arose hostility and the Thirty Years War, but later results included some toleration in religious and, by extension, in philosophical and scientific affairs. I do not argue that toleration prevailed in most European principalities, kingdoms, or states, because it often did not, but that Europe as a cultural entity became tolerant because of political and religious fragmentation. Almost any idea could find some place in Europe that was tolerant or hospitable.

The Reformation and Protestantism were important to the development of European civilization for another reason. Many Protestant denominations devalued priests as intermediaries between God and believers and insisted on the primacy of individual responsibility and consciences, or even on the priesthood of each believer. Britain and North America were affected by such ideas earlier and to a greater degree than most of continental Europe. It seems to be more than a coincidence that the Anglo-Saxon countries also pioneered the industrial revolution as well as the spread of democratic ideas and institutions. If the individual is directly responsible to God, if all believers are equal in front of him or equally at his mercy, then personal initiative as well as the restriction of wordly and priestly power is reinforced. Moreover, covenantal theologies and self-governing congregations also prepared people for later forms of democratic rule (Ostrom, 1991).

According to Weber's (1920/1972) famous proposition, Protestantism also contributed to capitalism and economic growth by delegitimizing *otherwordly* asceticism, by insisting on hard (and profitable) work as a way to find out whether one had been chosen by God, and by condemning luxury consumption of the fruits of one's labor. Instead the proceeds had to be reinvested; i.e., religion contributed to capital accumulation. Since the Weberian interpretation of Calvinism has come under vigorous attack (MacKinnon, 1988a; 1988b), I think that the obvious limitation of priestly authority by religious fragmentation deserves greater weight in an explanatory sketch of the European miracle than the disputed issue of the Protestant ethic and the spirit of capitalism.[7]

Political fragmentation also limited the power of governments to regulate prices. In almost all traditional societies there exist notions about "just" prices. By and large, just prices result from traditional price patterns. Just or traditional prices are incompatible with scarcity prices responding to changes in supply and demand. In order to allocate resources efficiently, economies need scarcity prices rather than just prices. In general, political and religious authorities tend to support what they believe to be just (but which are in fact inefficient) prices. Where trade crosses political borders, where neighboring political units compete rather than collude with each other, no authority can make just prices prevail. Again, political conflict undercuts the ability of governments (that control only part of the economically relevant area) to do much harm.

Within jurisdictions it was difficult to evade traditional pricing. Insofar as trade moved across political boundaries, however, there were no powerful guardians of traditional prices. The merchants, of course, preferred to buy cheap and to sell dear. In politically fragmented Europe nobody could effectively interfere with the self-seeking inclinations of merchants engaged in trade between jurisdictions. Markets first became liberated, i.e., free to respond to changes in demand and supply, at the interstate level. Later, pricing according to demand and supply spread to the domestic economies. But political fragmentation was important in creating an opening for rational pricing and ultimately for an efficient and growth-promoting allocation of resources.

Of course, interstate trade is not the only determinant of the liberation of prices from tradition. As Sombart (1917/1969, p. 197) has pointed out, the increased flow of silver and gold from the Americas to Western Europe in itself contributed to the undermining of traditional prices within Europe. A rapidly expanding amount of cash chased a less rapidly expanding amount of goods for long periods of time and thereby disturbed traditional pricing patterns. Moreover, the increasing number of merchants and of buyers and sellers and the increasing integration of previously localized markets because of slowly improving transport, communication, and information made it more difficult to defend traditional, or just, prices. For those benefiting from such prices, their maintenance is a collective good. But the procurement of collective goods becomes more and more difficult with increasing group size (Olson, 1965).

The liberation of prices and capitalist development were pushed by (overlapping) marginal groups that had sometimes been created, sometimes been tolerated, and often been harassed and persecuted by "legitimate authorities" (e.g., through expulsion or religious discrimination): for example, itinerant hawkers, strangers, heretics, and Jews. The very marginalization of these groups weakened their identification with the mainstream way of doing things. According to Sombart (1917/1969), these pockets of malintegration within Western societies contributed heavily to capitalist development. In addition, I want to underline that these insecure and free-floating groups could avoid extinction as a social phenomenon largely because the political and religious fragmentation of Europe prevented secular and spiritual leaders from imposing sterile conformity.

Compared to the great Asian civilizations, European development is special in several respects. Authority in Europe was always limited by conflict, disunity, and fragmentation. Individual responsibility and decision-making could slowly grow among vassals, in cities, and among Protestants. Limited government and fragmented religion contributed to the generation of the ideas of individualism, liberty, and personal responsibility. Fragmentation of authority has been the determinant of West European ideological developments. European political fragmentation and ideology contributed to capitalism and economic growth by dispersing economic decisionmaking in an environment of relatively secure property rights. It is important to recognize that individual self-determination contributed to scientific and economic innovation. Even perfectly democratic participation in collective decisionmaking could not serve as a substitute but as a barrier to innovation.

European progress in science and in the economy is rooted in the same political circumstances. The limitation of government by fragmentation generated room for experimentation, innovation, and unorthodox research. The market could reject bad products and reward innovative entrepreneurs. While some European governments and churches attempted to suppress certain ideas and even persecuted scholars, suppression and persecution could never be sustained and consistently applied throughout Europe. Ultimately, scientists could reject false theories even if they were favored by kings, governments, or churches.[8] Since the late nineteenth century scientific progress has itself become a major force of economic growth in the developed Western nations (Kuznets, 1966; Maddison, 1982; Rosenberg and Birdzell, 1986).

Interstate rivalry among comparatively small states does not prevent persecution of minorities within states, but it mitigates the effects of such persecution.[9] Jews and Christian heretics often had to leave their homes in order to escape such oppression. Often they found a new home in other European states or in North America. They took their knowledge with them and helped spread innovation across the West. The role of Protestant refugees from France in strengthening the economies of Holland and Prussia is probably the best-known example of the diffusion of productive techniques by refugees. Again, these beneficial effects derived from the limitation of power of European governments by conflict among relatively small states.

To summarize this analysis of European history: The point of departure is a system of competing states. Conflict among states constituted a forerunner to and a functional equivalent of constitutional limitations of governmental authority. Interstate rivalry provided "checks and balances" before constitutions did. Limited government, relatively safe property rights for the lower strata of society, and an *incapability* of suppressing scarcity prices or innovations from above and of suppressing the spread of innovations by refugees contributed to the rise of capitalism in the West. The creeping empowerment of producers and traders in West European history enabled Europe and North America to overcome mass poverty and mass starvation before the great Asian civilizations did.[10] The greater degree of freedom in Europe, the greater degree to which European producers and traders could make their own decisions (and reap most of the benefits therefrom), largely resulted from interstate competition in Europe and led to miraculous economic growth.

If political fragmentation and European disunity are as important determinants of the European miracle as I have argued, how could the United States, with its central government, avoid stagnation? After all, the United States did avoid involvement in European wars in the nineteenth century. International rivalry cannot have contributed significantly to limited government and safe property rights, but the United States benefited from two functional equivalents to the rivalries between European princes, states, and nations. First, there was the open western frontier, which allowed people to escape from governments they disliked. Second, the member states of the union jealously safeguarded states' rights. Since citizens, talent, and capital could easily move from one state to another, there was some kind of competition among states. As in Europe, this competition limited the capability of politicians to do harm.

Rosenberg and Birdzell (1986, p. 138) make this point and raise the question of whether constitutional developments, i.e., the shift of power from the states to Washington, might be a contributing factor in the decline of the United States:[11]

> It may be that a prerequisite to sustained economic growth is an economy trading across a geographical area divided among a number of rival states, each too small to dream of imperial wars and too fearful to impose massive exactions on its own sphere. The United States had a federal system in the nineteenth and early twentieth century in which political intervention by the national government was narrowly restricted by political tradition and

constitutional interpretation, while political intervention by the state governments was restricted by the fear of economic competition from other states. Whether the constitutional reconstruction of the United States as a classic empire is compatible with indefinitely sustained growth is, of course, a topical and controversial question.

The essentials are limited government and respect for producers' and merchants' property rights.

European principalities and kingdoms in the early modern age differed in the degree to which kings and princes could eliminate the privileges of the nobility and of city-based merchants and artisans. Some European states became more absolutist than others.[12] The Netherlands and England were less absolutist, Spain and France more so; i.e., the political power of the crown was most severely restricted in the Netherlands and in England, which led to capitalist economic development in the seventeenth and eighteenth centuries.[13] Once more we perceive the economic benefits of relatively limited government.

In England there was some rivalry between king and parliament and between the royal courts and common law courts. Neither king and royal courts nor parliament and common law courts could provide monopoly rights to producers and guilds. The royal courts could uphold special privileges granted by the king, but common law courts might disagree. Therefore, special privileges were hardly enforceable and of little if any value. Under such circumstances it does not pay for producers and merchants to obtain special privileges from a government divided against itself. By contrast, in absolutist France special privileges were enforceable and were an object of contention among economic actors. Whereas English entrepreneurs had to adapt to the market, French entrepreneurs could hope to escape from competition by buying royal favors. Therefore, England escaped early from the mercantilist rent-seeking society and its overregulated economy and outpaced the more populous France, where government officials found it much easier to interfere with the economy, to distort prices, and to reduce the efficiency of market allocations for the shortsighted benefit of the royal treasury (Ekelund and Tollison, 1981).

In this account the industrial revolution is a specific phase in the rise of the West. It began in Britain earlier than elsewhere. Mann (1993, p. 101) observes of early industrial Britain that "states had long regulated wages, apprenticeships, and prices, established monopolies, and granted licenses for large enterprises; but by 1820, wage, apprentice, and union restraints were removed, and most intranational trade was freed from monopolies." This observation is compatible with my causal claim about the benefits of limited government, deregulation, and free markets. Elsewhere, Mann

(1993, p. 96) makes another observation regarding the industrial revolution that is compatible with a Hayekian skepticism about large-scale planning and an endorsement of individual or family entrepreneurship:

> Bestriding this world were small masters, jobbers, traders, engineers, and independent artisans, mixing their own labor with small amounts of family capital—the classic petite bourgeoisie. It was their Industrial Revolution—perhaps the greatest class achievement in history—and yet they were not organized as a class. They did not need their own extensive organization. A civil society was already institutionalized in agriculture and commerce, its "invisible hand" promoting development intended by no one.

Finally, Mann (1993, p. 284) makes an observation about the industrial revolution that underlines the importance of initiative from below rather than guidance from the top: "From 1815, Western industrialization was inherently transnational. Such massive expansion of interregional commodity exchange could not be controlled by the feeble infrastructures of contemporary states. Not states but private property owners initiated economic growth, most of which emerged interstitially to state rule through fairly free markets."

In Europe, political and religious fragmentation generated limited government, relatively secure property rights for producers and merchants, and individualism as a generalized approach to life. Political philosophy and the nascent science of political economy (or economics) elaborated on, justified, and systematized these achievements. The French philosopher Montesquieu theorized about the separation of governmental powers and the autonomy of legislative, executive, and judicial functions. He recognized the importance of using power to check power and turned this idea into a constitutional principle. Montesquieu's writing was stimulated by observation of the English rather than the French system of government.[14] It has probably had some influence on the U.S. constitution, where checks and balances, i.e., the separation of governmental powers, have been taken most seriously. Montesquieu was largely interested in the limitation of the powers of an absolutist king, but for the framers of the U.S. constitution "the separation of powers was at least in part a means to protect property" (Riker, 1965, p. 139). One should not bemoan this concern with the security of property rights. In effect, it is a concern with the background conditions of economic development, growth, and prosperity.

My crude and short look at Montesquieu and the separation of powers serves to make two points. First, political ideas and theorizing depend on political experiences. The relatively limited character of some European governments led to the perception of the advantages of the limitation of governmental power. Second, Europe and even its North American daughter societies have been parts of a single civilization in which ideas could spread from country to country. Therefore, advances on the road to liberty in one European country could contribute to further advances elsewhere in Europe and even in European-settled North America.

The demise of absolutism and mercantilism in the late eighteenth century was accompanied by another important intellectual development. In 1776 Adam Smith published his book *An Inquiry into the Nature and Causes of the Wealth of Nations* and thereby founded the discipline of economics (or political economy). This theoretical breakthrough occurred only after the liberation of markets had already gone some way. But Smith and the other classical economists of his day, and later the neoclassical economists, or the monetarists, or the Austrian school, and the contemporary public choice theorists tirelessly attacked and continue to attack restrictive practices upheld by governmental authority,[15] such as protectionism and other follies favored first by royal and—it is sad but true—later by democratic governments. Mainstream economics from Adam Smith to the likes of Brunner (1985), Friedman (1962), or Hayek (1960) not only provided a theoretical analysis of what is but also campaigned for the limitation of government and the liberation of individuals from arbitrary rule.

2. War, Capitalism, and Democracy

In the Middle Ages and in the early modern age up to the French Revolution, interstate rivalry contributed to the limitation of governmental power, to securing property rights, and to the liberation of market forces. After the Revolutionary and Napoleonic Wars, nationalism—often wedded to democratic egalitarianism—became an important ideology and a determinant of the fighting spirit of troops. Widening popular participation in war increased the scale of warfare. Later, capitalist industrialization led to a further escalation in the cost, severity, and destructiveness of Western wars. The U.S. Civil War was a precursor of the bloody and protracted wars to come in the twentieth century. The escalating costs of war and its preparation even in peacetime, the conscription of able-bodied young men, and the ever-expanding mobilization of human and economic resources in the service of war began to undermine the autonomy of the economy. This undermining was not a smooth process affecting all European nations alike or at the same time. In the comparatively peaceful nineteenth century the process was much more muted than in the war-torn twentieth century. Continental Europe was affected earlier, more strongly, and more permanently than Britain or North America. But European war economies came to look like centrally planned economies. Indeed, some of them became models for centrally planned economies. Thus, war or the concern with national security even in peacetime, as well as Marxism and to a lesser degree even Keynesianism, contributed to the weakening of the autonomy of the market economy and to the legitimization of expanding state activities.

There is a complex argument in my explanatory sketch. For the period before the Revolutionary and Napoleonic Wars, I have credited interstate rivalry with the generation of the space for an autonomous market economy to develop. For the period after those wars, I charge interstate rivalry with contributing to the restriction of the operating space for the market economy or to the increase of state control over the human and material resources of society (Gurr, Jaggers, and Moore, 1990). In my view, the effects of interstate rivalry on economic performance are conditional on other factors. Given the oligarchical states and societies as well as fairly limited popular participation in fighting before the French Revolution, interstate rivalry was able to play a part in weakening the ruling elites vis-à-vis the rising capitalist merchants and entrepreneurs. Later, given nationalistic, egalitarian, and democratic ideologies and widening popular participation in war, interstate rivalry forced governments to penetrate economy and society, to prepare the economy for a semipermanent state of war, and even to mobilize for total war. After wars, state expenditures could come down but usually not to prewar levels. National security or the necessities of war served to legitimize protectionism and even the goal of autarky as well as national control of pivotal industries.

Actually, the relationships between risk of war, limited government, and democratization are so complex as to border on the confusing. While I do insist that interstate rivalry for centuries—at least until the French Revolution—promoted rulers' acceptance of subjects' property rights, I must admit that war-making and standing armies have had less beneficial effects as well.[16] Porter (1994, p. 10) describes some of them:

> The military power required to defend against foreign aggression can easily be turned to internal repression. A government at war is a juggernaut of centralization determined to crush any internal opposition that impedes the mobilization of militarily vital resources. This centralizing tendency of war has made the rise of the state throughout much of history a disaster for human liberty and rights, a triumph of raw power abetted by conditions of large-scale violence.

After the French Revolution, war-making in Europe tended to increase the power of the state, its rulers, and its agents at the expense of producers and subjects who were destined to suffer from higher taxation and conscription by ever stronger states. According to Porter (1994, p. 169) this extension of state power should be attributed not to industrialization per se but to its conjunction with war:

During the first century, the Industrial Revolution coincided almost everywhere with the *erosion* of mercantilist structures, the *elimination* of international barriers to trade, and the *reduction* of international tariffs. Only in the era of High Imperialism did pressures arise for the reintroduction of state economic regulation and higher tariffs; only after the two world wars did Europe witness the emergence of full-fledged regulatory states in which central command measures were as important as the market in mobilizing large-scale human effort. In short it was not industrialization per se that brought the state back into the economy—it was the industrialization of war.

Still, war-making and the preparation for war also promoted egalitarianism and to a lesser degree even democracy, as has already been noted by Weber (1923/1981, pp. 278–279, my translation): "Everywhere the basis of democratization is purely military in character. . . . Military discipline implied the triumph of democracy, because the participation of the non-noble masses was needed; once they had received arms, they also got political power." This argument has been carefully elaborated and illustrated by reference to a wide range of historical evidence by Andreski (1968a). Moreover, the relationship between military participation and egalitarianism in income distribution has received some, though not unqualified, support in a number of cross-national studies (Garnier and Hazelrigg, 1977; Weede and Jagodzinski, 1981/1987; Weede and Tiefenbach, 1981a; Dixon and Moon, 1986;[17] Chan, 1989; Weede, 1992c; 1993b).[18] In the late nineteenth century, Bismarck's simultaneous policy of the repression of social democrats and the laying of the foundation of the German welfare state demonstrated that preparation for war or concern about troop loyalty might be more effective in eliciting material concessions from the ruling classes to the masses than in fostering true democracy.[19]

The roots of democracy may be general military participation, as among Swiss men (Porter, 1994, pp. 50–53), or they might be the survival of the medieval "Ständestaat" and its representative institutions. Although absolutism replaced representative rule throughout most of continental Europe in the sixteenth and seventeenth centuries, remnants of the Ständestaat did survive in England and in Holland (Downing, 1992).[20] Because of England's privileged geopolitical location and its relative security behind the English Channel, English kings did not need to tax their subjects as heavily as, say, Prussia's. They did not need large standing armies and big administrations for taxation, conscription, and provisioning of large armed forces. Thus, representative institutions could survive, and later limit the prerogatives of the crown, and still later—in the nineteenth and twentieth centuries—become increasingly more encompassing.

While the military revolution of the sixteenth and seventeenth centuries reduced the number of states and increased the power of rulers over citizens, the impact of war on the slow process of democratization was not entirely negative even then. As Goldstone (1991, p. 479) has noticed, "the critical catalyst of democracy has most often been defeat in war." This observation is true for England in 1688; for France in 1870–1871; and of course for Germany, Italy, and Japan after World War II. In my view it is best, however, to put this observation into a much broader framework. By and large, lost wars undermine all regimes (see Bueno de Mesquita, Siverson, and Woller, 1992, for systematic evidence from the nineteenth and twentieth centuries).[21] Where and when most regimes are autocratic, the new regime may enter the path of democratization. One should, however, keep Huntington's (1991, p. 35) warning in mind: "Circumstances that contribute to the initial establishment of a democratic regime also may not contribute to its consolidation and long-term stability." The breakdown of the Weimar Republic in Germany, born out of defeat in World War I, provides a vivid illustration of this statement.

Whether democracy, once established, stands much of a chance of growing roots and surviving seems to depend very much on economic performance, as has been suggested by Lipset (1959; 1994). For example, British representative government became ever more encompassing in the nineteenth century when Britain was the economically dominant power. Except for black slavery, the United States was almost born democratic, and by the early twentieth century it had become a leading economic power whose wealth could easily underwrite democracy. Whether German, Italian, and Japanese democracy could have survived a protracted recession instead of economic miracles after World War II may well be doubted.

Some degree of rule of law, of safe property rights, and of individual liberty for broad categories of people preceded capitalism and was a prerequisite for its development. But capitalism itself preceded democracy, as we currently understand the term.[22] While England experienced representative government at least since 1689, only at the end of World War I were voting rights extended to most of the adult population. Thus, British capitalism preceded full democracy in Britain. The precedence of capitalism before democracy is even clearer in Germany. France is a more complicated case because of political instability and regime changes from more to less democratic regimes and back in the nineteenth century. Even in the United States we observe the temporal precedence of capitalism. Private property, some reasonable degree of rule of law, and production for the market existed under British colonial rule, i.e., before independence and the introduction of democracy.

So the temporal order of the "creeping" establishment of capitalism and the discrete, indeed often traumatic, steps toward the establishment of democracy is compatible with Berger's (1993, pp. 5–6) summary statements: "Capitalism is a necessary—though not sufficient—condition for democracy, but democracy is *not* a precondition for capitalism . . . it is the consequences of capitalism, *not* the motives of capitalists that create the space for democracy. . . . It opens the social space for civil society, and as people become more affluent they develop more ambitious political aspirations." In my view, there are essentially two reasons why capitalism "opens the social space for democracy." One has been widely recognized since Lipset's (1959) pathbreaking early work. The prosperity generated by capitalism makes the fulfillment of many different demands, i.e., compromise between the lower and upper strata of society, possible. Equally important is the fact that capitalism divorces political from economic power and thereby reduces the concentration of power within society. The capitalist separation of political power and economic power is essential in giving voice and choice to ordinary people who would be overawed if facing a unified ruling class commanding the army, the police, and the prisons as well as disposing of jobs (compare Bhagwati, 1993a, p. 34). Moreover, prosperous capitalism often provides electoral losers with an opportunity to make more money than they ever did while in office. Capitalism generates the foundations for the compatibility of government and participation from below.[23] Whether this compatibility is more than a transient achievement is an issue to be taken up in Chapter 6, Section 1, where the possibility, or even likelihood, of a decline of the West is discussed.

3. The Great Asian Civilizations

In the early Middle Ages there can be no doubt that China was a more advanced society than Western Europe economically, technologically, and scientifically. By the nineteenth century, however, the West had clearly overtaken China. As I argued earlier, property rights are the key to understanding these developments. In China producers', and even more merchants', property rights were very insecure. Where traders are harassed by the authorities, transaction costs are increased and the division of labor in society is restricted. Thus, restricting trade is tantamount to restricting productivity growth and economic development. But imperial China developed an ideology to justify this mistreatment of merchants. Yang (1987, p. 64) analyzes it in these terms:

> Confucianists tended to regard farm production as the "root" . . . of society, and commercial activity as the "branch" . . . to maintain a good society, the root must be strong. Accordingly, peasants were given a status next to literati, and merchants were denounced as speculators and given a lower status in the society. Because political power was controlled by the landed

literati, it is natural that taxation was designed to reinforce this belief in social order. The merchants were taxed but rarely protected in their rights. In fact, the commercial tax was used as a means to suppress commercial activities. . . . An individual . . . registered as merchant was ordered to pay twice as much poll tax. . . . In addition to these social discriminations, the merchant's property rights were not respected by imperial authorities. Not only the merchant's property was subject to arbitrarily high commercial taxes, but the imperial government frequently demanded "loans" from merchants, which sometimes caused them to fail. . . . The insecurity of merchants' property had the expected result of impeding trade.

To a somewhat lesser but still to a significant degree, peasants also suffered from insecure property rights. The Chinese emperor claimed to be the ultimate owner of the land.[24] This idea legitimated numerous imperial redistributions of land. By and large, the safety of property rights in land depended on political connections. Families with a degree-holder or, better still, an imperial official in their ranks were fairly safe. Families without political connections were likely to suffer and to lose their property. Thus, Confucian education, tenure of official positions, and de facto land ownership were strongly correlated. The idea of rights for those at the bottom of the social hierarchy was firmly resisted. Imperial orders or law were solely means to constrain the lower classes—i.e., peasants, artisans, and merchants—never means to protect them from their rulers.

In general, reliance on law was suspect in China.[25] Instead of law, the Chinese believed that custom and virtue should regulate social affairs. Confucius himself expressed the superiority of virtue over mere penal codes in these words (according to Fu, 1993, p. 31): "Lead the people by administrative measures and regulate them by penal punishment, the people will not commit crimes but have no sense of shame. Lead the people by virtue and regulate them by decorum, they will have a sense of shame and be upright." But virtue was a matter of status. A contract between a degree-holding land owner and his tenant would bind the tenant to a much greater degree than the land owner. Indeed, the land owner would not even have to sign the agreement. Nor would he be summoned to court if a tenant had a complaint against him (Yang, 1987, pp. 29–30). Insecure property rights for those actually engaged in production or trade must have significantly reduced the incentives to work hard.

The Confucian preference for custom over law has some advantages. Custom arises spontaneously rather than by conscious legislative action. It preserves the social capital or knowledge of previous generations without the need to make them conscious and publishable in law codes. Custom is enforced by diffuse social disapproval against those who do not respect it rather than by government and the police. Therefore, a custom-based society seems less likely to suffer from ever-expanding regimentation by a busy legislature, an exploding bureaucracy, and an overburdened police. The charm of custom compared with law is that it seems less disposable *because* custom is a gift from previous generations. It is found rather than invented or proclaimed (by the current generation). Therefore, most special-interest groups will prefer to write their own laws or to let legislators dependent upon their political support write them for them. A custom-based social order appears more likely to be compatible with limited government than a law-based order because the short-term disposability of law invites overregulation and the growth of government.[26]

But not all advantages rest with custom, nor do all disadvantages rest with law. According to William Graham Sumner (1906/1940), societies evolve. In the early stages of their development they primarily rely on folkways, then on mores or customs, and thereafter on stateways or laws. A major difference between these types of norms is that consciousness is minimized with folkways and maximized with laws. Moreover, law is much more likely to be internally consistent and coherent than folkways or even mores. If Sumner's evolutionary proposition is accepted, then it seems undesirable for a society to be stuck with a custom-based social order.

According to Max Weber (1922/1964), there are three types of authority or legitimate rule (i.e., Herrschaft). First, there is traditional authority; second, there is charismatic authority; third, there is rational or legal authority. Implicit in this typology is again some evolutionary conception. Rational or legal authority arrives last in human history. It has been fully developed only in the West. Moreover, in his economic history Weber (1923/1981, p. 240) insisted on capitalism's need for predictable law and adjudication. In the Weberian view, the development of the rule of law and of rational (in contrast to exploitative and speculative) capitalism are closely related to each other. Concerning the value of predictable law for the economy, i.e., for a private enterprise market economy, I see little difference between Weber and Hayek (1973-1976-1979) except that Hayek admires the common law tradition, in which the distinction between custom and law is somewhat blurred compared with the Roman and continental European tradition. Accepting Weber's judgment that predictable law and adjudication are indispensable for a modern and prosperous economy, we arrive at the question of whether custom is sufficient to order complex and rapidly changing societies. Since custom is a gift of the ancestors, the embodiment of their wisdom, it is hard to see how custom can avoid losing ground in a society undergoing rapid change. Since custom is less explicit and less coherent than law—this is Sumner's (1906/1940) point—customary regulation may suffer from a lack of consistency and therefore predictability. Admittedly, law and its application in adjudication are unlikely to achieve perfect consistency and predictability either. But law is likely to be both more adaptable to rapid social change and more coherent and predictable than custom, especially where custom denies rights to the lower strata of society.

I return now to the issue of why the Confucian social order of China under the Ming and Manchu dynasties did not promote economic growth and development more effectively. The Confucian classics say little about property rights and the function of scarcity prices in balancing demand and supply, nor do they praise competition. Taken together, these gaps in Confucianism provide a wide opening for bad administration and defective economic policies.

While the Western tradition for centuries tended to underscore equality before the law (or under the law), the Chinese tradition always attempted to achieve social harmony by the application of hierarchical principles of social organization. A young Chinese scholar (Yang 1987, p. 8) summarizes that tradition in the following way:

> Inequality was regarded by the Chinese as another fundamental value. Seeing the submission of persons in inferior positions as an important condition for achieving harmonious family relationships, the Chinese saw the principle of inequality as indispensable to a peaceful society. The emphasis on inequality in institutional arrangements implies that political authorities should not be bound by the same laws as bind other people. The "constitutionalism" developed in Western Europe was thus unknown to the Chinese. If this is the case, property rules developed by people at the bottom would have less effect in constraining the people above them . . . imperial law would be seen as a device less to protect individual rights than to regulate individual behavior.

So the substance of Chinese custom, with its stress on hierarchy and subordination, did little to constrain the degree-holding ruling class and little to protect private property rights. Over time the hierarchical nature of Chinese society became ever more pronounced. Peasants or merchants never had rights against rulers. As Fu (1993, p. 65) points out:

> The emperor could arbitrarily dismiss, punish, reward or execute any official at his pleasure. . . . During the Tang dynasty (618–907), senior ministers could sit together with the emperor when discussing matters of state. During the Song dynasty (960–1234), officials had to stand erect in the presence of his majesty. Beginning with the Ming dynasty (1368–1640), even grand councillors had to kneel in the austere presence of the Son of Heaven. . . . It was also during the Ming dynasty that the practice of having ministers beaten by eunuchs at the command of the emperor during court meetings was institutionalized. . . . During the Qing period (1644–1911), court officials had to prostrate themselves before the emperor, kow-tow, and call themselves "your Majesty's humble slave."

If this is the treatment members of the privileged classes have to face, then the position of the masses must be fairly desperate.

According to North (1981; 1990), it is the state that succeeds or fails in protecting the property rights of producers. The degree of success or failure influences transaction costs, which determine the effective size of the market and the degree of the division of labor that is feasible in society. Thus, failure to specify and protect the property rights of producers and merchants has far-reaching implications. State failure undermines incentives to work hard and to trade, i.e., to realize mutually beneficial exchanges; it undermines the incentive to save and invest; and it interferes with the ability of numerous people at the bottom of social hierarchies to put their own practical knowledge to its best use.

Against the odds and in spite of discrimination by officials, some Chinese merchants became very wealthy, but there was little incentive for them to remain in the dishonored business class. While China was never as open in practice as in theory, it was possible for a merchant to buy a Confucian education for his sons. They might become degree-holders and even imperial officials. If they succeeded, the family could become a respected and safe land-owning family. Thus, talent and capital were always diverted from business and channeled into land ownership and officialdom (Levy, 1953–1954; Chan, 1993, p. 18). In this way even the openness of Chinese social structures contributed to the prevention of capitalist development.

Traditional China suffered from arbitrary government, insecure property rights, meddlesome officials, and governmental brakes on the development of markets. If a European prince had insisted on this type of political framework, he would have suffered from an erosion of his tax base, from a flight of merchants and capital owners, possibly even from a flight of peasants. In politically unified China, neither merchants nor peasants could find refuge elsewhere. With Hall (1985, p. 102) one may summarize the explanation for China's failure in these terms: "In the West, the absence of empire removed the crucial bureaucratic block on the development of market forces; merchants persecuted in one place could always go with their capital elsewhere." Whereas the West prospered because of political disunity and the limitation of arbitrary rule that was thereby enforced, China failed to develop because of the burden of unlimited and arbitrary rule.

Whereas political and denominational fragmentation in Western Europe left room for curiosity, innovation, and the growth of knowledge—after the late nineteenth century this knowledge itself became an engine of economic growth—Chinese intellectual life was structured in such a way as to stifle innovation. One's social standing as an intellectual depended on passing state-administered examinations as well as on thereafter becoming an imperial official. While there were some private academies in imperial China, the imperial state was ultimately the sole employer of intellectuals and the arbiter of their social status. The state prescribed what young scholars had to learn and proscribed what they must not study. Such a system rewards conformity instead of innovation and progress.[27] Although there have been periods of history, such as the Warring States Period before the unification of China or the Southern Sung dynasty, when this state had to face equals (Rossabi, 1983), for much of the time the system worked to "stabilize" society. The Chinese scholar Fu (1993, p. 102) evaluates the system as follows:

> The social cost of imposing official orthodoxy and perpetuating autocracy was also tremendous. It barred intellectual innovation and discouraged genuine scholarship, especially during the Ming-Qing period, when the best intellects went into documentary research and historiography. The sterility and stalemate of Chinese scholarship after the establishment of official orthodox Confucianism since the Han dynasty was in glaring contrast to the period of the Warring States, when a hundred schools of thought were contending.

Although Pye (1985, p. 21) does not sympathize with rational choice, property rights, and transaction-cost approaches to development, he makes an observation about power and, implicitly, responsibility in Asia that permits an interpretation fitting well with the general thrust of this book: "In most of Asia . . . to have power was to be spared the chore of decision-making. In such Asian cultures the aspiration that impelled people up the ladder of power was that they might eventually rise above the need to trouble themselves with decisions. Decisions are what vex the minds of the weak and make life troublesome. In Asia, achieving power meant becoming free of care and having subordinates who themselves were taxed with the problems of decision-making." In my reading, such an attitude amounts to a systematic denial of responsibility, to an unwillingness to be held responsible. Such an attitude is helpful neither for good government, nor for running an economy, nor for attempting to correct market failure. In my view, such an attitude stands little chance of developing and spreading in a competitive interstate system such as those that have existed in Europe for centuries.[28]

Although Japan has been influenced by neighboring China, Japanese politics, society, and economy have always had distinctive characteristics. In some respects, Japan shared similarities with Western Europe; in other respects with China. Like China, Japan *seemed* to be a unified state ruled by a shogun during the Tokugawa period from the early seventeenth to the mid-nineteenth century. Like the Chinese emperor in the fifteenth century, the seventeenth-century Japanese shogun prohibited the construction of ocean-going vessels, forbade Japanese subjects to sail the high seas, and severely restricted trade with the Europeans (Kennedy, 1987, pp. 14–15). This isolationist policy nearly cut Japan off from the modernizing influences that cross-cultural contact is likely to bring. But the Tokugawa system of rule did not establish anything like a unified empire (Tominaga, 1989, p. 173; 1990, p. 43). Instead, one may regard Tokugawa Japan as a unipolar system of powers in which the shogun was the hegemon but other territorial rulers *(daimyos)* remained largely sovereign in running domestic affairs in their territories *(hans)*. According to Jones (1988, p. 165) this state of affairs struck just the right balance between promoting economic unity and a sizeable market on the one hand and limiting political power and the corresponding potential for abuse on the other hand: "Just enough seems to have been done to achieve national economies of scale while leaving the hans in competition with each other."

The large market, urbanization, and Tokugawa peace promoted commercialization and regional specialization in Japan. So did the shogun's requirement that daimyos reside in the capital city for part of the year and that they should leave family members as hostages in the capital at any time. This residence pattern generated a demand for liquidity and forced rulers into symbiotic relationships with merchants. Japanese merchants did not enjoy the prestige and autonomy that merchants in some West European cities had. They did not have the opportunity, as did rich Chinese merchants, to make their sons study the Confucian classics, to take imperial examinations, and to thereafter move the family from the despised merchant class to the gentry. Instead, they were forced to remain merchants to serve their political superiors and their customers in general. In contrast to the Chinese economy, the closure of the Japanese stratification system preserved talent and capital in a crucial sector of the economy (Levy, 1953–1954).

Although Japan was largely cut off from foreign ideas and imports during the Tokugawa period, its agriculture benefited from innovations and new plants acquired from Western traders in the sixteenth century, i.e., before Japan closed herself off: treadmills and Dutch pumps; sugarcane, sweet potatoes, and maize (Jones, 1988, p. 155). Moreover, Japanese agriculture benefited from institutional reforms. Communal farming was replaced by nuclear-family farms (Jones, 1988, p. 154), and taxpaying farmers had secure tenure on the land even though they could not freely dispose of it (Hall, 1964, p. 23). By and large, peasants faced incentives to produce.

Administration in Tokugawa Japan was effective and penetrated deep into society. At the end of the period, in the midnineteenth century, "there were rank and income registers, land registers, tax records, budgets, financial records, personnel records, religious inspection records, dossiers on adjucation of disputes, diaries of petitions, diaries of decisions—almost any conceivable administrative document. Every individual, whether samurai status or lower, was known to the government and registered on some official roster" (Hall, 1964, p. 35). Given the density of government and administration, Hall (1964, p. 27) concludes, "few people in pre-modern times have lived under such a heavy load of official regulation and supervision as the Tokugawa Japanese."[29]

From a Weberian perspective (1923/1981; aptly summarized by Collins,

1980), a *literate* administration may be a useful background condition for predictable rules, that is, law and order, and therefore for economic development. From a Hayekian or rent-seeking perspective, with its corresponding expectation of government failure, one has to look to what the Tokugawa government actually did and how it affected incentives and transaction costs. Many tollgates and checkpoints were abolished. Guild monopolies were broken. Trade was made freer than before (Jones, 1988, p. 162). Thus, the government turned *against* some restrictive practices and distributional coalitions. The government standardized measurements and unified scales and coinage (Jones, 1988, p. 164). Such measures do reduce transaction costs and thereby contribute to gains from trade.

Japan's outperformance of mainland Asia in fact predated the 1868 Meiji Restoration. By the midnineteenth century, the Japanese standard of living may have already been at a level similar to the British standard (Jones, 1988, pp. 36, 158). Moreover, the Japanese level of literacy was remarkable. Thus, Japan was uniquely positioned, among the non-Western societies, to join the modern industrial world.

While the burden of empire and the arbitrary rule that a huge empire permits can carry most of the burden in explaining the divergent developments in the West and in China, the burden of empire is a less satisfying explanation in the Indian and Islamic cases. True, property rights were insecure in these regions too (see Jones, 1981), but in India there was a long period of disunity and fragmentation between the Maurya and Mughal dynasties. In contrast to Western Europe, where states such as Portugal, Spain, France, England, Switzerland, the Netherlands, and to a lesser degree Austria and Prussia have been fairly stable over centuries, most Indian polities enjoyed a much shorter life span. According to Hall (1985), the very fact of political instability itself contributed to rulers' shortsightedness and limited horizons in calculating policy benefits. In the short run, preying on subjects and confiscation are always more profitable than concessions to producers and traders and the economic growth permitted thereby. The best political background for the development of safe property rights and low transaction costs is neither imperial stability—which India had for a while under the Mughals, though not for as long as China—nor long periods of turmoil and political instability. Instead the existence of a fairly stable interstate system is best where most major states have reason to expect survival and thus a chance to reap policy benefits that need some time to develop.

The failure of India to develop cannot be explained without reference to social structure and religion, i.e., the caste system[30] (Weber, 1921/1978). In traditional Hindu society, one is born into a caste and is therefore destined to do a certain type of work. Doing something different from one's caste duty will influence one's rebirth after death. If one dutifully performs one's tasks, then one will be reborn in a higher caste in the next life. If one fails to execute one's duties, one is reborn in a lower caste, or even as an animal. Since failure to fulfill one's caste obligations may magically affect the prospects of other caste members, caste members observe each other and enforce ritual conformity. Such a ritualistic understanding of work is obviously a powerful hindrance to innovation. A faithful Hindu never knows whether new techniques of work are compatible with his or her traditional duties. Therefore, it is safer to not even try to do things differently from one's parents. Since mobility in this life is out of the question in any case, the incentive to try something new is blunted.

The caste system may also be analyzed from an interest-group perspective because castes engage in restrictive practices and may gain from the monopolization of certain occupations. Olson (1982, p. 157) observes: "Castes traditionally have behaved like guilds and other distributional coalitions. . . . They controlled entry into occupations and lines of business, kept craft mysteries or secrets, set prices monopolistically, used boycotts and strikes, and often bargained on a group rather than individual basis." Even caste endogamy served an anticompetitive function because it limited the number of legitimate practioners of trades. Without such limitations, sons-in-law originating from other castes might inflate the number of workers in a trade and increase competition. Although such restrictive practices may serve the members of castes or cartels, they also interfere with efficient resource allocation and economic growth.

In India, the *political* implications of religion must also be considered. While artisans and merchants could acquire political power in many European cities, they never could do so in Asia. In India, the right to rule and to make war was reserved to the warrior and ruler castes. Other castes, i.e., producers and merchants, were destined to be disarmed and were therefore at the mercy of the rulers and warriors. This gap in political power between arms-carrying and disarmed castes was further reinforced by some heterodox religious developments in India. For Buddhists and Jainas, all killing is illegitimate. While Buddhism is no longer important in India, and Jainas are a very small percentage of India's population, there have been periods in Indian history when these religions were more important than they are now, especially in towns. By forbidding killing, Jainism and Buddhism reinforced the helplessness of merchants and artisans against the ruling castes.[31]

Many of the Islamic countries suffered from long periods of political instability and the predatory orientation of rulers that frequently existed under such circumstances. However, the Ottoman empire was fairly stable for about half a millennium. It was huge, extending at its peak from Algeria to the Persian Gulf, from the Crimea and the Balkans to the south of the Arabian peninsula. Again, this was an empire whose vastness itself reduced exit opportunities for subjects. Moreover, Ottoman rulers largely relied on administrators and soldiers who were recruited from among foreigners, minorities, or even slaves. Weber (1922/1964, p. 171) calls such a system of rule "sultanism." It is characterized by maximizing the arbitrary decision-making latitude of rulers. Because the government's staff is recruited from outsiders on the fringes of society, its members are absolutely dependent on the ruler's mercy and are therefore dependable instruments to enforce his will (Goldstone, 1991, p. 376).

In principle, Islam has some characteristics that seem to destine Islamic nations for the rule of law and that might therefore deliver the proper political and legal background conditions for capitalism and economic development. Gellner (1981, p. 42) analyzes the relationship between law and worldly rule under Islam in the following terms:

> A faith in which theology is scarcely distinguishable from law, and in which the central corpus of law is sacred, thereby also acquires a kind of built-in separation of powers. The legislature is distinct from the executive power, for the simple reason that legislation is in principle ready-made and in theory complete, and pertains to God alone. This also gives a certain measure of independence to the judiciary: though they may be appointed by the ruler, they apply a law which cannot be the ruler's. For if legislation is God's, it is not the sultan's. The entire corpus of the law, and not just the constitution (which is absent), stands above the ruler.

While the holy law of Islam could in principle provide some limitation to arbitrary rule, it did not in fact work this way. The political implications of sultanism overwhelmed it, and probably had to overwhelm it, for reasons similar to those that made Chinese customs a poor substitute for rational law. Indeed, the holy law is even less flexible than mere customs or traditional social norms. In the ninth century the four main schools of Islamic law had already closed the gates of independent judgment *(ijtihad)* that might readjust the law to social change. Given social and political change, there is some need to invent new, lawlike regulations, as did the Ottoman sultans and some other Muslim rulers (Arjomand, 1992). Therefore, most Muslim societies—and certainly the Ottoman empire—had a dualistic tradition of law in which part of the law was at the disposal of arbitrary rulers.[32]

Compared with the arbitrary exercise of political power in most Muslim societies, where a greater degree of arbitrariness existed than in the West, specific proscriptions in Muslim holy law—such as the prohibition of interest and usury—matter much less. Muslim merchants aided by scholars found ways to elude such proscriptions (Rodinson, 1966). Nevertheless, I argue that the necessity of avoiding even the impression of charging interest must increase some types of transaction costs. This increase is itself undesirable, although it is probably but a minor explanatory factor in evaluating why Muslim societies, including the mighty Ottoman empire, did not successfully compete with the West.

In my view, the lack of an autonomous development of capitalism under Islam should not be blamed on religious doctrine or holy law but on political practice in Muslim societies. Whereas many working inhabitants of many European towns had already achieved citizen status in the Middle Ages—of course, this status was related to their military roles in defending their cities—their Muslim counterparts had not. Instead, political power in Muslim societies tended to rest either with sultans and an extremely dependent staff (minorities, foreigners, slaves) or with comparatively backward tribes (see Ibn Khaldun, ca. 1377/1958; Weber, 1922/1964; Gellner, 1981). If Islam itself—rather than Muslim political traditions—is no major obstacle to the establishment of capitalism, it also need not be an insurmountable obstacle to the establishment of democracy (Zartman, 1992). But the political traditions of Muslim countries do not bode well for the establishment of property rights respected by the authorities and therefore for capitalism or for democracy in the near future.

Notes

1. Barry (1994) and Vanberg (1994) have pointed to some tensions between Hayek's arguments in favor of a "constitution of liberty" and his evolutionary theory. While I accept the former, I contend that Hayek's evolutionary approach needs significant modification in order to become empirically meaningful instead of tautological.

2. This comparison refers to the Ming and Manchu dynasties, not to earlier periods. The Southern Sung dynasty, for example, had to face equals (Rossabi, 1983) in something like an interstate system. Significantly, McNeill (1982, p. 24) labels the first half of the second millenium "the era of Chinese predominance."

3. Today we are used to taking sovereignty as an all-or-none affair. In the (European) Middle Ages and in early modern times, however, princes could owe loyalty to kings or emperors, but their command of their own military forces made their behavior a matter of choice. So "sovereignty" has been a matter of degree, and sovereignties have been nested. Here, autonomy in everyday decisionmaking matters, not the degree of legal sovereignty. The "Holy Roman Empire" had more existence in legal myth than on the battlefield or in providing services or disservices to the economy.

4. In this interpretation of European economic history, "exit" is more important than "voice." By contrast, Hirschman (1970) is inclined to regard (collective) voice as a frequently preferable alternative to (individual) exit.

5. Since early European trade consisted mostly of mass-consumption goods (such as salt, grain, or ordinary wine), the merchandise value of each convoy was lower than in Asia, where long-distance trade mostly concerned luxuries. Trade in commodities for mass consumption implies more frequent convoys than trade in commodities for ruling-class consumption. Low unit value, combined with frequent occasions to collect fees for safe-conduct, makes it easier for rulers to concede property rights to merchants than the Asian pattern of moving goods of high value less frequently.

6. While specific estimates vary between 80 and 500 distinct European political units for the late fifteenth century, by the late nineteenth century the number of independent European states had fallen to about 30 (Tilly, 1990, pp. 45–46).

7. According to MacKinnon (1988a; 1988b), Calvin's doctrine of predestination had already lost its influence in seventeenth-century England. Calvin's frightening God was transformed to a merciful God, and the threat of eternal damnation was pushed into the background. Anxiety about one's salvation receded and could no longer provide the Weberian stimulus for hard work in order to learn whether one has been chosen by God. Moreover, good deeds became more and more important tools to acquire salvation; i.e., crucial doctrinal differences between Catholicism and Calvinism had been very much reduced.

8. Liberty in markets and liberty in science are closely related to each other not only by common political prerequisites or by promoting growth in their respective fields but also by a common philosophical foundation that focuses on choice, human fallibility, and criticism as well as on the superiority of a spontaneous order over planning (Popper, 1959; Hayek, 1960; 1973-1976-1979; 1988; Radnitzky, 1987b).

9. The most murderous periods of European history were those in which a single ruler (temporarily) succeeded in subduing large parts of Europe. Hitler and Stalin provide pertinent examples.

10. For some documentation of arbitrary rule and confiscation in the great Asian civilizations (China, India, Islam) and in Russia, and the corollary distortion of incentives and the increase of transaction costs, see Jones (1981), Pipes (1974), and Yang (1987).

11. This book does not investigate the specific issue of U.S. decline compared to other nations, including, for example, Germany. Instead my topic in Chapter 6, Section 1 is the decline of the West relative to East Asia. On the specific issue of U.S. decline, see, for example, Baldwin (1993), Huntington (1988–1989), Russett (1985), and Sandholtz et al. (1992).

12. Compared to Asian despotism, European "absolutism" was still something like limited and orderly government (see Andreski, 1964, p. 312, on Louis XIV).

13. According to Maddison (1982, p. 35), the agricultural share of employment came down to ca. 40 percent for the Netherlands in 1700, for the United Kingdom in 1820, and for the United States in 1890.

14. Montesquieu seems to have overestimated the degree of separation of powers in England. My concern here is not the adequacy of his perceptions but the impact of his and related ideas.

15. In this context, I intentionally omit mention of the Keynesians. In contrast to the other schools of thought, they legitimated state interference with the economy beyond the classical tasks of government, which consist of safeguarding domestic order and property rights as well as external security. In asking the state to achieve more than these limited goals, the Keynesians departed from what I believe to be the mainstream of the economic tradition. In industrial societies the state has to face an additional task: pollution control, or the protection of the environment.

16. The analysis of the relationships among warfare, military organization, and political order was pioneered by Otto Hintze (1941). More recently Tilly (1990, p. 14) has reemphasized the basic point that "state structure appeared chiefly as a by-product of rulers' efforts to acquire the means of war."

17. Dixon and Moon's study (1986) analyzes not income distributions but basic human-needs fulfillment. It finds that the military participation ratio has some positive effects. Since an equal distribution of income should promote basic needs fulfillment, their study provides indirect but supportive evidence.

18. Strangely, my earlier studies have been more supportive of the idea than the more recent ones. Military participation effects should be distinguished from military expenditure effects. A volume edited by Chan and Mintz (1992) provides a diversity of views on the latter topic.

19. As Tilly (1990, p. 106) has pointed out, preparation for war also extended the scope of public administration: "The garrisoning of troops within the country involved military officials and their civilian counterparts in food supply, housing, and public order. Eventually the health and education of all young males, which affected their military effectiveness, became governmental concerns. Thus military reorganization entered a wedge for expansion of state activity into what had previously been local and private spheres."

20. In fact, medieval constitutionalism itself had military roots. Because of the frequency of war in politically fragmented Europe, rulers needed the cooperation, or at least acquiescence, of the people and the taxpayers. Downing (1992, p. 31) has observed: "In exchange for financial support, more often than not in time of war, estates assumed increasing control of law making."

21. Porter (1994, pp. 196, 298) argues that war is also closely related to the birth of totalitarianism.

22. Although Rueschemeyer, Stephens, and Stephens (1992) emphasize the role of the working class in achieving full democracy, their writing is compatible with the argument advanced here. In their model, economic development affects class structures, which in turn affect the prospects of democracy.

23. Even skeptics about the linkage between capitalism and democracy ultimately have to accept it. Take, for example, Fukuyama (1993, p. 102): "Capitalism in itself does not generate direct pressures for democracy. . . . But capitalism is a more efficient engine of economic growth than socialism, and thus is more likely to generate the rapid economic change that favors the emergence of stable democracy." For views that downplay the role of wealth or capitalism as prerequisites, or at least as strongly facilitating conditions of democracy, see the review article by Shin (1994) and the literature quoted there. By and large, I remain unconvinced by this alternative approach.

24. According to Fu (1993, p. 17), this claim dates back to the Zhou dynasty, i.e., the first millennium B.C.

25. Although specialists such as Fu (1993) and Yang (1987) disagree somewhat about the role of law and especially of so-called legalism in Chinese thought, they concur in the judgment that law never provided significant protection for politically powerless people against officials or rulers. This point is what matters most for my purposes. By and large, my views are based much more on Yang's work than on Fu's because the latter author is less interested in the economic consequences of law and politics than the former. According to Pye (1985, p. 296), suspicion of law still holds today in Mainland China: "The idea that everyone else is scrupulously observing the general regulations is simply too implausible for most Chinese to believe."

26. Obviously, this analysis of Confucianism has been inspired by Hayek's (1973-1976-1979) analysis of common law compared to statute law.

27. Given the arbitrary and whimsical standards of imperial rule in China, conformity was not easily achieved, however hard one might try. Although scholar-officials in imperial China were exempt from the corporal punishments meted out to peasants, even the highest-ranking scholar-officials were not safe from flogging, persecution, and execution (Fu, 1993, pp. 126–142). Moreover, even an official's sons or father could be executed for the official's crimes, and his wife and daughters could be given into slavery.

28. Kammler (1990) has pointed to other attitudinal effects of political author-

ity extending to the limits of civilization. It is much more difficult even to imagine an alternative social order if there exists only a single administration within one's civilization. Given political competition between units within a single civilization, comparison may promote criticism and ultimately change.

29. Tominaga (1989, p. 179) also points out that administration in Tokugawa Japan penetrated to the village level, very much in contrast to imperial China.

30. There are two types of castes, *varna* and *jati*. The broad scheme (varna) distinguishes between brahmins (scholars or priests), *kshatriyas* (warriors or rulers or land owners), *vaishyas* (commoners or businessmen), *sudras* (laborers or servants), and untouchables. These varna are subdivided into thousands of jati. Jati differ by occupation, and many are found only in some regions of India. Not even the untouchables (certainly more than one hundred million people) are a homogeneous group. Untouchable castes may be untouchable for each other.

31. According to Weber (1921/1978), Jainism had some characteristics that were good for business and that did contribute to the success of many Jaina merchants. By obliging merchants to be honest and trustworthy, Jainism made a positive contribution to economic development. Because Jainism extended the prohibition against killing to all living beings, including worms in the soil or insects in the air, however, the rational organization of production was impossible for Jainas.

32. Even the four great masters and founders of Islamic law schools were mistreated by secular authorities: Three of them were imprisoned and one died in prison; two of them were beaten or flogged (Ahmed, 1988, pp. 48–49).

WHY PEOPLE STAY POOR ELSEWHERE

1. Is Dependency the Answer?

For a long time dependency theorists have suggested that the persistence of Third World poverty is not accidental, that somebody makes or keeps poor people poor, and that Northern affluence and Southern poverty are just two sides of a single coin. While dependency theorists disagree among themselves on exactly which mechanisms maintain Third World poverty, they tend to shift responsibility for poverty from the poor to the privileged. Since the general idea that the privileged make or keep poor people poor is so plausible, criticism of dependency theories—all of which (like dependency theory) comes from more or less privileged persons—sounds implausible, self-serving, and even immoral. That is why I cannot imagine that dependency theories will lose their grip on the minds of people because of anomalies, falsification, or destructive criticism. Pointing to evidence that is incompatible with dependency theories is important because it forces dependency theorists to withdraw on this or on that intellectual front, but it does not suffice to overcome the paradigm. Only a competing paradigm can do so. The theory of the rent-seeking society offers such a competing paradigm, which will be discussed in detail in Sections 2 and 3 of this chapter.

Adherents of rent-seeking and dependency theories do agree on the general notion that the privileged make or keep poor people poor. Therefore, the rent-seeking approach looks as plausible as the dependency paradigm. Of course, dependency theories and the rent-seeking approach do differ in many important respects. At best, dependency theorists demonstrate "benign neglect" for microeconomic theory and the rational choice approach adopted in this book—despite the fact that economists find it easier to agree on microeconomic theory than on macroeconomic theory (see Bell and Kristol, 1981) and despite the widespread feeling that economics is the "queen of the social sciences." By contrast, the rent-seeking approach is not only compatible with microeconomic theory but should be conceived of as a broadening and deepening of the theory.

The issues to be discussed are what dependency and rent-seeking theories do assert, what evidence is available for a preliminary evaluation of these theories, what the policy implications of these theories are, and why I believe rent-seeking theory to be superior to dependency theories. Wherever possible, I shall give special attention to cross-national analyses of economic growth rates or income distribution. Given the scope and urgency of the global poverty problem, there is little hope of reducing it without more economic growth in poor countries (Ahluwalia, Carter, and Chenery, 1979) or without equalizing the distribution of income in many or most of them. Since I compare an older and—albeit only outside the discipline of economics!—more established paradigm, dependency, with a younger or even still nascent one, rent-seeking, the reader should not be surprised that there is more quantitative and cross-national evidence on dependency theories than on rent-seeking and that dependency theories tend to suffer from anomalies whereas the rent-seeking approach tends to suffer from a dearth of quantitative evidence. Such a state of affairs is typical when a new paradigm aspires to replace an older one (see Kuhn, 1962).

Dependency theorists agree with one another that poor people stay poor because privileged people contribute to and maintain their poverty and because privileged nations somehow benefit from the international economic order at the expense of poor nations. But they disagree with each other on exactly how worldwide inequity is created and maintained. I shall restrict myself to a discussion of those three dependency theories[1] that so far have received the most scrutiny in quantitative and cross-national research on economic growth and income inequality: Galtung's (1971) "structural theory of imperialism"; Wallerstein's (1974; 1979; 1980) world-system approach, which has been translated into quantitative research designs by an adherent of the theory (Rubinson, 1976; 1977); and Bornschier's (1980a; 1980b; Bornschier and Ballmer-Cao, 1979; Bornschier and Chase-Dunn, 1985) view that investment dependence and penetration of LDCs by multinational corporations contribute to stagnation and inequality.

According to Galtung (1971), developing countries suffer from vertical trade and feudal interaction patterns. Vertical trade refers to the fact that most rich, industrialized, and powerful countries tend to import raw materials but to export processed goods, while LDCs demonstrate the reverse pattern. In Galtung's (1971) view, the production of raw materials in LDCs creates few positive spin-offs; sometimes the eventual exhaustion of mineral deposits will leave nothing behind but a hole in the ground. But production of sophisticated processed goods in industrial societies necessarily contributes to human capital formation. Workers and managers learn new skills that tend to remain useful even when production is shifted from one good to another. In essence, the worldwide division of labor that concentrates manufacturing and processing, and in particular sophisticated processing, in some nations and extraction and agricultural raw-material production in others is the root cause of more privileged circumstances of life in wealthy industrial societies and of deprivation in LDCs. The need for a broad human-capital base in sophisticated industrial economies exerts some equalizing pressure in these countries. Since raw-material extraction or production favors landed property owners, the global division of labor permits a highly unequal distribution of income in LDCs.

Galtung's (1971) mechanism of vertical trade is supplemented by feudal interaction patterns. By and large, the export earnings of many LDCs derive from a very small number of products; sometimes a single product accounts for most export earnings. Moreover, commodity concentration is often accompanied by partner concentration. For example, some Central American "banana republics" not only depend on the export of bananas but also suffer from exporting most of them to the U.S. market, where those countries also buy most of their imports. Comparable degrees of dependency characterize the relationship between France and some former French colonies in Africa. Even where the pattern is less obvious, commodity concentration and partner concentration create opportunities for privileged nations to keep poor nations poor.

This crude sketch of Galtung's theory suffices to raise a number of questions. Countries like Australia or Canada and, most importantly, the United States do not really fit the theory. Australia, Canada, and even the United States do too well by exporting raw materials or agrarian products, as do some sparsely populated Organization of Petroleum Exporting Countries (OPEC) nations, which even enjoy (close to) tax-free welfare states. Moreover, the theory looks somewhat dated and ever less appealing the more the pattern of North-South trade shifts from the exchange of industrial goods for raw materials or agricultural goods toward trade in industrial goods produced by more or less skilled workers. While manufactures amounted to merely 5 percent of all Southern exports to the North in 1955 and only 15.2 percent in 1980, they had jumped to 53.5 percent by 1989 (Wood, 1994, p. 2).[2] But I do not want to evaluate Galtung's "structural theory of imperialism" by pointing to a couple of anomalies and its declining relevance over time. After all, "all theories are born refuted" (Lakatos, 1968–1969, p. 163; see also Kuhn, 1962). More important than the existence of anomalies is whether the independent variables of this theory, which Galtung already operationalized, do or do not contribute to the explanation of cross-national patterns of economic growth or income inequality. Do the import of (sophisticated) processed goods and the export of raw materials reduce the growth prospects of LDCs and simultaneously contribute to income inequality? Do export commodity concentration and partner concentration in trade decrease economic growth rates but increase income inequality?

Before I attempt to summarize the empirical evidence on Galtung's theory, I want to continue my sketch of various lines of reasoning within the dependency paradigm. According to Wallerstein (1974, p. 406), "the functioning of a capitalist world economy requires that groups pursue their economic interests within a single world-market while seeking to distort this market for their benefit by organizing to exert influence on states, some of which are more powerful than others but none of which controls the market in its entirety." In this view, some groups and nations succeed in distorting markets and rigging prices to their own benefit and at the expense of other groups and nations.[3]

In his effort to translate this general idea into quantitative research designs, Rubinson (1977, p. 7) argued that a strong state "is able to control the activities of the population within its boundaries . . . one indicator of state strength is the government revenues of a state as a proportion of GNP. . . . This indicator measures the degree to which the total economic resources of the country are available to the state." In addition to a domestic dimension of state strength, there is an international dimension. While Rubinson (1976; 1977) discusses and applies a variety of indicators, some of the most potent ones are trade, i.e., import and/or export, and shares of gross national product (GNP). To summarize the Wallerstein-Rubinson perspective: States are most likely and able to promote economic growth and income equalization if they exercise much control of economic activities within their borders, as indicated by the proportion of government revenue to gross domestic product (GDP) or GNP, and if they depend little on the vicissitudes of the world market, as indicated by low trade to GNP shares.

Finally, there is a third perspective. According to Bornschier (1980a; 1980b; Bornschier and Ballmer-Cao, 1979; Bornschier and Chase-Dunn, 1985), multinational corporations (MNCs) are the main culprits in Third World poverty. LDCs depend heavily on foreign investment, most of which is supplied by MNCs. In the short run, the inflow of MNC capital contributes to investment and growth. In the long run, however, MNCs succeed in getting more out of LDCs than they put in, i.e., in decapitalizing Third World economies. Rigging the terms of trade in *intra*-MNC, but simultaneously *inter*national, trade is one of the mechanisms whereby such decapitalization can be achieved. Moreover, given the strength of MNCs vis-à-vis LDCs, such corporations contribute to early market concentration and often enjoy monopoly power and monopoly profits. The more powerful MNCs are in a less developed economy, the worse that economy's growth prospects become. But MNCs do even more harm in LDCs. Since MNCs apply capital-intensive production technologies that do not need much local and unskilled labor input and since they tend to produce only for the more privileged classes in LDCs and ally themselves politically with those classes, MNC penetration reinforces income inequality as well.

This crude sketch of three dependency explanations of why poor people stay poor has yielded a list of six independent variables: vertical trade (or export of raw materials and import of processed goods), export commodity concentration, trade partner concentration, low government revenues as a proportion of GDP, high trade-to-GNP proportions, and strong MNC penetration. According to these dependency theories, all six variables should simultaneously reduce growth rates and increase inequality and thereby hurt the poor. Do they?

Adherents and opponents of dependency theories have done a lot of cross-national and cross-sectional work. So there is some evidence that LDCs that are extraordinarily dependent on exporting raw materials and importing processed goods or that suffer from severe export commodity concentration and trade partner concentration do indeed demonstrate greater income inequality and/or grow more slowly than other nations (Alschuler, 1976; Galtung, 1971; Rubinson, 1977; Stokes and Jaffee, 1982; Walleri, 1978a; 1978b). But there are also studies that cast a much less favorable light on Galtung's "structural theory of imperialism" (Bradshaw, 1985a;[4] Delacroix, 1977; Delacroix and Ragin, 1978; 1981;[5] Kaufmann, Chernotsky, and Geller, 1975; Pampel and Williamson, 1989, chapter 5; Ray and Webster, 1978; Weede and Tiefenbach, 1981a; 1981b). Similarly, there is some evidence of a relationship between low government-revenue/GDP or high-trade/GNP ratios on the one hand and less economic growth and more income inequality on the other hand (Bornschier, 1980a; Bornschier, Chase-Dunn, and Rubinson, 1978; Meyer and Hannan, 1979; Rubinson, 1976; 1977; Rubinson and Quinlan, 1977). But there are also other studies that call these findings, and thereby the Wallerstein-Rubinson line of reasoning, into question (Landau, 1983; Levine and Renelt, 1992; Marsden, 1983; Weede, 1980a; Weede and Tiefenbach, 1981a; 1981b; Wood, 1994, p. 223). Finally, there is some evidence for the negative impact of investment dependence, or MNC penetration, on economic growth and income equality (Bornschier, 1980a; 1980b; 1981a; 1982; Bornschier and Ballmer-Cao, 1979; Bornschier and Chase-Dunn, 1985; Chase-Dunn, 1975; Gobalet and Diamond, 1979). But again, there are studies that do not support these contentions (Bradshaw, 1985a, p. 202; 1985b, pp. 93–94; Delacroix and Ragin, 1981; Jackman, 1982; Muller, 1984; Pampel and Williamson, 1989, chapter 5; Weede and Tiefenbach, 1981a; 1981b). Even a study by Bornschier (1985) himself conceded that the negative effects of MNC penetration on economic growth were no longer significant in the late 1970s.

Since these studies differ in sample size, period of observation, operationalization of variables, and specification of regression equations, it is difficult to explain their inconsistent findings. In my view, it is not essential to do so for the purposes of this chapter. The mere fact of contradictory findings instead of robust support in favor of dependency theories justifies some doubt. One route of criticism starts with the observation that most studies neglect competing explanations of cross-national differences of growth rates or income inequality and thereby risk some specification error. If one takes into account that income inequality and economic growth demonstrate curvilinear and nonmonotonic relationships with the level of economic development;[6] that human-capital formation (as assessed by literacy, school enrollment ratios, or even military participation ratios) contributes to growth and equality; and that investment contributes to growth, then empirical support for dependency theories tends to wither away (Weede and Tiefenbach, 1981a; 1981b).[7] The list of control variables (except for the monotonicity problem discussed in note 6) is similar to the one used and confirmed recently by Levine and Renelt (1992). While the research strategy I have outlined suffices to call dependency theories into question, it is not necessary to employ it in order to arrive at similar conclusions (see Delacroix, 1977; Muller, 1984; Ray and Webster, 1978).

Firebaugh (1992; Firebaugh and Beck, 1994) staged an even more devastating attack on dependency research and its preferred research designs than empirically minded critics who by the nature of their approach could do little more than detect a lack of robustness in claimed dependency effects. According to Firebaugh and Beck (1994, p. 639) the single-equation stock and flow models used by Bornschier and Chase-Dunn (1985) "do not separate the long-run effects from short-run effects of dependence. A single equation has only one dependent variable, not one reflecting short-run effects and one reflecting long-run effects." Worse than attempting the impossible, the observable foreign-investment effects have been misinterpreted. According to Firebaugh and Beck (1994, p. 635) the negative effects of foreign-investment stocks on economic growth do not support the MNC or investment variant of dependency theory but instead call its validity into question:

> Investment rate is, in effect, the ratio of capital flow to capital stock. . . . With flow held constant, the greater the stock, the *lower* the ratio of capital flow to stock. So if investment boosts economic growth, then the greater the stock (holding flow constant) the *slower* the investment and therefore the *slower* the growth. In short, a negative coefficient for foreign stock indicates a *beneficial* effect of foreign investment in the dependency model. Researchers have simply misconstrued the effect of the denominator as a "dependence effect."

After this methodological criticism, the empirically minded critics (including me) seem to have produced results marginally more favorable to dependency theory than those produced by its advocates. Whereas dependency advocates unwittingly demonstrated significant benefits of foreign investment, critics were content with demonstrating that it did no harm.

In addition to cross-national studies of either economic growth rates or income inequality, there are some studies of the "physical quality of life" (Morris, 1979). This quality is assessed by (low) infant mortality, life expectancy at age one, and basic literacy rates. By and large, one should expect those variables that improve growth rates and equality to improve the physical quality of life as well. Growth generates higher incomes, and per capita GNP is strongly and monotonically related to the physical-quality-of-life index (Moon, 1991, pp. 55–56).[8] If the fruits of growth, i.e., income, are shared equally, then more children and adults should survive or obtain some education than under conditions of monopolization of wealth by a narrow and privileged ruling class.

Interestingly, a given income brought more quality of life in 1980 than it did twenty years earlier (Moon, 1991, p. 61). In my view, the most plausible explanation of this finding is medical progress, especially against contagious diseases. In my interpretation (and Bauer's, 1981), medical progress in the developed Western societies spills over to LDCs and improves the quality of life there. This relationship is quite contrary to the negative impact of industrialized societies on poor societies that dependency and world-system theorists perceive everywhere.

Moon's (1991, pp. 126, 179–213) cross-sectional study of about 120 countries contains some other findings relevant to the evaluation of dependency theories. First, the net effect of state size on the physical quality of life is not positive but mildly negative. Second, the core periphery distinction made by world-system theorists is hardly useful. Third, negative trade effects are restricted to the poorest countries. Fourth, there are no clear-cut supportive results on vertical trade,[9] commodity concentration, partner concentration, or penetration by MNCs. Thus, only a single finding (the one on trade) supports a dependency approach, but its validity does not cover all LDCs. Since this conditional negative trade effect on the physical quality of life does not fit with the previously discussed findings on economic growth rates or income distributions, it should not be given too much weight until it is replicated in further studies.

Firebaugh and Beck's (1994, p. 645) sophisticated study of caloric consumption, infant survival probability, and life expectancy rejected Wimberley and Bello's (1992) earlier claims concerning foreign investment and food consumption and arrived at the following conclusion: "There is no credible cross-national evidence that foreign investment is the leading cause of the 'immiseration' of the world's poor" (Firebaugh and Beck, 1994, p. 645). But they did find "some tantalizing support for the weak version of the theory," according to which the quality-of-life benefits of foreign investment are somewhat less than those of domestic investment (Firebaugh and Beck, 1994, p. 647). In my view, the contrast between capital returns accruing to citizens versus foreigners and the differential degrees of monopolization often coming with foreign versus domestic investment are plausible candidates for the interpretation of this finding.

To sum up: The dependency approach provides no reliable and valid answer to the question: Why do poor people stay poor? Although it is always conceivable that a research program in trouble—as dependency theory currently is—may recover and score better and more lasting explanatory success in the future than it has in the past, the search for alternative and possibly better explanations of why poor people stay poor seems justified.

2. Kleptocracy and Rent-Seeking at Home

As outlined in Section 3 of Chapter 3, rents are profits above opportunity costs. In a truly competitive market in which everyone is a price-taker, rents do not exist. Therefore, rent-seeking is an attempt to distort markets and to evade competition. Where rent-seeking is prevalent we refer to rent-seeking societies. The fundamental problem of rent-seeking societies is that they suffer from a serious distortion of incentives. There are strong incentives to engage in distributional struggles and to seek contrived transfers but comparatively weak incentives to engage in productive and growth-promoting activities. While rent-seeking decreases growth, there is no reason to expect the poor to be particularly successful in distributional struggles.

Rent-seeking aims at escaping from competition by monopolization, cartels, and barriers to entry. In Chapter 3, Section 3 the three effects of monopolies have already been discussed: regressive transfers, deadweight loss, and incentives for further monopolization elsewhere. Cartels are little better than monopolies. Their purpose is the same: to maximize profits by selling lower quantities at higher prices. In general, the regressive transfer from poorer buyers or consumers to richer cartel members still exists. The consumer surplus of those who are ready to pay competitive prices, but not cartel prices, still disappears. In particular where it is illegal, cartelization requires resources. But in contrast to monopolies, cartels require collective action. Seen from the perspective of a group of producers of some good, a cartel provides a collective good. If higher prices can be imposed on consumers, every producer receives some rent. For simplicity's sake, let us assume that cartelization is illegal and requires bribing politicians and bureaucrats to look the other way.[10] In that case, there is a freeriding tendency. Every producer would like to benefit from the cartel but to make other producers pay for it. According to Olson (1965; 1982), the prospects for the provision of collective goods and for overcoming freeriding tendencies are much better in small groups than in large groups,[11] which is why oligopolists should find cartelization easier than a multitude of small and scattered producers. Elitist interests always enjoy a head start in the cartelization game. Equalization by cartelization is extremely unlikely. Since cartelization consumes resources and interferes with efficient allocation and growth, it is a collective bad for society as a whole.

So far the discussion of rent-seeking has been rather abstract and removed from the problems of LDCs. This need not be so. Although not all of the quoted authors use the term *rent-seeking*, Lipton (1977) in his seminal book *Why Poor People Stay Poor*, Olson (1985; 1987), Bates (1988b), and Krueger (1992) analyze the phenomenon. In their view, there is a conflict of interest between urban and rural populations in LDCs that urban dwellers tend to decide in their own favor. In a conflict of interest between groups, the recipe for successful collective action and overcoming resistance is to generate concentrated gains for a relatively small group and diffused and preferably invisible losses for a much larger group (Olson, 1965). In most LDCs, by far the largest group is the rural population tilling the land. In general, this rural agrarian population is poorer than the urban population. If the smaller, relatively more privileged urban population can succeed in rigging the urban-rural terms of trade, the recipe of concentrated gains and diffused losses is realized,[12] which is why an incentive exists for urban exploitation of the rural population.

It is much easier for urban people to organize themselves for the promotion of their collective interests than for scattered rural agrarian people. Karl Marx (1852/1966) knew this fact, and Olson (1985) recently reaffirmed it. Urban interests are concentrated in small but densely populated areas. Rural interests in LDCs are widely scattered and often suffer from poor transportation and communication facilities. The higher cost of collective action in the underdeveloped countryside makes a rural defense of agrarian interest less likely. While Lipton (1977, p. 13) does not hesitate to refer to class struggle, he rejects traditional Marxist theories and neo-Marxist dependency and world-system theories alike:

> The most important class conflict in the poor countries of the world today is not between labour and capital. Nor is it between foreign and national interest. It is between the rural and urban classes. The rural sector contains most of the poverty, and most of the low-cost sources of potential advance; but the urban sector contains most of the articulateness, organisation and power. So the urban classes have been able to "win" most rounds of the struggle with the countryside; but in so doing they have made the development process needlessly slow and unfair.

A comparatively small number of urban producers in LDCs finds little difficulty in establishing an informal cartel where the law does not permit a formal one. It is much easier for urban factory workers to unionize than for scattered rural people, some of whom may be tenants or sharecroppers. Nevertheless, these rural people do share an interest in obtaining high prices for whatever they sell. Finally, the largely urban public sector with its bureaucratic structure tends to be born organized for collective action. Aggregation of these somewhat organized urban interests is relatively easy. Urban employers and manufacturers, urban workers, and largely urban civil servants and politicians do share an interest in cheap food to be supplied from the rural hinterland to the cities. Obviously, distorted urban-rural terms of trade—i.e., artificially low prices for food and artificially high prices for urban products—depend on governmental policies and some degree of state interference with international trade. If farmers were free to sell their products to the highest-bidding buyers from inside or outside the country, then food prices could not be distorted downward. But prohibition of exports or official monopsonies (marketing boards) may prevent such harmful interference with urban interests. Differing degrees of unionization and corresponding urban-rural terms of trade simultaneously decrease the labor-absorption capacity of unionized, urban sectors.

Why should ruling politicians contribute to, or at least tolerate, some distortion of urban-rural terms of trade in LDCs? There are a number of reasons. First, but possibly least important, such a distortion benefits them personally by reducing their cost of living. Second, it is much easier for a political entrepreneur to build a power base from better-organized groups than from amorphous groups. The costs of resource mobilization for political action can be dramatically cut by assembling a coalition of previously existing interest groups or organizations, compared with calling them into existence in the first place (Hechter, 1987; Oberschall, 1973; Chapter 3, Section 1 of this book). Third, most rulers prefer poverty, disorder, and violence to occur out of sight if they cannot prevent it. They prefer starvation in remote villages to an urban riot in front of the presidential palace. Fourth, since unorganized rural agrarian groups in remote parts of the country cannot effectively fight back (short of guerrilla warfare, which probably requires some foreign help; see Gurr, 1968; Gurr and Duvall, 1973), it may even be politically stabilizing to redistribute from the rural poor to somewhat better-off urban dwellers.

The size of urban bias, or the burden imposed on agriculture, can be very large. For five Latin American economies, Krueger et al. (1992, p. 3) report that "on average, the relative price of agricultural goods would have been 42 percent higher in the absence of government price intervention." Much of the distortion (about two-thirds) arises because of *indirect* intervention, i.e., as the result of high levels of protection of nonagricultural importables or of exchange-rate misalignment. Agricultural interest groups in less developed countries find it very hard to fight against the indirect interventions that put such heavy burdens on them. Krueger et al. (1992, p. 33) suspect "that the producer organizations of agriculture realize that the removal of indirect interventions would require an alignment of forces that goes far beyond their particular sectoral interests." In effect, they would have to attack most urban vested interests at the same time.

Sometimes low food prices and government action to achieve them are rationalized by state support for agriculture, such as subsidizing pesticides or fertilizers. In Latin America, such benefits compensate, at best, for about half of the burden (Krueger et al., 1992, pp. 4–5). Moreover, subsidization makes inputs appear cheaper than they are, so demand is bound to increase. In LDCs it usually cannot be met. Then somebody has to decide which farmers obtain the subsidized inputs and which ones do not. This somebody is likely to be a bureaucrat or a local politician. Even if the decisionmaker is honest—and that is a big if—allocation is likely to be discriminatory. Bureaucrats want to be properly approached. They like written applications or might even be legally required to insist on them. The smallest and poorest farmers in the remotest areas are least likely to pass this obstacle. Richer farmers are more likely to find somebody in their family or among their personal friends who is able to write an application or to fill out a form. Since Third World bureaucrats or local politicians rarely enjoy affluence, even though their incomes are much higher than those of ordinary peasants, tenants, or sharecroppers, there is a strong temptation to accept gifts or bribes for allocations of subsidized fertilizers or pesticides. If worst comes to worst, what has been intended as a subsidy for agriculture turns into a subsidy for bureaucrats and/or politicians and into an incentive for corruption. At best, when subsidy programs are competently and honestly administered, they still focus on "progressive farmers" and thereby deprive peasants of their natural leaders in the fight against harmful regulation by official marketing boards.

Urban bias in the economic policies of LDCs is married to a more general inclination in many such countries not to face the fact of their comparative disadvantage (relative to Western industrial societies) in large-scale organization, administration, and planning. Olson (1987, pp. 86, 91) points out that "the skills, attitudes and expectations of most people in these societies [are] . . . derived from and geared to small institutions rather than large ones" and that "in poor and truly underdeveloped areas the government must usually be either very small (as were medieval governments of individual manors or the governments of various primitive tribes) or else relatively ineffective, corrupt, or even merely nominal as many governments in underdeveloped regions now appear to be." Based on these considerations, one may conclude with Olson (1987, p. 96) but in contrast to many ambitious but unsuccessful Third World governments, that "whatever the optimal role of government may be in developed nations, it is smaller in developing countries."

Although subsidies are often justified by the need to serve the poor, they rarely do so. World Bank (1994, p. 81) officials have recently observed:

"Price subsidies to infrastructure almost always benefit the nonpoor dispro-portionately. In developing countries, the poor use kerosene or candles rather than electricity for lighting, they rely on private vendors or public standpipes rather than inhouse connections for water supply, and they are infrequently served by sewerage systems." Of course, infrastructure avail-ability and use is correlated not only with income but also with urban or rural residence. By and large, urban areas are better served than rural areas.

Overvaluation of the domestic currency is a useful tool for rigging urban-rural terms of trade. It automatically reduces farmers' export prospects and simultaneously benefits mostly urban consumers of imported goods. Since overvaluation necessarily reduces the competitiveness of urban industries and tends to suck in imports, a poor country with an overvalued currency is likely to experience some balance-of-payments problems. To handle the problem and to protect domestic industry, what an Indian news-paper once termed "permit, license, quota Raj" is created. Such regulations boost bureaucratic employment and promotion opportunities, to the benefit of some urban people. They provide gratifying rents for those who obtain them. Take an import license, for example. Even after illegal payments to bureaucrats or politicians, such a license may still be a source of nice prof-its. The licensed importer and bureaucrats or politicians in regulatory agen-cies share the rent that has been created by the regulation of foreign trade.

As Lipton (1977; 1984) has pointed out, the distortion of urban-rural terms of trade in LDCs is closely related to inefficient development strate-gies. Investment is often characterized by an urban bias that neglects factor scarcities in LDCs. Except for capital-surplus oil exporters, most LDCs suf-fer from a scarcity of capital but command an ample supply of unskilled or even semiskilled labor. Urban investments often outperform rural invest-ments in raising labor productivity, but rural investments generally outper-form urban ones in capital productivity. Where capital is scarce and labor is not, it is more important to maximize productivity per unit of capital than per unit of labor. Nevertheless, many LDCs prefer urban investments as a matter of principle and neglect rural ones. Therefore, they get lower rates of growth than they could. While a capital-intensive strategy of industrializa-tion retards development, it pleases some industrialists and unionized urban labor aristocracies that succeed in obtaining higher wages. At the same time, such higher wages slow down the labor-absorption capacity of the modern industrial sector and thereby condemn those not yet employed there to remain in the agricultural or in the urban informal sector, both of which con-tain the bulk of absolutely poor people in LDCs.

Although de Soto (1989) does not use the term *rent-seeking,* his *mer-cantilism* refers to the same facts. In the Peruvian rent-seeking society, many people are simply pushed out of the legal economy. According to de Soto (1989, p. 12) the informal sector employed 48 percent of the working population of Peru and contributed 61 percent of the hours worked and 39 percent to the GDP in the early 1980s. Since the informal sector grows rapidly, it might contribute as much as 61 percent to the Peruvian GDP by the year 2000. Estimates of the informal sector, or the shadow economy, imply that productivity in this sector is lower than in the formal sector, but people simply have no choice.

The weight of the informal sector in Peru can be explained by the shortcomings of government, administration, and the legal system. Many activities can be pursued legally not at all, or at best at a snail's pace. De Soto's (1989, pp. 134–135) associates needed 289 days to legalize a small textile factory in the Lima metropolitan area. The cost was thirty-two local minimum wages. Public officials attempted to extort bribes ten times. Twice the bribes had to be paid in order to continue the experiment. Obviously, this kind of legal barrier shuts many Peruvians out of the formal economy.

Housing in Lima faces similar problems. In principle, poor families might get legal access to urban wasteland for settlement purposes, but the bureaucratic process takes—according to de Soto (1989, pp. 136–137)—more than six years and consists of more than two hundred bureaucratic steps by forty-eight different offices. Given this bureaucratic nightmare, only illegal seizures of land and illegal housing can satisfy the urgent needs of 47 percent of the population. Even municipal housing projects involve illegal seizures of land. The informal sector provides housing and jobs and dominates local transport with buses, minibuses, and cabs. About 90,000 street vendors and about 40,000 additional traders in informal markets supply much of Lima's poor population and support the lives of about half a million inhabitants (de Soto, 1989, pp. 60–61).

Taxes constitute only about 22 percent of the cost of formal business, and compliance with legal and bureaucratic requirements amounts to 73 percent (de Soto, 1989, p. 148). This unproductive cost and the slowness and arbitrariness of the bureaucracy constitute the main reasons why so many Peruvians have to work in the informal sector. Of course, one cannot escape from corrupt officials even there. According to my calculations, de Soto's (1989, pp. 147, 154) account implies that petty entrepreneurs in the informal sector spend about two-thirds of what would have been taxes in the legal sector on bribes.

Informality is bad for business and for the national economy. First, informal businesses have to be small and hardly visible in order to evade punishment and repression. They have to remain small and to forgo economies of scale, whether or not it is efficient. They must not be capital intensive. They must not advertise. Second, informal business depends on cash payments and is severely affected by inflation, which tends to be high or exorbitant in Latin America and which results from the fiscal and monetary policies of the state. Third, informal possessions cannot easily be sold and bought. This limitation must interfere with the efficient allocation of resources. Fourth, informal businesspeople have to invest much time and effort in the defense of their possessions—primarily by belonging to political associations and making contact with politicians in order to persuade the authorities to "overlook" their activities. Fifth, the lack of safe property rights increases transaction costs and thereby reduces gains from trade.

According to de Soto (1989, p. 191) the main problem with the Peruvian administrative, political, and legal system is its redistributive orientation: "A legal system whose sole purpose is redistribution thus benefits neither rich nor poor, but only those best organized to establish close ties with the people in power. It ensures that the businesses that remain in the market are those which are most efficient politically, not economically."

Rent-seeking is bad for society and growth since it distorts incentives and interferes with efficient resource allocation. In LDCs most rents benefit urban groups and harm rural agrarian ones because the latter find it hard to organize themselves for collective action and to become included in prevailing distributional coalitions. In rent-seeking societies there is a protracted distributional struggle in which the poorest rural groups are destined to become losers. Equity is lost alongside efficiency.

The basic cross-nationally testable proposition advanced by Lipton (1977) holds that urban bias reduces growth rates. Lipton (1977, pp. 435–437) has himself published some data on the urban-rural disparity in output per person, i.e., incomes per person in the urban and rural sectors of the economy. Since Lipton's own data set covers only sixty-three LDCs ca. 1970, other researchers have operationalized urban bias or the disparity as a ratio of ratios from widely available data. Following Bradshaw's (1985b, p. 83) pioneering effort, the disparity is defined this way:

$$\text{Disparity} = \frac{\text{percent nonagricultural GDP/percent agricultural GDP}}{\text{percent nonagricultural labor/percent agricultural labor}}$$

With this kind of measure,[13] Bradshaw (1985a; 1985b; 1987),[14] Weede (1987b), and London and Smith (1988) could demonstrate that urban bias, or income disparities between the nonagricultural and agricultural sectors of the economy, does significantly reduce growth rates. In this context, it may be noted that earlier interpretations of English economic history, according to which discrimination against agriculture contributed to early industrialization, are now refuted (Bates, 1988a, p. 512). Of course, this insight into the negative effects of urban bias does little to reduce the political attractiveness of this type of rent-seeking in LDCs (see Bates, 1983).

In my view, all societies are to some degree afflicted by rent-seeking. After all, the generation and distribution of rents is what makes politics and government attractive for many (or most?) active participants.[15] But societies differ in the degree to which they tolerate or encourage rent-seeking. Is there any quantitative evidence beyond urban bias effects that those LDCs that permit more rent-seeking grow more slowly than others without at least generating a more equal distribution of income? While there is not much evidence, the existing evidence is fairly strong.

There is no rent-seeking without price distortion. Therefore, an index of price distortion is simultaneously an index of rent-seeking. For the 1970s and thirty-one LDCs, the World Bank (1983, pp. 57–63) provides such an index. The Bank's price distortion index "concentrates on distortions in the prices of foreign exchange, capital, labor, and infrastructural services (particularly power)." If the trade-weighted exchange rate of an LDC currency appreciates or does not depreciate despite higher inflation at home than abroad, if competitiveness is thereby eroded, this is simultaneously a cue to the presence of price distortions and a cause for protectionist interference with international trade, which is another cue to the existence of price distortions. Distortion of capital prices is assumed to exist wherever real interest rates are negative. Minimum-wage laws, high social security taxes, and cheap provision of infrastructural services by state agencies are further indications of price distortions and rent-seeking. The World Bank's (1983, pp. 57–63) price distortion index alone explained about one-third of the variance in GDP growth rates in the 1970s. Recently, the World Bank (1993b, p. 5) attributed the extraordinary economic performance of some East Asian economies to the fact that they "kept price distortions within reasonable bounds." But price distortion is not significantly correlated with income inequality. While certainly in need of replication in larger samples and for different periods of observation, the reported correlation between price distortion and reduced growth rates is much stronger than what dependency theory can offer. Moreover, if one introduces those control variables that make effects hypothesized by dependency theorists wither away, then the negative impact of price distortions on growth remains essentially as it was in bivariate analysis, and the relationship between price distortions and equality remains close to zero and insignificant (Weede, 1986a).

Closely related to price distortion is the issue of inward or outward orientation of the economy. According to Balassa (1981), an essential characteristic of outward orientation is the absence of discrimination against exports. A cross-national study of forty-one LDCs, which had 65 percent of the output of all LDCs, by Greenaway and Nam (1988) did demonstrate that there is a significant relationship between outward orientation and better economic performance. Recently, Dollar (1992, p. 523) analyzed data from ninety-five LDCs and reaffirmed that "outward-oriented developing economies really do grow more rapidly." Unfortunately, the robustness of this finding may be questioned (Levine and Renelt, 1992, p. 954). Often the extraordinary success of high-performing East Asian economies is attributed to their outward orientation. Critics of this explanatory approach (such as Amsden, 1985; or Wade, 1990; 1992) stress that governments in Japan, South Korea, and Taiwan engaged not in laissez-faire politics but in the promotion of specific industries. Although the fact of a lot of government intervention must be admitted, industrial policies did *not* invariably succeed even in these countries (Chan, 1993, p. 62; Porter, 1990, pp. 4, 414, 475; World Bank, 1993b, p. 86). Moreover, government intervention seems to do much less harm when the goal is national competitiveness in global markets rather than meeting redistributional targets or serving special-interest groups.[16] In a summary of the East Asian experience, World Bank analysts (1993b, p. 355) argue: "Thus the seeming success of industrial policy in these three economies probably rests not on picking winners . . . but on the setting of export targets for promoted industries and the use of export performance to assess policies." The best thing about outward orientation is that it forces enterprises to compete fiercely. As Porter (1990, p. 174) emphasizes: "Competitive advantage emerges from pressure, challenge, and adversity, rarely from an easy life."

3. Rent-Seeking and International Relations

Even when a discussion of rent-seeking focuses on the domestic context, reference to the world economy as a whole is unavoidable. The deadliest blow to the rent-seeking society that I can imagine is to throw the doors wide open to foreign competition. In essence, rent-seeking requires barriers to entry in order to avoid competition. While international borders are not the only conceivable barriers to entry, they constitute probably the most powerful and persistent ones that actually exist. International borders enable some domestic distributional coalitions to capture rents not only at the expense of other groups at home but also at the expense of other groups abroad. Moreover, the winning group at home may be fairly inclusive, whereas the losers or losses may be scattered worldwide, or nearly so.

Some core insights that were first developed by a dependency theorist, Emmanuel (1972), may be retained if one replaces his Marxist or theory-of-value assumptions with a rent-seeking perspective. Emmanuel makes four major observations. First, wages in industrialized democracies are much higher than in the Third World, even when different skill levels or work intensities are accounted for. Second, capital is fairly mobile from country to country. That mobility is why capital yields similar returns everywhere, leaving out risk premiums in some politically unstable places. Third, labor is much less mobile than capital, despite such phenomena as the influx of Mexicans into the United States, Algerians into France, Indians or Pakistanis into Britain, and Turks into Germany. Fourth, labor is much better organized in the more developed countries than in the LDCs. As Emmanuel claimed, these facts are interdependent.

One may improve one's understanding of worldwide rent-seeking if one applies a line of reasoning similar to Emmanuel's (1972) major observations, as Becker (1971) did in his work on the economics of discrimination or as Krauss (1983) did more recently. From a global perspective the most efficient solution would be to overlook the Northern (or Organization for Economic Cooperation and Development [OECD]) or Southern (or Third World) origin of capital and labor; i.e., no nation-state would interfere with movements of capital or labor, and newly arrived laborers could compete on an equal footing with others.[17] Capital and labor would move to places where the outlook for high returns is best. Obviously, much Southern labor would move to the North and some Northern capital would move to the South. These movements of capital and labor would exert globally equalizing pressures on capital and labor returns. In this scenario, some people would gain and others would lose, compared with the status quo. By and large, unskilled and semiskilled Northern labor would suffer great losses and Southern labor would score major gains. Just imagine the pain in Chicago or Paris and the joy in Calcutta or Lagos if the gap in wages for, say, garbage collection began to close, since no one would prevent garbage collectors from poor countries from threatening the job security of garbage collectors in rich countries.

Whether Southern capital would lose and Northern capital would win depends on one's assessment of the effectiveness of current restrictions on international capital movements. I am inclined to accept Emmanuel's (1972) belief that current restrictions on capital movements are by and large ineffective—even more so now than at the time of his writing. Dismantling such restrictions would not make much of a difference. So, it is evident that the overriding effect of abolishing all state interference with capital and labor movements would be beneficial for Southern labor (or parts of it) and harmful for unskilled Northern labor.[18]

This scenario, if it ever came true, would do much more to fight absolute poverty on a global scale than do welfare states in industrialized democracies. As Tullock (1983, p. 64) and Krauss (1983) observed, Northern welfare states cater to or redistribute within the most privileged decile or quintile of mankind; at the same time, their redistributive efforts depend on keeping the less fortunate majority of mankind out. But the scenario I have just sketched is unlikely ever to become true, for the obvious reason that relatively well-organized and unionized workers in the North will prevent it from happening.[19] They are likely to succeed in protecting their rents.

A short look at South Africa before majority rule may clarify the general issue. Until the late 1980s jobs were reserved for the benefit of white citizens and tight control was exerted over the influx of blacks and others into the "white areas" of South Africa. Certainly unskilled and semiskilled whites gained from these practices at the expense of about equally skilled but much poorer blacks. While the South African economy grew more slowly than it conceivably could have done without such discrimination, a bigger slice of the cake easily compensated whites for the slower expansion of the cake. OECD citizens may be more like their white South African brethren (before recent reforms) than most care to admit.

OECD welfare states do little to help the poor in LDCs, and the efficiency of their aid is questionable (Bauer, 1981; Bornschier, Chase-Dunn, and Rubinson, 1978; Krauss, 1983; Mosley, 1987; Singh, 1985). Of course, there are some studies that demonstrate the positive impact of certain projects on economic development. But one must keep in mind that most projects are not rigorously evaluated; that evaluated projects are not a representative sample of all projects; and that, most importantly, cross-nationally there is no relationship between aid and economic growth rates (Mosley, 1987, p. 135). Already there is little evidence at the project level that aid succeeds in reaching the poorest strata of society. Moreover, many of the biggest economies are niggardly donors who do not concentrate their aid on the poorest countries.

Even international organizations such as the World Health Organization (WHO) spend their money in ways that cannot be justified on humanitarian grounds. According to Tollison and Wagner (1993, p. 16), the WHO spends on the inhabitants of poor Ethiopia only a quarter of the amount that it spends on the inhabitants of Kuwait, which enjoys more than a hundred times the per capita income of Ethiopia. On top of this misallocation of aid, one may even argue with Krauss (1983) that OECD welfare states slow down LDC growth rates *by being welfare states*. First, the welfare state distorts incentives and reduces allocative efficiency and growth (Bernholz, 1982; 1986; Pampel and Williamson, 1989; Weede, 1984a; 1986c; 1991; Chapter 6, Section 1 of this book). Less growth in rich countries simultaneously hurts the growth prospects of poor countries. Second, the transformation of a capitalist country into a welfare state affects the structure of demand as public demand partially replaces private demand. Public demand is less likely than private demand to improve the export prospects of LDCs. American and Japanese hesitation to become full welfare states according to the Scandinavian model may help LDCs more than generous Scandinavian aid does.

The very existence of a multitude of states on the globe and state interference with the world economy is closely related to the problem of why poor people stay poor. State-supported or -tolerated price distortions within domestic economies are supplemented by state-generated price distortions within the world economy. Both kinds of distortions keep poor people poor. Now I find myself in partial agreement with a dependency theorist whom I critically evaluated above. Therefore, I quote Wallerstein (1974, p. 406) once more: "The functioning of the capitalist world economy requires that groups pursue their economic interests within a single world-market while seeking to distort this market for their benefit by organizing to exert influence on states, some of which are more powerful than others but none of which controls the market in its entirety." I agree with Wallerstein on the harmful impact of price distortions and on the state's role in generating these distortions, although I do not regard these observable aberrations as functional requisites of a capitalist world economy. Nor can I conceive of avoiding the negative effects of price distortions by manipulating these distortions to the benefit of the poor, as Wallerstein (1974; 1979; 1980) seems to imagine.

Olson (1982, p. 175) deplored the fact that "in these days it takes an enormous amount of stupid policies or bad or unstable institutions to prevent economic development. Unfortunately, growth-retarding regimes, policies, and institutions are the rule rather than the exception, and the majority of the world's population lives in poverty." From a global perspective, rent-seeking at the expense of other groups at home or abroad is indeed incredibly wasteful and—if one wants to call it so—stupid. Losers always lose much more than winners gain. Still, the game looks gratifying to those who win it. The "stupidity" of the game serves winners well. Privileged people keep poor people poor, and must do so if they want to protect their rental incomes, because rents rest on barriers to entry. Of course, inequality and poverty would persist even without rent-seeking, but there would probably be less inequality and almost certainly less poverty.

What can be done? In theory, providing a list of policy recommendations is deceptively simple. LDC governments should stop distorting prices for domestic currencies, for food, for capital, and for labor. They should open their economies and be less tolerant of the efforts of monopolies and distributional coalitions to distort prices. Industrialized democracies should improve the prospects of the poor by eliminating agrarian and industrial protectionism and discrimination against low-wage exporters, by interfering less with worldwide capital and labor flows, and by eliminating discrimination between citizens and foreign labor and discrimination between those who have held a job for some time and new and possibly foreign and usually poorer applicants. Such reforms are incompatible with welfare states for the most privileged quintile of humankind (Krauss, 1983; Tullock, 1983), but they could help the truly poor, almost all of whom live in the Third World.[20]

In the 1970s dependency and world-systems theorists blamed international trade and North-South economic cooperation in general for the persistence of poverty in most LDCs. Recently, free trade has been attacked for almost the opposite reason. Some analysts have argued (Allais, 1994; The Economist, 1994c; Wood, 1994)[21] that trade in the manufacturing sector between rich industrial democracies on the one hand and the more success-ful LDCs such as South Korea, Taiwan, Hong Kong, Singapore, or even China on the other hand threatens unskilled jobs in the rich countries. Lower trade barriers reduce the demand for the factor of production that is used intensively in imported goods, i.e., low-skilled labor in rich-country imports, and increases the demand for the factor of production that is used intensively in exports, i.e., high-skilled labor in rich-country exports.[22] There is even some cross-national evidence (*The Economist,* 1994c, p. 20; Wood, 1994, pp. 206, 208, 268) to support the view that increases in manu-factured imports from LDCs are related to declining manufacturing employ-ment shares and rising differentials between the wages of low- and high-skilled laborers in Western societies. Whereas many European welfare states have succeeded in limiting wage differentials, failure on the employment front is obvious. By contrast, the United States reigns in unemployment but suffers from increasing wage differentials.[23] Thus, the West may face a stark choice: either turn protectionist or accept rising unemployment or accept increasing inequality. According to Allais (1994), a French Nobel laureate in economics and a frequent commentator in newspapers, Western politicians are obliged to choose protectionism in order to prevent the other two evils.

The protectionist prescription is not convincing for a number of rea-sons. First, it is by no means generally accepted that rising wage differen-tials and unemployment in Western countries depend largely or mainly on Asian competition. Second, even if one concedes this argument, protection-ist policies need not follow. Competition from successful Asian economies with Europe or the United States is speeding up the "creative destruction" visualized by Schumpeter (1942). Europe and the United States lose some low-skilled jobs but may generate other and better-paid jobs. It is not obvi-ous that Western societies should try to evade or postpone adjustment or that they benefit in the case of "successful" postponement. After all, consumers benefit from cheap imports. According to Wood (1994, p. 346) many "goods would typically cost about three times as much if they were made in the North."

Third, the political economy of protectionism has to be considered. Even if one imagined that an *omniscient* government motivated *only* by the *public* interest could reduce adjustment costs by intelligently applied pro-tectionism, in the real world governments are likely to lack information, may turn to special-interest groups for information, may succumb to lobby-ism, and may end up with an economic policy that serves not the national interest but a winning coalition of log-rolling interest groups. Unfortunately,

Western protectionism in the service of special-interest groups would not improve the prospects of LDCs but would merely hurt the West itself.

Fourth, protectionism in order to buy peace at home would exact a price abroad. Is it in the Western interest to contribute by protectionism to the preservation of poverty and unstable and often repressive governments in the Third World? In the concluding chapter of this book I shall return to these issues. Moreover, is it compatible with Western *moral* ideals to contribute to the preservation of poverty in the Third World by protectionism? Do we really want a world in which nationality or citizenship and income are highly correlated and in which political power becomes more, rather than less, important than it currently is?

Fifth, one should remember that international trade is also a substitute for international migration. If the West closes its markets to Third World products, the incentive to migrate from poor countries to rich countries will increase. Race riots and crimes by natives against immigrants demonstrate that reducing emigration pressure in poor countries by permitting those economies to grow by trade might be in the selfish interest of rich countries (which might otherwise face a flood of economic refugees who can be neither absorbed nor humanely turned back).

In my view, the sum of all these arguments against protectionism is convincing enough to survive even the demolition of one or another of the arguments. The demolition of all or most of them seems inconceivable, so the case for free trade stands. But contemporary arguments about the harmful effects of free trade on equality and employment in the West are likely to make rent-seeking easier for groups that suffer from poor-country competition.

While I do not know how to overcome the rent-seeking society, or how to achieve the equivalent of general disarmament in distributional struggles, I do think that one obvious strategy does not work. The poor cannot as easily unite, exert political pressure, or compel revolutionary change and obtain a better deal as more privileged groups.[24] Meanwhile, the predicament of the poor facilitates rent-seeking by some privileged persons. As Bauer (1981, p. 13) has observed, "Most beneficiaries of redistribution include its advocates, organizers and administrators, notably politicians and civil servants, who are not among the poor."[25] Politics and the price distortions thereby created are related at least as much, if not more closely, to the causes of poverty than to their cure. If the poor only unite, they have no chance to prevail. If some poor groups receive an offer to participate in a winning coalition, they will accept it. The winning coalition will aim at concentrated gains for its members, including previously poor ones, and dispersed and preferably invisible losses for others who cannot fight back—for example, because they are yet not organized and still poor.

It is possible that the true heroes of human history and improvement are those who aim for minor but useful reforms, who never get tired in the uphill struggle against rent-seeking. But to ask for this kind of work is to ask for a kind of altruism, and the trouble with altruism is that it is so rare that we should not trust one self-confident group to enforce it in others. Most guardians of morality are likely to defect and to look for rents in the end.

Notes

1. There are other dependency approaches. One of them is incompatible with rent-seeking theory in its economic foundations but similar in its analysis of distributional conflicts (Emmanuel, 1972). This approach is discussed later in the chapter.

2. Of course, one might modify Galtung's theory. After all, vertical trade looks bad to him because it concentrates the pressure to upgrade human capital on developed societies. Such a modification might lead one toward Wood's (1994) recent work, but then it would be difficult to maintain the argument that the Third World suffers from international trade.

3. Wallerstein's (1974; 1979; 1980) focus on government-sponsored distortion of markets is compatible with rent-seeking theory. Much of his theorizing, however, as well as Rubinson's (1976; 1977) interpretation of it, is not.

4. Bradshaw (1985a, p. 202) does not even refer to Galtung or his theory, but he reports a weak positive effect of primary product specialization on growth and an equally weak negative effect of commodity concentration on growth in black Africa. While the former result flatly contradicts Galtung's expectations, the latter provides some extremely weak support for it.

5. Some readers may object to my listing the studies by Delacroix and Ragin (1978; 1981) among those that call Galtung's ideas into question. The older study was mainly concerned with different issues, but it did control for human capital formation, i.e., secondary school enrollment. In my view, this control is useful, and other studies should have done so as well. Therefore, one should note that the older study does not find a negative effect of primary product exports and manufactured imports. The more recent study maintains that the export of primary products and commodity concentration obstructs development in "advanced peripheral countries." Most LDCs are not classified in this category by Delacroix and Ragin, but countries such as Japan, Israel, Italy, Austria, the Soviet Union, Poland, Czechoslovakia, East Germany, and some true LDCs are. Given the heterogeneity of the "advanced" category, the important result seems to be that neither the export of primary products nor commodity concentration hurts the growth prospects of the so-called poor periphery that still contains nations such as Brazil, Turkey, or South Korea among its members.

6. It is hard to say whether the relationship between the level of economic development and growth rates is nonmonotonic or not. In most of my earlier work with data from the 1960s and 1970s, it seemed to be nonmonotonic. In some of my recent work with later data, it seems to be monotonic. I suggest proceeding pragmatically: Let the goodness of fit decide which specification is superior, even if this suggestion implies different specifications for different periods of observation. Since almost all of the studies surveyed here refer to data from the 1960s or 1970s, a nonmonotonic specification seems appropriate. Concerning the relationship between the level of economic development and income inequality, Muller (1994) has recently

called the general acceptance of Kuznets's theorizing into question. In his view, the curvilinear relationship between the level of economic development and inequality is spurious. It disappears if one controls for agrarian inequality, i.e., the geometric mean of land ownership concentration (Gini) and the (logged) percentage of the labor force in agriculture. One of my students, Nicol Hansen, however, could not confirm the disappearance of the nonmonotonic relationship between economic development and income inequality through controls for agrarian inequality for a different inequality data set. Another recent study (Nielson, 1994) does not criticize the Kuznets curve but explains it by "dualism." Technically, controlling for "dualism" also reduces the curvilinear effect of economic development to insignificance. So far, all sides in the dependency debate have not controlled for agrarian inequality or "dualism" as potential substitutes for the curvilinear level of development effect in their work.

7. The relationship between military participation and human capital formation is discussed in Weede (1983b). By and large, negative findings on dependency propositions do not depend on inclusion or exclusion of military participation ratios as control variables. Still, some results are fairly sensitive to one's point of view on a number of technical issues. See the debate between Bornschier (1981b; 1982) on the one hand and Weede and Tiefenbach (1981a; 1981b; 1982) on the other hand. My most recent work on the effects of military participation (Weede, 1993b) finds that these effects are conditional on the level of economic development. The lower the level of economic development, the stronger the positive effects of military participation on growth rates. For highly developed societies, military participation no longer produces any growth benefits.

8. Moon (1991, p. 88) also points out that "the share of labor force in agriculture is more closely related to the physical quality of life index than is overall GNP per capita."

9. Moon (1991, p. 258) argues that "development centered around the plantation and the factory produces relatively more effective basic needs provision than development centered around the mine and subsistence agriculture." The negative evaluation of mines and subsistence agriculture as well as the positive evaluation of the factory fits with Galtung's (1971) ideas on vertical trade, but the positive evaluation of the plantation certainly does not fit his ideas.

10. It may be that reality is sometimes even worse when there are no bribes. Lobbying, dining with bureaucrats, entertaining legislators, and offering electoral support may be even more costly than outright bribes (and do some recipients less good) and still result in similar policies.

11. Unequal resourcefulness of group members also makes the provision of collective goods more likely. At the same time, it may occasionally create the interesting phenomenon of the exploitation of the strong by the weak.

12. By and large, we can observe a mirror-image phenomenon in contemporary industrialized democracies. Here rural agrarian minorities succeed in distorting the urban-rural terms of trade in their favor and at the expense of urban consumers and taxpayers. Again, the recipe of concentrated gains and dispersed losses is met.

13. Essentially this measure of urban bias assumes (rather than demonstrates) that the disparity results from distortions rather than from productivity differentials. If this assumption were false and its opposite true, however, one would find no plausible reason why the disparity should have some negative impact on growth rates.

14. Unfortunately, Bradshaw's work has been focused on urbanization rather than on growth or inequality. While the direct effect of urban bias on growth appears weak and sometimes insignificant in Bradshaw's regressions, he does support the

idea of a positive effect of urban bias on overurbanization, which indirectly contributes to lower growth rates. For the purposes of this chapter, a summary measure of direct and indirect effects of urban bias on growth rates would be more interesting than the information Bradshaw provides.

15. One may dispute this statement insofar as rich industrialized democracies are concerned. In the United States, entering public service or politics often implies major income losses. Not so in LDCs, where politics or state employment come close to being the only available paths to personal advancement. That is why politics in poor countries without vigorous private enterprises so easily degenerates into what Andreski (1969, p. 64) aptly termed "kleptocracy." One may possibly minimize (though not abolish) kleptocracy by limiting government revenues or governmental control of the economy.

16. Moreover, South Korea and Taiwan had fairly competitive labor markets and weak trade unions during their early and authoritarian phases of economic development.

17. In this scenario nobody would enjoy job security or tenure because such privileges are inherently discriminatory.

18. As Emmanuel (1972) claimed, worldwide unity of labor movements is unrealistic. Whatever the declaratory policy of Northern unions is, their factual policy must aim at defending their privileges against Southern competition whether by protectionism, migration control, or impeding the outflow of capital and technology. For a more recent treatment, see Krauss (1983).

19. It is hard to imagine how one can make a humanitarian case for local welfare states in rich countries without implicit or explicit recourse to ethnocentric or racist arguments. Why should rich people in OECD countries be taxed in order to enable their less fortunate fellow citizens to buy used cars or to enjoy Mediterranean holidays instead of saving truly poor fellow men and women in LDCs from abject poverty and starvation?

20. The Hungarian philosopher and politician G. M. Tamas (1993, p. 74) provides the most devastating indictment of this state of affairs: "We are all national socialists. . . . Some combination of ethnic nationalism and collective welfarism characterizes most of the states in the world today." An open door for Third World exports and emigration to the rich countries are substitutes: The more exports the rich countries admit, the less migration pressure there will be.

21. While Allais favors European protectionism, neither *The Economist* nor Wood does. But they agree on some consequences of North-South trade in manufactures.

22. Although there should be some convergence, the factor price *equalization* theorem need not apply. Specialization, transport costs, and differences in infrastructure prevent it (see Wood, 1994, pp. 28–30, 41).

23. For numerical information about unemployment and pay differentials, see OECD (1993). The OECD also discusses dependency traps generated by the tax and welfare state and unduly high worker protection as determinants of (long-term) unemployment. Although the OECD does mention global competition as a conceivable source of unemployment and increasing pay differentials, it does not not commit itself to naming global competition as a primary or dominant cause of these events. Instead, the OECD pays more attention to technological change (which, of course, may interact with global competition) or even to demographic trends, such as large numbers of young people entering the labor market in the 1980s, putting pressure on it and widening pay differentials. According to Allais (1994, pp. 187, 197), free trade may have generated unemployment in the European Union in the

order of magnitude of 10 or 20 million, and it may necessitate 50 to 70 percent lower wages for workers with few skills if they have to compete with Third World producers. In Allais's (1994, pp. 361–362, 422) view, social policies in France contributed 32 to 38 percent to unemployment (in 1993), free trade 28 to 34 percent, technological progress 13 to 15 percent, and business cycles 10 to 13 percent. The smaller numbers apply if some unemployment is attributed to non-European immigration into France.

24. For a systematic treatment of revolutions from an economic perspective, see Tullock (1974) or Weede (1992a, chapter 21).

25. A useful illustration is the budget of the World Health Organization. About three-quarters of it goes to paying the salaries of its own staff members, many of whom live comfortably in Geneva (Tollison and Wagner, 1993, p. 19).

6

THE WEST IN DECLINE
AND THE RISE OF EAST ASIA

1. Distributional Coalitions
and the Welfare State in the West

According to the World Bank (1994, pp. 162–163), high-income economies averaged an annual per capita GNP growth rate of 2.3 percent in the 1980–1992 period. Except for the United Arab Emirates, all of the high-income economies are either Western (i.e., European or countries primarily settled by Europeans) or East Asian. There are only three East Asian societies in the select group of twenty-three high-income economies, but they monopolize the first three ranks in economic performance. Hong Kong is number one, with 5.5 percent annual per capita growth; Singapore number two, with 5.3 percent; and Japan number three, with 3.6 percent. By contrast, the economies of the United States and France grew 1.7 percent, Germany and Britain 2.4 percent. While all of the West is in the high-income group, most of East Asia is not yet. If one looks at other East Asian societies, one finds South Korea with 8.5 percent, Thailand with 6.0 percent, and China with 7.6 percent per capita growth rates. In spite of the sorry state of the North Korean economy and the persisting problems in the Philippines or parts of Indochina, there can be no reasonable doubt that East Asia outperforms the West. Why?

The most obvious answer refers to "opportunities of backwardness" (Gerschenkron, 1962, chapter 1; Maddison, 1969, p. xxiii). According to Kuznets (1966, p. 10), "since the second half of the nineteenth century, the major source of economic growth in the developed countries has been science-based technology." If advances in knowledge and scientific progress fuel economic growth, then comparatively backward economies can borrow from the leaders and apply imported technology to their own benefit. Imitation can be faster and cheaper than the exploration of technological frontiers and the development of entirely new products. This argument may be applied to the contrast between East Asia and the West as well as to the explanation of different performances among the industrial societies. It may

91

be supplemented by the observation that comparatively backward societies tend to have a larger pool of labor in agriculture. Therefore, they have a much better chance of reallocating labor from agriculture to more productive pursuits in industry or services than countries where agriculture employs less than 5 percent of the work force. The advantages-of-backwardness explanation of different economic performances is powerful and has repeatedly been confirmed in cross-national studies (for example, Bornschier, 1989; Pryor, 1984; Weede, 1991 [for industrial societies]; Dollar, 1992; Weede, 1993b; World Bank, 1993b, p. 51 [for global comparisons]). While there is some reason to doubt whether the advantages of backwardness extend all the way to the lowest levels of economic development, this doubt does not refute the applicability of the argument to the explanation of intra-Western variation or to the divergent experiences of the West and East Asia.[1]

Another obvious answer starts from a growth-accounting perspective. Here, rapid growth in output is attributed either to growth in inputs—such as more employment, improvements in education, or massive investment in physical capital—or to gains in efficiency, i.e., increases in the output per unit of input. Where growth is primarily input driven, it must run into diminishing returns and therefore be inevitably limited. Singapore's spectacular economic performance is primarily input driven (Krugman, 1994b, pp. 70–71; Young, 1994). Between 1966 and 1990 the city-state roughly doubled per capita incomes every decade. To achieve this result, the employed share of the population grew from 27 to 51 percent. Such a near doubling of employment cannot be repeated. Educational standards were also dramatically improved, but since two-thirds of the work force had already completed secondary education by 1990, further equally dramatic improvements seem unlikely. Finally, investment rose from 11 to 40 percent of output. It is hard to imagine that rising investment can underpin future growth as vigorously as it did with past growth. If Singaporean growth remains input driven, as it was in the past, and if there are no dramatic efficiency gains in the future, then future growth rates will compare poorly with those in the past. Similar arguments may apply to South Korea and Taiwan and, to a much lesser degree, even to Japan.

The "advantages-of-backwardness" and the "growth-accounting" perspectives share a common implication: The West need not worry too much because advantages of backwardness are soon exhausted, or because economic growth by increasing inputs must run out of steam and meet diminishing returns quite soon. One should nevertheless not become too complacent. Mainland China's giant population implies an economic size more than twice as large as that of the United States, even before per capita incomes reach half of the average U.S. income. There is no reason to believe that advantages of backwardness, or input-driven growth, meet their inherent limits so early. Moreover, the gap between East Asian and Western growth rates exists not only because of conceivably transient Asian miracle growth rates but also because of faltering Western performance, which is the main topic of this section.

According to Olson (1982), we should look for a different explanation. In his view, the nature of collective action exerts the strongest influence on growth rates. In all societies there are latent interest groups, i.e., groups of people with similar interests who could gain from collusion and avoidance of competition among themselves. Established producers of some good share an interest in erecting barriers to entry for new producers, in limiting competitive imports, in market-sharing arrangements, and in cartel prices higher than those that can be realized in a competitive market. In other words, established producers would like to obtain rents. Similarly, workers or professionals in a given branch of the economy share an interest in unions or professional associations, in controlling and limiting the supply of labor, and in excessive pay for their services or in comfortable working conditions. While all kinds of latent interest groups could gain substantial advantages for themselves if they succeeded in getting organized and becoming capable of collective action, not all of them capture these advantages. By and large, restrictive practices and collusion constitute collective goods, so the freerider problem arises. In Olson's view, small groups such as oligopolists should be the first to overcome it.[2] Others depend on selective incentives and coercion, where the applicability of coercion demands at least government acquiescence or, better still, complicity.

The purpose of interest groups or distributional coalitions is to distort prices in favor of their members. Distorted prices convey misleading signals and interfere with the efficiency of resource allocation. If distributional coalitions accumulate over time, if their impact on the economy grows ever more pervasive, then growth rates should decline. In Olson's opinion, a stable institutional framework provides a fertile ground for the establishment of distributional coalitions. Although such coalitions in communist-ruled societies differ in style from Western distributional coalitions, they seem to have given a helping hand even in the economic decline of the Soviet Union (Murrell and Olson, 1991; Faith and Short, 1995). The general proposition about the effects of political stability on distributional coalitions and growth may also be specifically applied to Western democracies. Olson (1982, p. 77) posits "that countries that have had democratic freedom of organization without upheaval or invasion the longest will suffer the most from growth-repressing organizations and combinations." The hypothesized relationship between the age of democracy and growth-repressing distributional coalitions depends upon the difficulty of overcoming the freeriding tendency—some groups succeed quickly, others need more time; therefore, there is an accumulation of growth-repressing organizations over time—and upon the lack of respect for established interest groups shown by successful revolutionaries, totalitarian governments, or foreign armies of occupation.

Distributional coalitions do so much harm because they undermine some prerequisites of capitalism. Capitalism and the market need scarcity prices in order to allocate resources efficiently. In signaling scarcity of goods or services, high prices induce efforts to reduce scarcity. This inducement is the positive function of high prices. Since prices reflect only scarcity, not whether it is natural or contrived scarcity, high prices, or the hope of obtaining them, may have two different effects. First, they may induce some expansion of production. From a producer's point of view, this route tends to be ultimately self-defeating because expanded production reduces scarcity rents. Second, the hope for high prices induces efforts to restrict competition, to preserve scarcity, and to obtain rents, because competition has been reduced or eliminated.

The task of state and government should be to nurture competition and to combat restrictive practices. A very crude first approach to this issue makes one expect that government should rarely succeed in doing so. After all, fair and fierce competition instead of rigged and restricted competition is a collective good at the societal level of analysis. Restrictive practices and price distortions tend to be collective goods at less highly aggregated or subsocietal levels of analysis, i.e., for the members of distributional coalitions. Since a society is by definition a larger group than its components, since group size reduces the probability of procurement of public goods, it is to be expected that subnational groups are more successful in reducing competition than society is in maintaining it.

A more refined analysis specifically tailored to democracies leads to a similar conclusion and to the expectation that the democratic permissiveness toward rent-seeking is simultaneously bad for growth and for income inequality. The starting point is a standard assumption in public choice theorizing. Democratic politicians are neither better nor worse than ordinary citizens; like anyone else, they are self-seeking utility maximizers. Parties are associations of political entrepreneurs (and their supporters) who want to get enough votes to control political and administrative offices and decisionmaking. Ideologies and party programs are instruments in the struggle for power. If all voters were fully informed about politics, then politicians would be equally responsive to the preferences of all voters. However, if some voters are ignorant of the policies that affect them, then there are no incentives for politicians to take the policy preferences of these voters into account. Thus, the existence of information deficits, uncertainty, and even rational ignorance severely qualifies the responsiveness of democratic politicians to the electorate (for similar views, see Brunner, 1978; Demsetz, 1982; Downs, 1957; and Schumpeter, 1942).

There are a lot of reasons why the distribution of information among voters should be highly unequal. Some people find politics entertaining; others find it boring. Some people receive political information by pursuing their administrative, business, or professional careers; others don't. Leaders of interest groups may even make a job out of the observation of those governmental decisions that affect their clientele and, ultimately, themselves. Unequal levels of information and interest in certain decisions generate opinion leadership. Parties may become coalitions of attentive interest groups as well as *prisoners of these groups* (see Bernholz, 1977; or Brunner, 1978).[3]

Under the assumption of equal information and attentiveness, democratic redistribution has to be egalitarian. Under this assumption, a relatively poor majority could benefit itself by redistributing away from a relatively rich minority. The result would be some equalization of the size distribution of income. If one thinks that the equality of the vote is a more important determinant of political decisionmaking than the inequality in attention, information, and organization, then one expects egalitarian redistribution within democracies, as do Korpi (1983) or Muller (1988). The more time a democracy has had for correcting or equalizing income distributions by political interventions, the less inequality should still exist. In my view, however, this is a false perspective on the problem.

Where equal votes are combined with highly unequal levels of political attention and information, something different is to be expected. While the rhetoric of equalization may still prevail, actual policies benefit well-informed minorities at the expense of ignorant majorities. Since the level of political attention and information is correlated with socioeconomic status (Nie and Verba, 1975), there is no reason to expect any bias of actual policies in favor of the lower classes or the poor.

Given unequal levels of information and often very restricted attention spans of opinion leaders and organizations on specific issues, a proliferation of political interventions in the economy, and the growing complexity resulting therefrom, is to be expected. Since political information is unequally distributed and is focused on different special issues in different parts of the electorate, the main result of competition among politicians in a democracy is the expansion of state power and state interference with the economy. Of course, this contention in no way implies that political competition and efforts to obtain special privileges are the only important sources of government expenditure growth (see Borcherding, 1985; North, 1985, for other reasons).

The distribution of political attention, information, and interest in society is not random. Attention and information are likely to result from individuals' concentrated interests and organization. Those whose interests are concentrated on some specific issue have much stronger incentives to collect the relevant information and to get organized than those whose interests are only marginally affected and are widely scattered. By and large, producers benefit from interest concentration. Their income, profit, and standard of living largely depend on the price they get for their few products. If some politicians promise them protection from foreign competitors (who cannot vote), they will certainly notice it. Moreover, the politicians will tell them about their good deeds. If producers get such protection, they will use it for raising prices at the expense of consumers. Since most consumers are hardly affected by the prices of most of the items they buy, consumers will not notice what politicians do to them. Even if they do notice, other issues are likely to dominate their (political) intentions. Such political intervention in the economy interferes with the efficiency of resource allocation and thereby reduces average incomes and growth rates. At best, the impact on income distribution is merely arbitrary.

Reality is likely to be somewhat worse. Typically, politicians and policies are not influenced by single voters separately attempting to exercise political influence. Instead, there are mediating organizations between the income earner, voter, and consumer on the one hand and state or government on the other hand. According to Olson (1965; 1982), some people with equal or similar interests find it easy to turn a latent interest group into a distributional coalition capable of procuring collective goods for the members of the coalition, while other people never overcome their freeriding tendencies. By and large, small groups find the procurement of public goods (for themselves) easier than do large groups. Large groups have to rely on the availability of selective incentives and coercion. Of course, coercion depends very much on the facilitating behavior of the government.

Since politicians urgently need the political support of distributional coalitions and their leaders (Bernholz, 1977), and since elitist groups find the establishment of distributional coalitions easier than do large and deprived groups (Olson, 1965; Tilly, 1978), the political process in a democracy should be biased toward better-organized and more privileged groups. According to Olson (1982, p. 175), "government and other institutions that invervene in markets are not in general any less inegalitarian than competitive markets" because "there is greater inequality . . . in the opportunity to create distributional coalitions than there is in the inherent productive abilities of people." In his work on East Asian societies, Steve Chan (1987a; 1987b, p. 138) took statements like these as his point of departure and argued that there should be "a negative relationship between the strength and number of distributional coalitions in society and its level of socioeconomic equity. The poor, the uneducated, and the unemployed lack the skills, the time, the information, and the selective incentives that make collective action possible."

According to another line of reasoning, neither catch-up opportunities nor input mobilization nor distributional coalitions exert the strongest influence on economic growth rates: Too much government does. Friedman and Friedman (1981) and Hayek (1960) praise the growth-promoting virtues of economic freedom and limited government and simultaneously deplore the consequences of government interference with the economy. Bernholz (1986, p. 675) has listed the efficiency-reducing effects of state interference with the economy:

> Firstly, it becomes relatively more and more rewarding under these conditions to expend time and effort in reducing the tax burden and in attempting to gain welfare benefits instead of doing productive work. Secondly, productive work which can escape taxation, i.e., the underground economy, tends to be more and more attractive; the benefits become greater and greater compared to the risks involved. Thirdly, at given gross rates of profit and interest saving and investment become less and less attractive relative to consumption. Moreover, much saving will be invested unproductively in precious metals, works of art, private homes and other property in order to gain speculative profits, which are either not taxable or taxable at lower rates or which are more difficult to tax. Finally, risky investment in projects aiming at product and process innovation will decline, since the high profits arising if the project is successful will be taxed at high marginal rates, whereas the losses which may be incurred if the project fails can only be deducted from profits for a limited period of time.

For these reasons the increasing power of the state should be a contributing cause to the retardation of growth rates in Western economies.

While Bernholz's arguments focus on the negative impact of taxation, Frum (1994, pp. 28–29) focuses on the "benefits" that the welfare state seems to provide and charges that it "is a colossal lure tempting citizens to reckless behavior. . . . Welfare can never be reformed in a way that simultaneously encourages people to work and provides them with a decent livelihood if they do not." From this perspective, the welfare state undercuts responsibility and the virtues that a capitalist economy requires: thrift, diligence, prudence, and orderliness. Although there is a long tradition in the social sciences according to which the market may undermine its moral foundations, here it is argued that the welfare state rather than the market undermines the moral foundations of capitalism. If this idea should be true, then more "perfect" welfare states should grow more slowly than less perfect ones.

Expanding government size or social transfers are generally justified by the need to provide infrastructure and public goods and to serve the poor. Given what I have just said about concentrated interests, the distribution of political information and attention among voters, and the head start of the privileged strata of society in collective action, it is by no means obvious, however, that the poor will benefit from the expansion of government and the welfare state. Conceivably, they even lose twice: first because the expansion of government and of social transfers reduces economic growth rates and thereby the future size of the pie; second because the lower classes lose the rent-seeking and political redistribution game in spite of their numbers.

Bornschier (1989), Korpi (1985), and Pryor (1984) provide empirical evidence that advantages of backwardness or catch-up opportunities are major determinants of cross-national differences in growth rates. Bernholz (1982; 1986), Choi (1983a; 1983b), McCallum and Blais (1987), Lane and Errson (1986), and Weede (1984a; 1986b; 1986c; 1987a; 1991) support Olson's claim that "institutional sclerosis" or "age of democracy" reduces growth rates. Bernholz (1982; 1986), Dudley and Montmarquette (1992); Weede (1986b; 1986c; 1991), and to a lesser degree Cameron (1985) confirm a negative relationship between public sector size or social security transfers and reduced growth rates.[4] Of course, it is not true that there has been no dissent and controversy. Quite to the contrary, Pryor (1984) found no evidence in favor of Olson's proposition and has been severely criticized by Weede (1987a). Korpi (1985) argued that the welfare state may constitute an "irrigation system" instead of a "leaky bucket." His argument has been rebutted by Weede (1986c) in a work that demonstrated that inclusion of Olson's age-of-democracy effects makes this contention untenable. More recently, Castles and Dowrick (1990) rejected the proposition that government expenditures reduce growth rates in pooled cross-time, cross-national regressions. But they achieved this result by inserting atheoretical and post hoc dummy variables. In my view (Weede, 1991), this insertion is exactly what should *not* be done.

Summarizing this set of findings, one has to admit that there is some evidence in favor of differential catch-up opportunities, of negative age-of-democracy or institutional-sclerosis effects, and of public sector size or social security transfers being important determinants of growth rates. But none of these supposed determinants of growth is uncontroversial. Moreover, a technical issue is important: whether dummy variables for periods in pooled regressions and some country dummies, especially for Japan, should be included. In my view (Weede, 1991), they should not be included. If they are excluded, then "advantages of backwardness" count for little in explaining growth differences among highly developed nations, but age of democracy and public sector size or social security transfers still can be shown to do much harm.

There has been surprisingly little research on the relationship between distributional coalitions and age of democracy or institutional sclerosis on the one hand and income distribution on the other hand. The reason is that Olson (1982) himself did not suggest testing of this implication of his theory. Chan (1987a; 1987b) pioneered this effort, but he focused on East Asian societies rather than the largely Western high-income nations where data are probably more available than elsewhere. According to Muller's (1988, p. 58) *global* study of income distributions, the oldest democracies do not succeed in minimizing income inequality. Instead his "relatively old democracies"— labeled by comparison with young Third World democracies—do best. Although Muller's global focus leads him to a different interpretation (criticized in Weede, 1989a), some of his results actually are not so far from my own conclusions (Weede, 1990c; 1990d). According to these results, the permissiveness of old democracies toward interest groups results in less rather than more equality.[5] Therefore, distributional coalitions—supported by politicians who serve special-interest groups and by rationally ignorant voters—hurt the poorest strata twice: first by reducing growth, second by even less egalitarian sharing than the market.

In their massive investigation of the welfare state, Pampel and Williamson (1989) evaluate and criticize alternative theoretical perspectives—from pluralism and industrial society via the social democratic perspective to dependency—and arrive at rather similar conclusions. One of their suggestions and two of their conclusions complement the approach I have taken. First this suggestion: "To the extent that it directs resources away from production and discourages upward mobility, welfare spending may retard the progress toward greater equality coming from economic growth" (Pampel and Williamson, 1989, p. 107). Then these findings: "In addition to reducing inequality, then, rising income reduces the effect that income inequality has on the physical quality of life" (p. 159). And: "The empirical results reveal an apparent contradiction in the functioning of democratic polities: It raises spending but not equality" (p. 172).[6]

The establishment of the Common Market in Europe *might have* increased the size of the market, *might have* reinforced competition, *might have* undermined restrictive practices, and thereby *might have* promoted growth. In principle, a European Union on the one hand and limited government, private property rights, and market exchange at freely established scarcity prices on the other hand could be compatible with each other. Observation of political practice makes one suspicious, however. The common agricultural policy is still the most costly endeavor of the European Union. This policy has always been an orgy of interventionism, inefficiency, and injustice. By establishing minimum prices, the European Union guarantees overproduction. Price supports benefit rich farmers more than poor farmers. Simultaneously, high food prices hurt poor consumers more than rich consumers. Moreover, exports of European farm products at subsidized prices hurt U.S. farmers, and thereby burden transatlantic relations, as well as Third World or East European farmers, thereby reducing the chances of poor countries catching up with the rich countries. In a nutshell, professional economists would be hard pressed to invent a policy that does as much harm and as little good as the European common agricultural policy. The more general point is that the Europeanization of economic policy-making establishes the opportunity to commit policy errors on a much grander scale than has been possible in most of European history. Politicians do not hesitate to exploit such opportunities.[7]

European agricultural policies are also useful in making another point. Decisions are made to serve special-interest groups or distributional coalitions, not to serve anything like national, European, or cosmopolitan interests. Recently, the common agricultural policy and other interest-group-serving policies accounted for about 73 percent of European Community expenditure and 78 percent of its legislation in terms of number of pages (Vaubel, 1994, p. 174).

According to Olson (1982), aging political regimes in general, and aging democracies in particular, are likely to become prisoners of interest groups and to pursue ever less efficient economic policies. Governments intervene in the market, distort prices, transfer income, and interfere with efficient resource allocation. The older an established regime—for example, a democracy—becomes, the more it suffers from institutional sclerosis and reduced economic growth. Although empirical support for this proposition has been quite weak when U.S. states have been compared with each other (Gray and Lowery, 1988; Nardinelli, Wallace, and Warner, 1986; Vedder and Gallaway, 1988), Olson's proposition has received fairly strong and consistent support when industrialized democracies have been analyzed (Bernholz, 1986; Choi, 1983a; 1983b; Lane and Errson, 1986; Weede, 1991). Moreover, economic decline has been further reinforced by high government revenues, expenditures, or transfer payments (Bernholz, 1986; Pampel and Williamson, 1989; Weede, 1991). Some Western countries, such as Britain and Sweden, suffer both from being old democracies (and therefore afflicted with strong distributional coalitions) and having high government expenditures, while others (such as the United States) suffer from at least one of these ailments. Since Western nations are close to the leading edge in technology, there is also little room to boost growth rates by capturing the "advantages of backwardness." Thus, the West is likely to be outperformed by more dynamic regions.[8]

In Chapter 4, Section 1 I attributed the rise of the West to political disunity and competition between Western states and their ruling classes. Disunity and competition have provided an opening for individual liberty and private efforts to improve material well-being. Politicians—such as the German Social Democrat Rudolf Scharping (1994, p. 193)—resent the package of interstate competition and economic interdependence and, rightly, point out: "The ability of national economies to apply policy controls decreases with their interdependence with other economies." Scharping is also worried by interstate competition to cut taxes—or one may put the same point somewhat differently: to respect private property rights.[9] Without the chains on politicians provided by interstate competition, the future of capitalism, prosperity, and the West would look very bleak.

The state interventionism inspired by distributional coalitions or vote-seeking politicians and the welfare state may be understood as constraints on economic development or brakes on growth. Recently there have been some econometric investigations of the relationship between economic freedom and growth rates. Scully (1992, p. 179) concludes from his investigation that "the average growth rate in societies where these freedoms are restricted is one-third of that of free societies." Although I subscribe to the same theoretical proposition linking freedom and growth as Scully, his econometric evidence looks rather weak to me. First, the institutional variables that he presumes to affect growth rates actually refer to the end rather than the beginning of the growth period (Scully, 1992, p. 235). This is unfortunate, because the proposition that good economic performance promotes liberty is not altogether unreasonable (compare Lipset, 1959; 1994). Torstensson's (1994) econometric study of property rights and economic growth builds on Scully's previous work but refers to a later growth period and therefore escapes the criticism just raised against Scully's work. Torstensson reports that arbitrary seizures of property (by the state) do significantly retard growth. Moreover, he carefully establishes the robustness of this effect.

In Scully's work, it makes little difference whether one focuses on economic freedom, civil liberty, or political rights. Since Western democracies cluster at one end of all of these scales, communist-ruled societies at the opposite end, and much of the Third World in between, this finding is not astonishing. If one accepts the idea that political freedom or democracy and economic freedom have been hardly distinguishable during the Cold War era, then Scully's (1992) results should also be compared with the much larger number of studies relating democracy to economic growth rates. These studies have recently been summarized by Sirowy and Inkeles (1990), Przeworski (1993, p. 46), and Weede (1993a). Since these reviews of the literature concur in reporting that the number of studies favoring the idea that authoritarianism promotes growth is similar to the number of studies arguing that democracy promotes growth, one may either stress the inconclusiveness of these studies or conclude that neither democracy nor authoritarianism makes a major difference to average growth rates. I incline toward the latter interpretation. In my view, the seeming inconclusiveness of the findings results from the weakness and lack of robustness of regime effects.

Unfortunately, the quantitative evidence from cross-national studies does not fit easily with the qualitative evidence from other investigations. Fukuyama (1993, p. 99) provides an example: He arrives at the conclusion that many of the most impressive economic growth records in the last 150 years have been compiled not by democracies, but by authoritarian states with more or less capitalist economic systems. This was true of both Meiji Japan and the German Second Reich in the latter half of the nineteenth century, as well as any number of more recent modernizing authoritarian regimes such as Franco's Spain, post-1953 South Korea, Taiwan, Brazil, Singapore, or Thailand.

In my view, there are essentially three ways to account for the divergence between the qualitative and the quantitative evidence. First, one may dismiss the qualitative evidence because it lacks rigor. Although I favor quantitative studies wherever feasible, I would not recommend this easy way out. Second, one may point to the fact that quantitative studies tend to focus on quite narrow and recent time periods, such as the 1960s or 1970s. Therefore, one may even give greater credibility to the qualitative studies. Again, I hesitate to do so. Third, one may note that cross-national studies focus on comparing *average* growth rates of more and less democratic regimes. Now, it is conceivable that growth rates of democracies and authoritarian regimes are quite similar *on average* but that the variance among authoritarian regimes is much larger than among democracies. An unpublished reanalysis of my recent study (Weede, 1993a) indicates that this is indeed true: Some authoritarian regimes do much worse than even poorly performing democracies. Some other authoritarian regimes do much better than even strongly performing democracies. If this interpretation is accepted, then Fukuyama's claim and the evidence from quantitative studies are compatible and, indeed, complementary parts of the full story.

In Chapter 4, Sections 1 and 2 I have argued that capitalism precedes democracy and lays the foundations for it. Part of this relationship is due to the conflict-mitigating effects of the high incomes that only capitalism can generate (Lipset 1959; 1994). Another part of this relationship is the fact that only the capitalist divergence of economic and political power permits dissent. Obviously, democracy without opportunities for dissent is a sham at best. Whether people will dare to dissent depends on the cost. According to Bhagwati (1993a, p. 34): "The cost of dissent is immense when those who hold political authority also control the means of production." While capitalism is a necessary (but not sufficient) condition of democracy, democracy may well undermine liberty, efficiency, and prosperity. It is *not* the level of democracy that does harm—otherwise the empirical evidence should consistently demonstrate superior growth in autocratically governed societies, and it does not do so—but democratic permissiveness toward distributional coalitions and the welfare state. This point brings us back to Olson (1982) and the literature supporting his ideas that has been discussed earlier. In my view, Przeworski (1993, p. 47), who wants democracy not to be constrained by capitalism, has properly diagnosed the root of the troubles of the West: "Democracy inevitably threatens 'property rights.'" Unless we overcome this inclination, democracy might threaten itself by attacking its own economic base.[10]

I have argued that the welfare state reduces economic growth and thereby the means to pay its own way. More generally, one may point out (following Crozier, 1975, p. 13) that "the more decisions the modern state has to handle, the more helpless it becomes. Decisions do not only bring power; they also bring vulnerability." The welfare burden on Western societies grows inexorably. According to a causal model (Wilensky, 1975, p. 25), its most important determinants are the percentage of people aged sixty-five or more and the age of the social security system. Recent research (Pampel and Williamson, 1989, pp. 62–67) has corroborated the impact of the aged and even demonstrated that their political effectiveness seems to expand over time. The "graying" of the West, especially of Europe, and the bureaucratic inertia of social security systems together make a sustainable rollback of the welfare state unlikely.

Compared to Europe, the United States has always been a laggard in social security expenditure. Since the 1960s, however, even the United States has undergone its own "welfare shift." Huntington (1975, p. 70) deplores that "the tendency was for massive increases in governmental expenditures to provide cash and benefits for particular individuals and groups within society rather than in expenditures designed to serve national purposes vis-à-vis the external environment." While war and its preparation have fueled the growth of the state in the nineteenth and much of the twentieth century, by now interest-group politics, rent-seeking, and the welfare state generate ever more bloated and rudderless governments.[11]

Western economic decline is promoted by distributional coalitions and the price distortions they "achieve" because of governmental assistance. It is also promoted by legislated refusal to learn (Pejovich, 1990; 1995, pp. 198–207). Since 1976, we have had a codetermination law (Mitbestimmung) in (West) Germany. According to this law, enterprises employing two thousand or more workers have to grant them (or their unions) some representation on enterprise boards as well as codetermination rights. I do not want to argue that codetermination is inefficient. Maybe it is efficient, maybe it is not. It is even conceivable that it is efficient in some sectors of the economy but inefficient in others. But the German law makes it almost impossible to find out—of course, a prohibition of codetermination by law would also constitute a barrier to learning. Elsewhere, we observe competition not only between enterprises but indirectly also between ways to organize enterprises because enterprises suffering from inefficient constitutions suffer the fate of maladapted species, whereas enterprises benefiting from efficient constitutions grow and expand. A legislated monopoly for any specific enterprise constitution abolishes this valuable competition and thereby the resulting incentives to organize enterprises ever more efficiently. Only if one could be absolutely confident that democratically elected parliaments somehow overcome the human tendency to submit to error could one not worry.

In the 1960s Huntington (1968) theorized about political decay in LDCs and traced decay to deficient political institutionalization. This variable consists of four components, one of which is autonomy. Huntington (1968, p. 20) defined that component as follows: "Political institutionalization, in the sense of autonomy, means the development of political organizations and procedures that are not simply expressions of the interests of particular groups." As narrow and special-interest groups enjoy an advantage over wider or even nationwide interests in their capacity for collective action, autonomy is hard to achieve. Western governments have largely lost it.

The instrumentalization of the state by interest groups, or the loss of governmental autonomy, goes hand in hand with a declining willingness to face the hard facts of life that even capitalism cannot overcome. In the early part of this century, Max Weber (1923/1981, p. 240) defined capitalism by a list of characteristics including formally free labor and workers selling their services under the compulsion of the whip of hunger. In my view, one should generalize and say not only employees but self-employed persons offer their services under the compulsion of the whip of hunger. Certainly such a statement is at least descriptively as accurate for "self-employed" Indian shoeshine boys or sharecroppers in many LDCs as it is for McDonald's employees in the United States or anyplace else. Acceptance of the whip of hunger as a fact that is older than capitalism but has not yet been overcome by capitalism has become "politically incorrect."

There are still some authors, such as Murray (1984, p. 177), who dare to oppose the spirit of the time in writing: "The tangible benefits that any society can realistically hold out to the poor youth of average abilities and average industriousness are mostly penalties, mostly disincentives. 'Do not study, and we will throw you out; commit crimes, and we will put you in jail; do not work, and we will make sure that your existence is so uncomfortable that any job will be preferable to it.' To promise much more is a fraud." I am confident—admittedly, without a basis in survey data—that this type of statement would get a ringing endorsement in East Asia, whether capitalist or nominally still communist, but would be rejected as too crude or inhumane in the West.

2. National Purpose and Competition in the East

As I have outlined in Chapter 4, Section 3, Japan had a head start over the other great Asian civilizations. It excelled in productivity and standard of living, literacy, and administration. In 1854 U.S. warships forced the

Japanese government to end its long-standing policy of isolation. In the late 1860s and early 1870s the political system was reformed and rationalized according to Western models. The Meiji Restoration was a revolution from above rather than from below. One may deplore this fact and relate it to authoritarianism, militarism, aggression, or "Asian fascism" (as Moore, 1966, has done), or one may admire the comparatively peaceful change[12] in Japan and point out (Scalapino, 1964, pp. 64, 85):

> The nation as a whole did not waste its energies or resources in the mass liquidation of persons and institutions. . . . It is questionable whether the limited social mobility that has characterized twentieth century Japan has served as a barrier to modernization, especially in its early and middle stages. The principle of hierarchy conserved the traditions of a committed and well-qualified elite on the one hand, and a disciplined and malleable people on the other. In a society so ordered, there is little waste through violence and there is a heightened capacity for sacrifice.

One may regard Japanese customs or traditions and their focus on authority, deference, consultation, and consent as a kind of social capital that promotes efficiency in the polity as well as in the economy.

After the Meiji Restoration the Japanese economy grew fast. From 1880 to 1913 agricultural production increased by two-thirds of the baseline; industrial production multiplied by a factor of five; national income doubled and even tripled until 1935 (Lockwood, 1964, pp. 119, 137). While the standard of living of the rural population, especially of tenants, remained low and increased only slowly, real industrial wages improved by one-third between 1897 and 1914 (Lockwood, 1964, p. 124). After opening its economy to the world then dominated by the West, Japan performed well almost from the beginning. Why? Part of the answer has already been provided: Because of comparatively high standards of literacy, the country was better endowed with human capital than any other non-Western country. Social capital was preserved rather than destroyed. But there must be additional determinants of the Japanese miracle.

Friedman and Friedman (1981, p. 53) point to the fact that Japan relied on markets and the corresponding incentives. Indeed, the Western powers had forced the country not to impose customs duties higher than 5 percent. Therefore, big price distortions were avoided, development could proceed according to comparative advantage rather than political whims, and efficient resource allocation was possible. This "growth by free trade" interpretation of the Japanese success story points to a stark contrast between early Japanese industrialization and later industrialization of other Asian economies, such as India, which focused on import substitution and wide-ranging regulation of foreign trade and industrial policy. Nevertheless, economic freedom is certainly not the full story.[13]

The Japanese state had an industrial policy from the beginning

(Fingleton, 1995; Johnson, 1982; Samuels, 1994).[14] It promoted certain industries and even established some of them as state-run pioneer enterprises, subsidized them, and protected them in formal and informal ways: "buy Japanese" campaigns, social pressure, and government procurement. From a theoretical perspective that regards economic freedom and decentralized decisionmaking by entrepreneurs as sources of growth and views government intervention as a likely brake—and this is the view endorsed in this book—the Japanese success story poses an explanatory problem: Why was government intervention less harmful in Japan than elsewhere?

Here, elite motivation matters. The driving force behind the modernization of Japan was the desire to avoid the fate of China and other Asian nations that had either lost independence altogether (such as India, Indonesia, the Philippines, or Indochina) or had accepted bridgeheads under effective foreign control (as did China, with Hong Kong, Macao, Tsingtao, and the treaty ports such as Shanghai). As the Opium War clearly demonstrated—it was fought for the British "right" to push drugs in China—Western rule in Asia was not benign. The Japanese elites determined that only a "rich nation (and) strong army" (Samuels, 1994; Tominaga, 1990, p. 42) could maintain national autonomy and dignity. Whereas industrial policies and state intervention in the economy in the contemporary democratic West almost always aim at satisfying the interests of comparatively narrow groups—whether by agricultural subsidies, tariff walls, "voluntary export restraint" agreements, minimum-wage laws, or social security transfers—the overriding driving force of Japanese economic policymaking has been not redistribution but national interest.[15] This situation is quite similar to the later success stories of South Korea and Taiwan.

I do not deny that the Japanese state in the late nineteenth century and the twentieth century guided the economy with a sometimes rather heavy and visible hand. Instead, I claim that perceived threats to national security made government guidance less divisive, more acceptable, and more efficient than state guidance of the economy for the sake of distributional targets. Since the role of the state among late industrializers (including Germany) tends to be much larger than in the Anglo-American model, one may even argue with Herman Kahn (1979, pp. 334, 457) that "one of the real difficulties that many developing nations labor under today is that they have no clear and present danger which they must face up to." He also attributed the economic miracles of South Korea and Taiwan to "very unforgiving external political environments." Put crudely and clearly, external threats are an important means of imposing discipline on ruling elites.[16] Indirectly, external threats and the conscription they necessitate also affect mass discipline, as Dahrendorf (1965, p. 68, my translation) has recognized: "Military training on the Prussian pattern might be much more useful as a preparation for industrialism than Calvinist creeds might be even under optimal circumstances." In my view (Weede, 1983b; 1993b), the concept of human capital should be extended to cover not only intelligence and cognitive and trade skills but also discipline and willingness to obey orders. After all, not all jobs require innovation. Sometimes obedience will do.

With ideas like these in mind, the Polish-British sociologist Stanislav Andreski (1968b, p. 75) has suggested:

> The sentiments of national solidarity, the habits of co-operation in a large mass and the concern for efficiency have undoubtedly been stimulated, if not created, by the wars which the European nations have waged during several centuries. And it may not be due to solely material advantages that the nations renowned for efficient military organization, like the Germans and the Japanese, have also been successful in catching up in the industrial race.

Such ideas may be tested with cross-national regressions in which the military participation ratio is one (out of many) explanatory variable for growth rates, where the level of economic development, investment, and other aspects of human capital formation can be and have been controlled (Weede and Jagodzinski, 1981/1987; Weede, 1983b; 1992c; 1993b). These studies demonstrate that countries with high military participation ratios do grow more rapidly than others, but this effect is conditional on the level of economic development. It is no longer useful for the United States, Germany, or contemporary Japan, but it seems to have been useful for less developed countries such as Taiwan or South Korea from the 1960s to the 1980s.[17]

The guiding hand of the Japanese government proved to be more helpful than government interference with the economy usually is, not only because of its national-security rather than special-interest orientation but also because there have been limits to government guidance. The international treaties putting a cap on Japanese customs duties in the late nineteenth century are just one example. Samuels (1994, p. 39) refers to another with his remarks about "the largest noncoerced privatization of industrial facilities in history" in late-nineteenth-century Japan. Thus, the state attempted to make private interests its servants rather than trying to improve on human nature by proscribing the profit motive. Finally, small competitive industries, particularly textiles, reflecting Japan's comparative advantage in the world economy of the late nineteenth century, played an important part in generating the foreign currency to pay for imported technology and machinery (Samuels, 1994, p. 39). Obviously, Japan is a mixed case of state guidance (by and large exceptionally competent guidance) and markets.

Before World War II, and afterward even until the 1960s, Japan's economy was neither admired nor feared in the West. Now it is both. Since the end of World War II, it has outperformed all other industrialized economies.

By now the Japanese economy is larger than any Western one except the U.S. economy. Trend extrapolation seems to give Japan some chance of overtaking the United States early in the twenty-first century. Nevertheless, one might suspect that Japan cannot sustain its past performance: Some of its past success must be attributed to opportunities of backwardness. Japan could imitate the best practices from more advanced countries, especially the United States, and therefore grow faster than other developed countries. Moreover, Japan still had a large agricultural sector in the 1950s and 1960s. By reallocating labor from less productive agriculture to more productive industry, Japan could boost its growth rate. But these sources of enhanced growth are largely exhausted, as is the comparative weakness of distributional coalitions. In the post–World War II world, Japan's democracy was one of the youngest. According to Olson's (1982) theory, institutional sclerosis should have been a less effective brake on growth in Japan than elsewhere.[18] Over time, this Japanese advantage should diminish. Finally, Japan largely avoided the welfare-state trap.[19] The grayer Japan becomes, the more difficult it will be to avoid this European disease. Therefore, I think that trend extrapolation overestimates Japan's potential. But from the 1950s to 1980s, Japan was the only industrial democracy in which growth was simultaneously promoted by catch-up opportunities, by being a young democracy, and by the existence of a small welfare state. As an outlier (or nearly so) in all of these variables, Japan should have been an outlier in economic performance. It was.[20]

Japan's spectacular post–World War II performance deserves two more comments. One concerns saving and investment. De Long and Summers (1991, p. 455) argue that "differences in equipment investment account for essentially all of the extraordinary growth performance of Japan relative to other countries." In my view this statement is compatible with what I said about the effects of catch-up opportunities, comparatively weak distributional coalitions in young democracies, and avoidance of the tax and welfare state. These conditions provide a setting in which equipment investment makes sense. Recently Sandholtz et al. (1992, p. 8) even pointed out that "the absolute level of industrial investment in the United States has fallen below that of Japan." Such facts should certainly make alarm bells ring in the West—and lead to breast-beating rather than to blaming Japan.[21]

The other comment concerns government guidance of the economy or industrial policy. I do not doubt that the Japanese government has done so (and still does, although to a lesser degree). But government intervention has not always been successful. For example, it did *not* work in the chemical, aircraft, and software industries (Porter, 1990, p. 414).[22] The most important feature of government guidance in Japan may well be that it does not reduce, overcome, or abolish competition. Competition is often fierce (Porter, 1990, pp. 417, 421; Samuels, 1994, p. 51), occasionally even dirty (Samuels, 1994,

p. 72). Referring to Japan as well as South Korea and Taiwan, World Bank analysts (1993b, p. 355) write: "Thus the seeming success of industrial policy in these three economies probably rests not on picking winners . . . but on the setting of export targets for promoted industries and the use of export performance to assess policies." By contrast, industrial policy in the West tends to fall prey to special-interest groups that want to overcome competition. The more a country is already a rent-seeking society, the less it can afford an industrial policy. Even if the East Asian industrial policies were less controversial than they are, I would not expect comparable results if the old democracies of the West were to emulate them.[23]

Ultimately, the difference between the contemporary West and East Asia might be that the Japanese, Korean, and Taiwanese governments interfere with the economy because they want to compete in global markets, whereas Western governments interfere because they feel that their constituents no longer want to stand competition. They forget what Porter (1990, p. 174) has stated so forcefully: "Competitive advantage emerges from pressure, challenge, and adversity, rarely from an easy life."

One of the most serious critics of free-market or "getting-the-prices-right" explanations of East Asian success stories is Wade (1990, pp. 157–158; 1992; see also Amsden, 1985), who has specifically focused his investigations on Taiwan; he writes:

> The state has interfered in trade not less, but differently, than in many other developing countries. As gatekeeper for the national economy, it has scrutinized inflows and outflows and affected the terms of transactions in line with national objectives. It has balanced the need to bring international market pressures to bear on domestic producers with the need to build up supply capacity in an increasing range of industries. It has accomplished this feat by avoiding both free trade and high, unselective, and unconditional protection, and by welcoming foreign investment while placing constraints on its role in the domestic economy.

One could criticize this statement by arguing that of course state interference with the economy is ubiquitous, that the real issue concerns the kind and degree of state interference in Taiwan and elsewhere, and that only quantitative information about Taiwanese and other countries' interventions would provide a solid basis for judgment. Wade (1990, p. 72) is aware of this type of argument and its power. I shall desist from invoking it because it is good only for reminding us of our lack of solid knowledge and the provisional character of any conclusions. We know that already from Popper's (1959) philosophy of science and do not need specific arguments to demonstrate the obvious.

Instead I shall accept the qualitative statements by Wade on the Taiwanese economy and underline where that economy differs from the declining West. The quotation from Wade in the preceding paragraph under-lines the government's concern with national interest rather than special-interest-group objectives; it also refers to international market pressure on domestic producers rather than protectionism in the service of rent-seeking groups. Wade (1990, p. 55) points out: "The labor market in Taiwan is as close to a textbook model of a competitive labor market as one is likely to find." If one regards the price of labor as the single most important price and the labor market as the single most important market, then the idea that Taiwan got the most important price right receives support even from a the-orist who tends to put little weight on this type of explanation.

Ultimately, Wade (1990, p. 375) concludes his thorough study of Taiwan and his shorter excursions into the South Korean and Japanese economies with a statement that comes very close to Huntington's (1968) praise for autonomy and my own earlier writing (Weede and Jagodzinski, 1981/1987; Weede, 1986a), where I argue that threats to national security[24] reduce rent-seeking and thereby promote growth:

> State effectiveness . . . is therefore a function of the degree of insulation (or "autonomy") from the surrounding social structure. Insulation is a function of, among other things (1) officials' dependence on the state for their incomes, not on interest groups; (2) officials' expertise, which gives them grounds for asserting their own preferences for state actions against those of interest groups; and (3) the extent to which the nation faces a threat to "national interest" from other states, in response to which nonstate groups are likely to confer substantial autonomy on state officials.[25]

While I do admit the existence of industrial policies in East Asia, and I do believe that industrial policies in East Asia did less harm than govern-ment interventionism in the West, I still do not concede that interventionism in East Asia has achieved something that markets cannot achieve. With Krugman (1994b, p. 78) one may reject the superiority of Asian industrial policies over laissez-faire approaches by the following argument: "But in any case, if Asian success reflects the benefits of strategic trade and indus-trial policies, those benefits should surely be manifested in an unusual and impressive rate of growth in the efficiency of the economy. And there is no sign of exceptional efficiency growth."

According to the World Bank and The Economist (1993c, p. 63), China in 1991 was already number three in the world GDP league, placed about halfway between Japan and Germany. Of course, its per capita GDP was only between 8 and 9 percent of Japanese or German incomes and less than 8 percent of U.S. incomes. But three characteristics do make China a seri-ous contender: first, the sheer weight of numbers; second, its spectacular economic growth rate; and third, its military power base (see *The Economist,* 1993a), which already includes nuclear weapons.

Since China has about 4.55 times the population of the United States and 0.091 times the per capita GDP, in 1992 it was already about 41 percent of the economic size of the United States (World Bank, 1994, pp. 162–163, 220–221). This quantity is about 2.6 times the size of the Russian economy and 96 percent of the size of the Japanese economy. While 1994 data are not yet available, the size of the Chinese economy might already equal or exceed the size of the Japanese economy. Other sources estimate the size of the Chinese economy as between 45 and 60 percent of the U.S. economy (*The Economist,* 1992, p. 5). Still, even this would be a poor economic base from which to challenge the United States if Chinese and U.S. growth rates were similar in order of magnitude and if Chinese and U.S. state capabilities and willingness to impose burdens on their peoples were closely matched. None of these conditions applies. For the 1980–1992 period, the World Bank (1994, pp. 162-163) reports a Chinese per capita growth rate of 7.6 percent and a U.S. growth rate of 1.7 percent. Looking to GDP growth rates, China scores 9.1 percent, while the United States scores 2.7 percent. If the Chinese advantage in growth rates persists, *The Economist* (1993e, p. 16) expects the Chinese economy to match the U.S. economy in size by 2010.[26]

Of course, it is risky to make growth predictions nearly two decades ahead. Political turmoil after Deng Xiaoping's death may throw the Chinese economy back for decades. After all, communist-ruled China suffered from terrible policy mistakes and turmoil in the past. The great leap forward in the late 1950s, the people's communes, and the mass starvation that resulted cost between fifteen million and forty million lives. Later, the cultural revolution killed another two million or more people. Adding up all those who lost their lives under Chinese communism yields estimates to the order of magnitude of sixty to eighty million victims (Domes, 1985; Domes and Näth, 1992).[27] Thus, persistent communist rule does permit the repetition of tragedy. But I am more optimistic. Charismatic, powerful, and evil dictators who murder people by the millions—such as Adolf Hitler, Joseph Stalin, and Mao Zedong—are rare. If it can avoid being struck by calamitous leadership twice in a short period of history, China stands a chance of catching up with the United States in economic size within a generation or less.

China's prospects depend mainly on two factors. First, will China be capable of continuing its spectacular economic growth for another decade or two? Ruling out another period of government-imposed folly, as during the great leap forward or the cultural revolution, the prospects are good. Part of China's extraordinary economic growth rate may be accounted for by the advantages of backwardness, i.e., by the possibilities of imitating the best practices already applied in more advanced countries and reallocating labor from agriculture to more productive industries. This source of growth is unlikely to be exhausted soon. Another widely agreed-upon source of economic growth is human capital formation. Primary school enrollment is universal in China, and secondary school enrollment is better than it was in South Korea in 1970 or than it currently is in Thailand. Thus, human capital formation is sufficient to underwrite a continuation of the Chinese economic miracle. Another widely recognized source of growth is investment. Chinese gross domestic investment was significantly higher than other countries' in the 1980s, and its growth rate has been surpassed only by South Korea (World Bank, 1993a, pp. 252–253). Again, investment provides no reason why the Chinese economic miracle should run out of steam soon.

The more difficult issues affecting the growth prospects of China are private property rights, competition, innovation, the size of the public sector, price distortions, and the openness and export orientation of the economy. In Chapter 4, Section 3 I argued that a chief reason why imperial China was overtaken by the West during the past five hundred years was the insecurity of property rights in China caused by an arbitrary government (see Jones, 1981; Yang, 1987). The communists, of course, did not respect private property rights in the first decades of their rule. Their rule perpetuated and reinforced the Chinese tradition of arbitrary government[28] in which law is a disposable tool of the rulers instead of being above the rulers and acting as a constraint on rulers and ruled alike (see Fu, 1993). They expropriated and massacred millions of rich peasants and capitalists who were deemed to be adversaries of the revolution. Then they forced peasants into cooperatives and later into people's communes, thereby thinning out property rights and reducing incentives to work. After 1979, however, the ruling communists under the competent stewardship of Deng Xiaoping did again decentralize property rights and return rights to work the land to individuals, families, or small groups of families (Domes, 1985; Domes and Näth, 1992). Thus, work incentives were reestablished in the countryside. Since the overwhelming majority of the Chinese population lived in the countryside and worked the fields in the 1980s, and since rural incomes grew threefold in only eight years (*The Economist,* 1992, p. 4), these actions were the beginning of the Chinese economic miracle. While later reforms even permitted the establishment of private manufacturing enterprises, while private enterprises have significantly outperformed state-owned industrial giants,[29] the security of private property rights must remain at risk in a regime still nominally committed to socialism.

Concerning competition, the situation is much better for two reasons. First, the weight of agriculture in the economy does guarantee competition among many producers, i.e., peasants. Second, the devolution of economic power to the provincial, township, or village levels also reinforces competition. For example, when a township, village, or rural district owns a textile factory, it must compete with similar enterprises owned by other local governments, collectives, or private entrepreneurs. Often the competition is ferocious. In contrast to central government–owned enterprises, local government–owned enterprises are subject to hard budget constraints. The weight of township and rural enterprises in the Chinese economy is considerable. They "employ more than 100 million people and produce more than one-third of gross national output" (World Bank, 1994, p. 80).

To some degree, private property rights and competition foster innovation. Moreover, China can adopt innovations from elsewhere. The large population of overseas Chinese in Southeast Asia, Taiwan, and Hong Kong may serve as a transmission mechanism. Private property, competition, and openness tend to undermine price distortions. Although China still suffers from state-controlled prices and distortions, and although there is not yet a free (i.e., hire-and-fire) labor market, the situation did move in this direction over the past fifteen years. The economic retrenchment of 1989–1990 led to layoffs in the collective and private sectors, especially in small cities and rural areas (Chan, 1991, p. 128), thereby demonstrating not only human suffering but also some flexibility in labor markets.

The most successful economies in the Chinese neighborhood, including Mainland China's hostile small brother, Taiwan, grew by export orientation (Dollar, 1992; World Bank, 1987; 1991; 1993b). How export oriented is China? According to World Bank data, the Chinese GDP in 1991 was 1.67 times the size of the Indian GDP. In general, larger economies trade less than smaller ones. Nevertheless, the ratio of Chinese and Indian exports in the same year was not somewhat less than 1.67 but 3.12. By this measure, China's orientation toward global markets is nearly twice as strong as India's. India is the only country comparable to China in population, poverty, and potential market size. Moreover, the growth rate of China's exports in the 1970s was already twice as high as India's, although only about half as high as Taiwan's. In the 1980–1991 period, however, the gap (ratio) between China's and India's export growth rates narrowed somewhat because of a significant Indian improvement and a lesser, although still encouraging, Chinese improvement. In this more recent period the Chinese export growth rate was between the Taiwanese and South Korean rates. Moreover, in 1991 China was the second-largest recipient of foreign direct investment, after Mexico, which of course benefits from the closeness of the United States. By contrast, India received less than the World Bank's (1993a) reporting threshold of one million dollars. Moreover, investors' interest in China seems to continue to grow. In the first half of 1993 direct foreign investment pledges were four times as high as they were in the corresponding period of 1992 (*The Economist,* 1993d, pp. 53–54). While these are all fairly crude indicators, they provide no reason to doubt that China can sustain the growth rates that it experienced in the 1980s.

Since Deng's reforms in the late 1970s, China has experienced "creeping capitalism" and begun its long march toward prosperity. While the establishment of democracy is still very remote, and even the dominant aspiration is nothing more than a "benevolent dictatorship" (Goodman, 1991, p. 16), I do endorse Kim's (1993, p. 22) view that "the communist regime in China is transforming itself into a de facto authoritarian-pluralist system in order to meet the demands of modernization." This transformation alone does not guarantee that democracy is the ultimate destination, but Kim's (1993, pp. 23–24) propositions about the effects of capitalism and prosperity are compatible with the South Korean and Taiwanese experience and may acquire future relevance for the case of Mainland China: "It is in the nature of capitalism that it secretly nurtures and eventually unleashes democratic forces."[30]

In the short run, democracy in China is unlikely. Instead, China's army is likely to determine China's future. The main task of the Chinese army is to maintain its unity. This task was not easy in spring 1989, but the army succeeded because its leaders "recognized that a unified, disciplined, national army enforcing bad policy is better than a divided army at war with itself, even for the best of reasons" (Jencks, 1991, p. 154). Economic success will make it easier to maintain military unity, and military unity may contribute to political stability and the economic growth that ultimately should make China ripe for democracy.

In economic size, two giants dominate Asia: Japan and China. In population size, again two giants dominate Asia: China and India. Although India has miraculously maintained democracy in spite of abject poverty and thereby demonstrated that economic development or high incomes are not absolutely necessary prerequisites of democracy, India has been a comparative failure economically—at least by East Asian standards. This failure may be blamed on "Fabian politics and English economics" (Bhagwati, 1993b, p. 21), and it may change. But it is still too early to predict whether Indian economic reforms will continue or whether and when the country will become a great economic power.

The West in general, and Western Europe in particular, seems strangely unaware of what is happening in the global economy. Social justice is still a more popular topic than meeting the Asian challenge. The size of this challenge has recently been outlined by *The Economist* (1994c, p. 4) in an extrapolation of what the rank order of the largest economies might look like in 2020, a mere quarter-century in the future. By then, the Chinese economy may be about 40 percent larger than the U.S. economy. Among the "great seven," there will remain only two Western economies: the United States and Germany (as number six, barely ahead of South Korea) but five Asian countries: China, Japan, India, Indonesia, and South Korea. Beyond that, Thailand may be economically larger than France, and Taiwan may outdistance Italy, Russia, and Britain.[31] Chapter 8 returns to the issue of how the *still* dominant West can accommodate and possibly postpone this challenge, which will affect international security as well.

Notes

1. Certainly there is no automaticity in catch-up and convergence. See Abramovitz (1986), Baumol (1986), and De Long (1986). While there is strong evidence in favor of convergence in total factor productivity, some countries fail to catch up in per capita incomes because of insufficient investment (Dowrick and Nguyen, 1989).

2. While I accept the objections by Oliver and Marwell (1988) against Olson's generalization in principle—as has been discussed in Chapter 3, Section 1—I do think that Olson's simple rule of thumb is valid over a wide range of circumstances and that it fits the case of cartels very well.

3. Worse still, political parties in general, and the opposition in particular, may even substitute for distributional coalitions. Political entrepreneurs may look for pockets of discontent, promise remedies at the taxpayers' or consumers' expense, and hope thereby to win votes. See Bernholz and Breyer (1994, p. 184).

4. Since government consumption and investment are part of GDP, one may argue that it is more appropriate to analyze the effect of government spending on the rate of productivity growth in the nongovernment sector than its effect on GDP or GDP per capita growth rates. Hansson and Henrekson (1994, p. 396) have done so and arrive at the following conclusion: "The level of total outlays, consumption and transfers invariably have a negative impact on the rate of growth of total factor productivity. . . . On the other hand, educational expenditure exerts a positive influence on TFP-growth."

5. Muller's (1994) most recent work takes a position in between his earlier views and my own views. On the one hand, he points to some equalization of income in young or reestablished (after World War II) democracies, such as France, Germany, or Italy; on the other hand, he observes the least top-to-bottom redistribution of income in the oldest democracies, such as the United States or Britain.

6. Earlier in the text, I referred to studies that document the negative impact of spending on growth rates.

7. The reasons that European economic policymakers are so error prone are analyzed by Vaubel (1995). In his abstract, he summarizes as follows: "The European Commission, Parliament and Court of Justice have a vested interest in European social regulation. This is also true for the governments and producers of the highly regulated member countries." High-cost producers must be interested in raising rivals' costs by social regulation.

8. The EC share in world manufacturing exports has been falling since 1980. Then it was above 22 percent. Now it is below 18 percent (*The Economist,* 1993b).

9. Taxation is a question of more or less. It may become confiscatory. Inevitably, it interferes with private property rights, including the right to enjoy the results of one's efforts.

10. Pejovich (1995, p. 68) neatly summarizes why and how private property rights promote prosperity and a separation of powers: "Exclusivity provides incentives for owners to put secure assets into the highest-valued uses; transferability provides incentives for resources to move from less productive to more productive owners; and the constitutional guarantee of ownership separates the accumulation of economic wealth from the accumulation of political power."

11. Of course, Western governments are rudderless only if one considers the task of government to be the realization of national rather than parochial interests.

12. Obviously, the standard of comparison is provided by the Russian and Chinese revolutions and their bloody consequences.

13. Although Johnson (1982) underlines the role of industrial policy in later Japanese development, he is quite close to Friedman and Friedman regarding the early decades of the twentieth century.

14. While there are major disagreements in the specialized literature, they are beyond the scope of this book. Johnson (1982), for example, focuses on the role of MITI in guiding the Japanese economy. By contrast, Fingleton (1995) insists on the dominance of the ministry of finance.

15. Of course, government policies in Japan had distributional effects, but this was not their main point.

16. Japanese civil service entrance examinations for top careers are extremely difficult. Johnson (1982, p. 57) reports failure rates between 90 and 98 percent for different periods of observation.

17. My references to positive effects of threats to national security or of high military participation ratios should not be misread as saying anything about the effects of high defense expenditures. On the latter topic see, for example, Chan and Mintz (1992), Deger (1986), and Grobar and Porter (1989).

18. Since Olson (1982) is not a specialist on Japanese society, it may be useful to quote Johnson's (1982, pp. 315–316) description of the legislative and judicial branches of Japanese government. Their functions include the responsibility "to fend off the numerous interest groups in the society" and "to create space for bureaucratic initiative unconstrained by political power."

19. Johnson (1982, p. 240) refers to "a tax system that made Japan a businessman's paradise" and "a system of forced savings due to weak or nonexistent welfare commitments."

20. The argument that not only was Japan an outlier in economic performance but that it was predictably one has been made before (Weede, 1991, p. 432). Since I have argued that controlling for age of democracy and social security spending (but not for country and period dummies) reduces the catch-up effect *sometimes* to insignificance, one may wonder why I still refer to it in the main text. This is not only because of its theoretical plausibility but also because of the strong support I obtained where GDP growth per person employed has been analyzed.

21. Bhagwati (1991), a native of India who teaches economics in the United States, provides a strong defense of Japan against the charges of unfair trade that are popular in the United States and in some European countries. An example of "Japan bashing" is Dornbusch (1993).

22. Concerning the aircraft industry, Samuels (1994, pp. 260–266) severely qualifies this widely accepted judgment.

23. In principle, external economies provide some justification for an industrial policy. In practice, there is reason for skepticism. Krugman (1993b, p. 177) simultaneously makes a case for industrial policy and is afraid of its misapplication: "The point is that it is in fact easy to offer a justification for industrial policy, and not even very hard to specify plausible targets for such a policy. The difficult questions are how to implement such a policy in practice, and how to manage the political economy of such a policy in such a way as to avoid the usual mistakes." In my view, the "usual mistakes" refer to governments becoming tools of rent-seeking distributional coalitions. Moreover, industrial policies aimed at promoting some activities often discriminate against other firms or industries (Cooper, 1993, p. 142).

24. A Korean scholar (Moon, 1991, p. 35) adds that "bitter historical memories of Japanese colonial domination" reinforce the desire to catch up with Japan in its former colonies, i.e., Taiwan and Korea. In my view, this is a complementary, not a competing, argument.

25. Kim and Huang (1991, p. 105) argue that there are significant differences between South Korea and Taiwan in state strength, i.e., "fundamental limits on state capacity prevented the KMT government from intervening in the market as directly and extensively as its Korean counterpart."

26. If you add Hong Kong and Taiwan to the People's Republic of China (PRC), then the economic size of China may match that of the United States by 2002 (*The Economist*, 1993e). Other optimistic evaluations of China's economic future are Kristof (1993) and Overholt (1993). More pessimistic evaluations are reported by The Economist (1994a) or Krugman (1994b, p. 76), who still gives China a chance to achieve 82 percent of the economic size of the United States by 2010. While Hong Kong is bound to become the most special economic zone of China, the future relationship between the PRC and Taiwan is less predictable. On the one hand, Taiwan's "one country, two governments" policy (Lee, 1991) may be a prelude to independence; on the other hand, Taiwanese investment in the PRC exceeded that of the United States and Japan in 1990 (Ledic, 1991).

27. The lower estimates come from the earlier book (pp. 38, 49, 212); the higher numbers come from the more recent book (pp. 46, 62, 121). For the mass starvation after the great leap forward, Fu (1993, pp. 235, 304) reports an even wider set of estimates than does Domes, ranging from 16.5 to fifty million victims. Fu himself seems to believe in a number larger than thirty million. Rummel (1994b, chapter 5) distinguishes between more than thirty-five million victims of democide and an about equal number of victims of policy-induced famine. His sum hits the midpoint of the Domes and Näth estimates.

28. Mao Zedong seems to have been aware of this continuity. He had a special admiration for the founder of the unified Chinese empire, who ruled in the third century B.C. (Fu 1993, pp. 188–189). This favorite of Mao also excelled in cruelty.

29. Inefficient and loss-making state firms still employ about 107 million people. Moreover, these firms also constitute welfare systems for workers. Their deficits contribute to the central government's deteriorating finances and inflationary pressure (see *The Economist*, 1993d, pp. 53–54). In contrast to Soviet-type economies, at least some managers of Chinese state-owned enterprises are rewarded or punished for their performance. If unsuccessful, they may lose about half of their salary. While factory workers have jobs for life, managers may be demoted or fired (see *The Economist*, 1992, p. 15). The actual decision latitude of managers varies widely from place to place (Blecher, 1991, p. 44). There even exists the famous case of a manager who fired his Party secretary (Sullivan, 1991, p. 89). Moreover, the size of the public sector in total employment in the PRC should not be exaggerated. It is in the same order of magnitude as in Britain or France, not Russia (see *The Economist*, 1993f, p. 75). On the other hand, the bureaucracy actually grew faster during the 1980s than before. A partial explanation of this fact refers to the rehabilitation of cadres who lost their positions during the cultural revolution (Blecher, 1991, pp. 36–40).

30. Lipset (1993, p. 128) concurs: "As Bhagwati asserts, Deng Xiaoping's emphasis on economic development in China may yet lead to freedom for that country, while Gorbachev's efforts in the old USSR failed decisively." A rejection of the proposition that "Asian values" are incompatible with democracy is provided by Kim (1994).

31. Those who are not ready even to consider such possibilities should remember some Japanese achievements. Although I find the report somewhat exaggerated, Tsuru (1993, p. 182) has claimed that from 1950 to 1988 Japanese per capita output multiplied by a factor of 152. Even from 1970 to 1988, output still rose tenfold.

Concerning the smaller Asian countries, such as South Korea, Thailand, and Taiwan, Krugman (1994b) provides some reasons why these forecasts may be exaggerated. In essence, it is dubious whether these countries can switch from largely input-driven growth to efficiency-driven growth fast enough to maintain their past growth rates.

7

WAR AND PEACE IN THE CONTEMPORARY WORLD

1. National Decisionmaking Under Systemic Constraints

In the first two sections of Chapter 4, I analyzed interstate rivalry and the resulting risk of war as determinants of the European miracle, or the rise of the West. At that time, war or its background conditions were independent variables. Now war is the dependent variable. In Chapters 2 and 3, rational action was ascribed to individuals, but the discussions of the problems of preference aggregation, of obstacles to the procurement of public goods, of agency, of rational ignorance, and of the strong tendencies toward government failure imply that the idea of *rational and unitary* action by corporate actors and governments has to be rejected. This rejection is in stark contrast to standard procedures (Grieco, 1990; Stein, 1990) and to one of the leading contemporary theories of war (Bueno de Mesquita, 1981a; Bueno de Mesquita and Lalman, 1992).

The idea that states are rational and unitary actors—or at least that they act as if they were such actors—has been defended by Bueno de Mesquita (1981a, pp. 19ff.) by reference to the fact that most wars in the nineteenth and twentieth centuries were won by the initiators. In my view, this is an extremely weak defense of an unrealistic assumption. First, there is a plausible alternative explanation. If surprise and initiative are force multipliers—as they are (Betts, 1985; Dupuy, 1987)—then there should be some relationship between taking the initiative and winning, even if wars were started by a nonrational process. Second, the relationship between initiative and winning is much weaker than Bueno de Mesquita believes. According to Wang and Ray (1994), such a relationship is supported only for the nineteenth and twentieth centuries, not for the preceding three centuries. Worse still, even within the nineteenth and twentieth centuries only one out of four wars between great powers has been won by initiators. Thus, the "supportive" relationship between initiative and war neither holds across time nor is true for the most important recent wars. A unitary-rational-actor approach to war fails to account for these phenomena.[1]

The unitary actor assumption actually depends on overlooking the internal divisions and conflicts within nations and states, or, as Stein (1993) has elaborated, the "incoherence of grand strategy" resulting therefrom. Stein (1993, p. 97) points to two specific examples from U.S. history:

> Roosevelt and many members of his administration clearly understood the security challenge posed by Germany (and Japan) and expanded the nation's military to deal with the threat. Yet domestic political opposition prevented the administration both from making the military commitments that might have prevented war and, once hostilities broke out in Europe, from becoming a cobelligerent until the United States was attacked. In contrast, the Truman administration could extend peacetime security commitments to a host of countries, but found itself unable to procure the requisite military capability to fulfill those obligations until after the invasion of South Korea.

In essence, d'Lugo and Rogowski (1993) point to a similar incoherence of German naval policies before World War I. The German naval buildup strained Anglo-German relations, but the German taxation system could not back up the challenge by providing sufficient resources for winning the arms race. So internal disunity, cumbersome coalition-building, and log-rolling rather than unitary rational planning was behind the German challenge to the British navy. Although Rosecrance and Steiner's (1993, p. 150) analysis of British grand strategy before World War II does not focus on internal disunity, it is also not easily compatible with the image of states as unitary and rational actors because it arrives at the conclusion "that nations sometimes decide to commit themselves to military goals that they cannot possibly achieve."

If one accepts historical analyses like these, then one may regard the unitary-actor assumption as already falsified. According to Popper (1959), falsified assumptions should be rejected because reliance on false assumption rules out valid explanations. Valid explanations arise only from three requirements being met at the same time. First, the logic connecting premises and conclusions must be valid. Second, empirical observations or measurements of variables must be reasonably reliable and valid. Third, the theoretical assumptions must be valid. The state-as-unitary-actor assumption is generally invalid and therefore incompatible with the third requirement.

It is a poor defense of rational decisionmaking models based on the state-as-unitary-actor assumption to point to their ability to support some manifestly true and observable conclusions. Faulty logic, too, is compatible with arriving at true conclusions. While valid logic and true premises guarantee true conclusions, invalid logic guarantees nothing, not even false conclusions. Similarly, invalid observations or measurements guarantee nothing, not even false conclusions about the validity of theoretical claims.

Similarly—and this is the point under dispute here—false assumptions about collective decisionmaking guarantee nothing, not even false statements about world politics. Therefore, explanatory success at this level, as in the work of Bueno de Mesquita (1981a) and Bueno de Mesquita and Lalman (1992), is insufficient to justify assumptions about unitary and rational decisionmaking at the nation-state level that must be false for reasons discussed above. If we have to buy more valid and rigorous reasoning connecting premises and conclusions by less realistic theoretical assumptions, then little has been achieved.

Rational action is a specific type of decisionmaking under constraints. Although I reject the idea of rational choice by corporate actors or governments, I stick to the idea that constraints largely determine what happens. A ubiquitous constraint is the scarcity of resources relative to wants or desires. This constraint applies to collective decisionmaking as much or more[2] than to individual decisionmaking. Decisionmakers on national security issues are not exempt from this fact. A specific constraint in international politics (in contrast to domestic politics) results from the "anarchical order of power" in the international system (Aron, 1966; Bernholz, 1985; Herz, 1950; Lieber, 1993; 1995; McNeill, 1982; Waltz, 1979; Weede, 1975). Not even the invention and proliferation of nuclear bombs and intercontinental missiles has overcome international anarchy and the corresponding necessity of self-help.[3]

As long as collectives, states, or nations are capable of waging war against each other, as long as no effective superior authority is capable of imposing either the status quo or some specific change on even the most powerful states within the international system, decisionmakers will have to face the prospect of war. Waltz (1979, p. 113) maintains: "In international politics force serves, not only as the *ultima ratio,* but indeed as the first and constant one." Those who do not prepare for waging war may have to face abdication and capitulation. Since the latter course of action is not attractive to privileged and ruling classes, it should generally rank quite low in individual as well as in collective preference orders. I shall assume that foreign and defense policymakers everywhere want to maintain sovereignty, national security, and at least the current level of decision latitude and influence. In this respect, heterogeneity of preferences among decisionmakers is simply assumed away.[4]

Under international anarchy and given technical capabilities for waging war among states and societies, there exists a security dilemma for strategically interdependent nations or states, i.e., a conflict of interest between their respective decisionmakers. Decisionmakers of, say, two neighboring states know that the armed forces of the other state might attack their nation, defeat it, occupy territory, dismember the country, or even extinguish it as a sovereign political entity. They know—in the two-state world of our mental experiment—that there is but one way to achieve security: namely, superiority, preferably overwhelming superiority. Sometimes this conceivable way out of the security dilemma is labeled "peace by strength." In the two-state world of our imagination, it is easy to see that "security by superiority" generally cannot work for both contenders. Unless military technology and the state of the art in warfare are such that the defender has a huge military advantage, even under surprise attack, superiority by one must imply the inferiority and hence insecurity of the other one.[5]

According to Grieco (1990, p. 28), "the major effect of anarchy is . . . the recognition by states [or by their decisionmaking elites] that others might seek to destroy and enslave them." Grieco continues "to identify a major constraint on the willingness to cooperate, one which is generated by anarchy and which is identified by realism: the concern of states that others may achieve relatively greater gains. . . . Realists do not believe that anarchy causes states to be rational egoists, but instead to be defensive positionalists." So the struggle for superiority and relatively greater gains generates irreconcilable conflicts of interest between states. Interstate relations are in some respects even worse than a prisoners' dilemma (Grieco, 1990; Stein, 1990). In the prisoners' dilemma, both sides can agree that mutual cooperation is preferable to mutual defection because both sides can obtain greater gains by cooperation than by defection. What impedes cooperation is primarily the fear of being exploited if one side cooperates but the other side defects. Where relative gains or positional goods are the goal, one might forgo substantial benefits if one could thereby reduce the benefits to one's opponent to an even greater degree.

Given international anarchy and the security dilemma, cooperation becomes much more difficult than in iterative games in which the players know that they will survive and will face each other again and again.[6] Stein (1990, pp. 101–102) points to two reasons why cooperation may be too dangerous: First, "if the consequences of even once being taken advantage of are disastrous, expectation of future gains will not ensure its initial cooperation"; second, "in cases when others can be profitably bankrupted a concern with future payoffs makes conflict rather than cooperation more likely in the short term."

So far I have been guilty of the mistake, which should be avoided, of lapsing into a unitary-actor assumption. Once one introduces strategic disagreements and bargaining within the ruling classes of both nations, the likely direction of the policy consensus on both sides, or even the possibility of arriving at some consensus, seems obscure. It may even be argued that "groupthink" replaces serious efforts at utility maximization (Janis, 1972); i.e., the goal of achieving consent within some decisionmaking groups pushes other goals into the background. In an attempt to develop some general theory of international politics, we have to substitute assumptions for detailed information about the variety of preferences or arguments accepted and agreed upon by various members of the decisionmaking elite.[7]

Instead of seriously attempting to maximize benefits and to minimize costs, the main concern of national security decisionmakers will be to achieve some unity of purpose. National decisionmaking bodies have to solve a problem of internal coordination first. The most likely solutions are perceptually prominent, obvious, unique, simple, or traditional. As Schelling (1960, p. 68), who as an economist is not totally disinclined toward relying on the economic model of man, has suggested:

> It often seems that a cynic could have predicted the outcome on the basis of some "obvious" focus for agreement, some strong suggestion contained in the situation itself, without much regard to the merits of the case, the arguments to be made, or the pressures to be applied during the bargaining. The "obvious" place to compromise frequently seems to win by some kind of default, as though there is simply no rationale for settling anywhere else.

If "security by superiority," or "peace by strength," is the most obvious "solution" to the security dilemma (although it makes it worse), then any deviation from the unitary-actor assumption or any move toward collective decisionmaking will reinforce rather than mitigate the dilemma. A better solution, if it should exist, will not necessarily be simple, will not immediately sound familiar and therefore look reasonable, and need not be obvious. In essence, I suggest that some general agreement on "security by superiority" is more likely than any other agreement. The immediate corollary of "peace by strength" is *"si vis pacem, para bellum"*: If you want peace, prepare for war. This corollary has not lost its obviousness or attractiveness since the time of Roman antiquity, although preparation for war frequently did not prevent its outbreak.[8]

Although I underline the importance of relative gains or the positional good of superiority as driving forces behind security policies, Glaser's (1994–1995, p. 76) strong objection must be faced: "If cooperation increases a country's security, then increases in the adversary's security are usually desirable, whether or not they exceed increases in the defender's security." Admittedly, it is hard to see how and why *unitary rational actors* should worry[9] if another state's security is enhanced even more than their own security, say by a global and verifiable shift from offensive to defensive armaments. In my view, the emphasis on relative gains and superiority goals can be best explained by explicitly rejecting the *unitary*-rational-action assumption regarding state behavior. Groups of national decisionmakers may predictably agree on the desirability of relative gains even when a single rational decisionmaker could see their irrelevance. In essence, I claim that group decisionmaking within states and nations itself generates a focus on relative gains, although such a focus often represents a misplaced emphasis on means, such as relative gains or superiority, that do not always serve their putative end, i.e., security.

There is another complication. International systems typically contain a multitude of states rather than just two. A weak state may balance a stronger neighbor by relying on allies. But allies may be unavailable, or insufficient, or undependable in the long run. Therefore, the "look for allies" prescription seems less obvious or attractive than "security by superiority" and its "para bellum" corollary. When some states do find credible allies, these alliances necessarily reduce the perceived security of others and may reinforce rather than reduce the perceived and domestically agreed-upon need for "security by superiority."

But "security by superiority" is not an equally obvious solution everywhere. The more military power a nation already commands, the more obvious "peace by strength" and the "para bellum" corollary appear. The more powerful you are, the more you attract the hostility and suspicion of those who are less powerful. In a hostile world where future wars are expected, it is even rational to attack first in order to exploit the advantages of surprise, to defeat your conceivable opponents, or to add to your resource base by annexation of economically or strategically valuable territory (see Kaplan, 1957; Bueno de Mesquita, 1981a). Under international anarchy, even wars of aggression may be perceived by their initiators as ultimately defensive because preventive. The interpretation of many initial steps toward war as effective, even if immoral from a humane perspective, fits the fact that initiators tend to win battles, campaigns, and *in some periods of observation* even some types of wars more frequently than do their victims (Betts, 1985; Bueno de Mesquita, 1981a; Dupuy, 1987; Epstein, 1988; for serious qualifications, see Wang and Ray, 1994).

So far, international anarchy has carried the main burden of explaining why states attempt to gain "security by superiority," or "peace by strength." But the dynamics of domestic politics and governmental decisionmaking may contribute to the same result. Expansionist policies are likely to affect individuals and interest groups in a society in different ways. Some may benefit, or seem to benefit, in the short run before the policy has produced disaster. Others know from the beginning—or at least could know if they overcame rational ignorance—that a bellicose policy is likely to result in nothing better than conscription, higher taxes, and the risk of being maimed or killed in war. Although it seems obvious that a majority of citizens and interest groups in most nations most of the time have good reason to be worried about bellicose and expansionist policies, it is misleading to conclude from this that nations—at least democratic nations—are never bellicose and expansionist. Snyder (1991, pp. 15, 18) explains how even self-defeating expansionist policies can be agreed upon:

> Though overexpansion hurts the society as a whole, it is attractive to some groups within society. The benefits of expansion are disproportionately concentrated in their hands, while the costs of expansion are largely borne by the state and thus diffused throughout the society. . . . Since interests in expansion and militarism are typically more concentrated than the interests opposed to them, logrolling is inherently more apt to produce overexpansion than underexpansion.

My focus on the security dilemma, anarchy, and self-help puts me close to the Realist, or mainstream, tradition of theorizing on international politics. Until recently, the mainstream of U.S. scholarship tended to neglect the other and equally serious dilemma in international politics, i.e., territorial delimitation.[10] In an international system without some effective superordinate organization to enforce either the territorial status quo or specific changes to it, states are on their own in voicing as well as enforcing territorial claims. Again, the interaction of domestic and interstate politics exacerbates the problem. Since territory has been an asset for centuries, state elites have tried to expand the territories under their control in their efforts to maximize power and security. Territorial aggrandizement has been an essential component of the attempt to achieve "security by superiority." It is easy and "obvious" for the decisionmakers of a victorious state to agree that annexation is desirable. But it appears to be quite difficult for the decisionmakers of the victim state to reconcile themselves to their losses: Any forced territorial change underlines the possibility of future forced changes. As long as territory is a strategic asset, the desirability of expansion is always obvious and beyond dispute. Moreover, some people in the losing state will be personally and strongly affected by the territorial loss. They may be influential or form a special-interest group and agitate for the recovery of the lost territories. From a domestic politics point of view, it usually seems safest not to confront those who aim for territorial expansion or reexpansion.[11]

The rise of the ideology of nationalism—i.e., the idea that people who speak the same language, are bound together by a common history, and share culture and often religion should live in one and only one state—tends to fuel rather than to overcome territorial conflicts. In some places it is simply impossible to generate frontiers that seem "just" to all participants. Domestic politics on both sides tends to favor agreement on the "obvious" solution of maximizing one's own claims, even at the expense of generating irreconcilable conflicts of interest. Moreover, in order to be accepted as "obvious," frontiers must appear to be natural. This criterion rules out the acceptance of enclaves or exclaves as legitimate by all parties concerned.

I am aware that I am dangerously close to accepting the idea of some free-floating "national interest" in territorial possessions that cannot be derived from the interests of at least the majority of a nation's citizens.

Actually, I do accept the idea that such definitions of "national interest" resulting from domestic political processes have a tendency to affect policies and to become causes of war. Luard (1970, p. 7) has made this point very forcefully:

> It is commonplace that territory has a psychological importance for nations that is quite out of proportion to its intrinsic value, strategic or economic. Sentiments of national pride and national honour are aroused by threats to territory more rapidly and intensely perhaps than over any other type of issue. Longstanding resentments and long-cherished desires to recover territory may be harboured, whether the territory in question is an economic asset or economic burden, and whether it is inhabited by ethnically related people or not. In consequence, disputes over territory have been perhaps the most important single cause of war between states in the last two or three centuries.

My rejection of the unitary-rational-decisionmaker assumption and my long-standing focus on territorial conflicts of interest (Weede, 1975) put my ideas close to those of Vasquez (1993). Indeed, my previous data analyses of war for the period between 1900 and 1970 are strongly supportive of his claim that territorial disputes are the most important source of war. According to Vasquez (1993, p. 147), "the very idea of power politics and its practices are derived from the inability to settle territorial questions. Power politics is not the key fact of existence, as the realist paradigm would have us believe, but may simply be an epiphenomenon of territoriality." In my view, this notion goes too far. While disagreements about territorial claims are the most powerful source of war, they are not the only one. The security dilemma often affects even nations that advance no territorial claims against each other.

It is important to underline that the pursuit of "collective interests" by groups may interfere with the rational pursuit of individual interests. The pursuit of the "national interest" in territorial expansion may well be incompatible with the individual interest of large numbers of individuals in war avoidance, survival, and prosperity. Similarly, we may observe in almost all industrial democracies—except Australia and New Zealand—agricultural policies that benefit about 5 percent of the population at the expense of overwhelming majorities of taxpayers and consumers.

To summarize the main arguments made so far: The anarchical character of the international system as well as the security dilemma and the territorial-delimitation dilemma that must arise in such an anarchical system constitute fundamental constraints for national decisionmakers. The need to achieve some kind of intranational consensus, to get some support at home, constitutes another powerful constraint. This domestic constraint tends to interfere with consistency and tends to subject foreign policymaking to some "law of least mental effort" (Deutsch, 1968, p. 124). The international and domestic constraints together generate "solutions" to the security dilemma as well as to the territorial-delimitation dilemma that generate irreconcilable conflicts of interest. If nations (i.e., their decisionmakers), or at least the great powers, pursue "security by superiority" and territorial expansion, then war is placed on the agenda, and little more than a trigger is needed for it to break out.

The general constraints for national security decisionmaking are also influenced by the polarity of the international system. What is perceived as possible and necessary depends on the systemwide distribution of power. By and large, we distinguish between unipolar, bipolar, and multipolar systems.[12] By definition, a unipolar system is dominated by a single and hegemonic power, and all other political units are severely constrained in their decision latitude. Their sovereignty may approach the purely nominal. In a unipolar system, war serves to make, to maintain, or to break the preponderance of the hegemon. Given the immense superiority of the hegemon, the risk and difficulty of building a countercoalition that stands a chance of prevailing, and the obvious imbalance of power, unipolar systems should be characterized by less war than other systems (Gilpin, 1981; Modelski, 1983; 1987; Modelski and Thompson, 1993; Organski, 1958; Kugler and Organski, 1993).

Bipolar systems are characterized by the existence of two dominant states with approximately equal military power, whereas multipolar systems are characterized by at least three major powers. Whether bipolar or multipolar systems are more war prone is very much disputed (Deutsch and Singer, 1964; Kaplan, 1957; Singer, Bremer, and Stuckey, 1972; Waltz, 1964; 1979). Those who favor multipolarity argue that such systems enforce some dilution of foreign policy attention that tends to mitigate conflicts of interest. In addition, they argue that a large number of militarily significant states generates much uncertainty about who will fight with whom and against whom and that this uncertainty has some pacifying impact.[13] This argument seems implicitly to ascribe risk aversion to national decisionmakers. If one were to assume risk acceptance, however, then multipolar systems should be more rather than less war prone. Obviously, implicit or explicit auxiliary assumptions about risk acceptance or risk aversion loom large in theory development. According to Waltz (1979) and Blainey (1973), it is the certainty about power relations and pecking orders that makes bipolar systems less war prone than multipolar systems.

The controversy between the adherents of multipolarity and bipolarity has not been empirically resolved. According to Singer and Small (1968, p. 283), "alliance aggregation and bipolarity predict strongly away from war in the nineteenth century and even more strongly toward it in the twentieth." This finding is not helpful because it presents different results for different periods of observation without anything better than an ad hoc explanation, because the intercentury difference is not robust (Moul, 1992), and because the measure of bipolarity confounds the distribution of power and alliance bonds. Another study from the "correlates of war" project (Singer, Bremer, and Stuckey, 1972) again reports different results for the nineteenth and twentieth centuries (and is also criticized by Moul, 1992): During the nineteenth century, multipolarity and uncertainty seem to have had some pacifying impact, whereas during the twentieth century, power concentration and certainty about the pecking order seem to be the better pacifier.[14] If one replaces Singer, Bremer, and Stuckey's nation-months-of-war variable with a simple dichotomization (major-power war or not in five-year periods), then the intercentury difference disappears altogether. Moreover, no particular distribution of power, neither power concentration nor balance, thereafter predicts the likelihood of major-power war (Bueno de Mesquita, 1981b). Another complicating factor is that the best example of bipolarity has one specific characteristic; i.e., the bipolarity during the Cold War was characterized by a nuclear balance of terror in which "mutual assured destruction" was perceived as the likely outcome of war. As far as U.S. decisionmakers were concerned, the expectation of "mutual assured destruction" even preceded Russian capabilities to do their part in this scenario (Betts, 1987). The comparatively peaceful record of the Cold War period may be due either to bipolarity or to capabilities for and fears of "mutual assured destruction."

Recently Mansfield (1994) has argued that polarity distinguishes merely between the existence of one, two, or many great powers but that power concentration (as defined by Singer, Bremer, and Stuckey, 1972, and taking account of demographic, industrial, and military characteristics of nation-states) permits a more complete analysis of the impact of structural characteristics of the international system on its war proneness, especially its proneness to major-power war, by also being sensitive to power differentials between all major powers. Indeed, his quantitative analyses of nineteenth- and twentieth-century data from a variety of sources support the contention that "an inverted U-shaped relationship exists between concentration and the frequency of wars involving the major powers" (Mansfield, 1994, p. 229). In Mansfield's (1994, p. 230) view, balance-of-power and power-preponderance theories contain merely partial insights:

> Those balance-of-power theorists who have argued that approximately uniform distributions of power deter war seem to be correct. So too are those power preponderance theorists who have maintained that highly skewed distributions of power lead to few major-power wars. . . . Both of these leading explanations have failed to appreciate the extent to which *moderate imbalances* among the major powers disproportionately encourage the outbreak of wars involving these states.

Whatever the effect of power distributions (or polarity) may be,[15] there is little reason to expect that collective security may work. Given unipolarity, peace depends upon nobody challenging the hegemon and on the hegemon enforcing peace among the lesser states. Collective security is not needed, and at most it confers some legitimacy upon the hegemon and his actions. Given bipolarity, collective security would require that neither of the two dominant powers be aggressive or want to overcome the status quo, that they always act together. Historically this is not the way bipolar systems have worked for any significant period of time. It is hard to imagine how two dominant powers capable of threatening each other can escape the security dilemma and the "obvious" response to it, namely, attempts to gain "security by superiority," or "peace by strength," which results in hostility and suspicion. So collective security stands little chance of working under bipolar systems.

The real issue is whether collective security can work under conditions of multipolarity. According to Organski (1958, pp. 373–384), collective security first requires general agreement about the identity of the aggressor, second a general interest in denying success to the aggressor, and third that everybody be able and willing to do something against aggression. If these three conditions are fulfilled, then the power of the peaceful bystanders and the victim of the aggressor together would suffice to defeat the aggressor. Since the would-be aggressor would know the results, it would not initiate the aggression in the first place. Unfortunately, the three requirements are unlikely to be met even one at a time and are almost impossible to meet simultaneously.

The aggressor will probably attempt to hide and justify its aggression. More importantly, decisionmakers in other states who contemplate aggression themselves may be positively interested in the failure of collective security rather than being interested in defeating and deterring aggression as a matter of principle. So Organski's second requirement comes close to demanding that all states, or at least the overwhelming majority of militarily significant states, be satisfied with the status quo. If my arguments about territorial conflicts are true, if forced transfers of territory almost always cause resentment, then general enthusiasm about the status quo is extremely unlikely ever to exist.

The third requirement presupposes that a lot of collective-action problems are solved and that freeriding is curtailed everywhere. This problem exists at the level of cooperation among states as well as at the level of cooperation within states. Waging a "collective-security" war against an aggressor implies carrying some burden. Within states it must be agreed who takes what part. Even if an interest group is not against participation in a collective-security campaign, this agreement alone does not make the group volunteer for a tax increase to be imposed on its members. If everybody tries to make others carry the necessary burden, then participation in the collective-security campaign may be impossible or ineffective. For domestic policy reasons, some states may be incapable of helping the victims of aggression. Even if nation-states were unified actors and capable of helping, their cooperation may still fail because too many of them will try to freeride. It is hard to imagine how states can simultaneously renounce fighting wars of self-interest and endorse fighting wars of global or collective interest.

Since so many collective-action problems have to be overcome in order to get "collective-security" campaigns started, it is unlikely that an unbroken series of successful campaigns will be conducted so that future aggressors will ultimately be deterred. Token successes do not suffice to make collective security an effective deterrent. The dismal record of collective security—Mearsheimer (1994–1995, p. 33) counts three failures in the 1920s and another six failures in the 1930s—is fully compatible with these skeptical statements. Moreover, even if collective security could work under prenuclear or nonnuclear conditions, it is hard to imagine that other nuclear powers will be ready to confront a nuclear-armed aggressor that threatens a minor and helpless target state in its neighborhood (see Claude, 1962, p. 194).

As I have already mentioned, important constraints on national security decisionmaking depend on geography: for example, on good or bad luck concerning the quantity and quality of neighbors. Since military power tends to decrease the further away from its home base a power is engaged (Boulding, 1962), a central location in a configuration of powers is much worse than a peripheral location (Bernholz, 1985; Collins, 1986; McNeill, 1963).[16] The surrounding states can easily project power against the central state, and all of its neighbors are suspicious of it, but only some states worry about geographically peripheral states and deploy forces against them. Moreover, any expansion of a central power soon becomes a threat to many other states, whereas a similar expansion at the periphery will cause worries much later or even go unnoticed. Therefore, geographically peripheral states stand a much better chance of transforming a multipolar system into a unipolar system with themselves as the hegemon or of becoming one of the dominant powers in a bipolar system. Ancient examples of a peripheral state ultimately becoming the hegemon are Akkad, which overran all of the Mesopotamian city-states, or Qin (Chin), which unified China more than 2,200 years ago.

A recent example are the two peripheral states in the Eurocentric international system of the first part of the twentieth century that became the two superpowers of the Cold War period. The centrally located power, Germany, was vanquished and dismembered. Moreover, based on geopolitical reasoning and pointing to the Russian loss of peripheral territory advantage,

Collins (1986, p. 186) predicted the "future decline of the Russian Empire," or, as it then was called, the Soviet Union.

Capabilities are another important kind of constraint. Some theorists (Gilpin, 1981; Organski, 1958; Organski and Kugler, 1980; Kugler and Organski, 1993; Modelski, 1983; 1987; Thompson, 1983; 1992; Modelski and Thompson, 1993) argue that the rise and decline of great powers determines great-power war. In these accounts, major powers fight for hegemony. Vasquez (1993, p. 95) objects "that the hegemonic wars that do occur do not evolve in the manner that the explanation leads one to expect." The United Kingdom was surpassed not only by Germany but also by the United States before 1914. But the United Kingdom and the United States did not fight each other. Moreover, World War I started not as an Anglo-German war but because of the linkages between the Serbian-Austrian, Austrian-Russian, and French-German conflicts. Similarly, World War II began in Europe as a war between Germany and Poland, with the latter country backed by Britain and France. It became a world war only after Japan attacked the United States and Germany attacked Russia, i.e., the strongest state (the United States) was brought into the war by a then still rather weak one (Japan).

Concerning power-transition theory, Organski and Kugler (1980) provide some quantitative tests and find that among contenders war breaks out only when a power transition has occurred and that the rapidity of the transition increases the risk of war. But the power-transition explanation seems applicable only to the strongest two or three states (called "contenders") in the European center of the international system (before 1945) and not elsewhere. This unexplained restriction of power-transition effects has been criticized as rather odd (Vasquez, 1993, p. 99). But Geller's (1992) study goes a long way toward meeting this criticism. Its starting point is the proposition that power concentration and movements toward unipolarity should reduce the risk of war. Of course, this reduction should be most clearly visible when there is a substantial risk of war to begin with. Here, Geller (1992, pp. 275–279) demonstrated for so-called contender dyads, i.e., dyads consisting of the most powerful nations of their time, and for the 1820–1976 period, that war occurred in five out of fifty-three cases (five-year-period dyads) where power was grossly unequal but in eight out of thirty-two cases where power was about equal. In dyads where power was unequal (and therefore concentrated in one contender), the risk of war was 5/53 or 0.09. Where power was approximately equal, the risk of war was 8/32 or 0.25, i.e., nearly three times as high. This difference is significant at the 0.01 level.[17]

Power concentration within the dyad interacts with power concentration at the level of the international system. Where the system is characterized by a trend toward increasing concentration, or where the system moves from anarchy toward hegemony, the dyadic power balance matters much less than where the system is characterized by decreasing concentration. If there is a nation ascending toward hegemony, then equal dyadic power balances do not increase the risk of war (balance or imbalance, the risk is about the same), but where the systemwide power concentration is in the process of being reduced or where anarchy reasserts itself, dyadic balances do matter. Summarizing Geller's results, it is clear that dyadic power concentration prevents war among contenders where there is no ascending hegemon. Where there is an ascending hegemon, the "local" balance loses its importance. It seems to depend on the hegemon whether there is war or peace. It is capable of constraining others.

2. Patterns of International Conflict During the Cold War and the Contemporary Challenge

For analytical purposes the international system of the 1950s to 1980s may be decomposed into a number of subsystems.[18] The dominant subsystem consisted of the superpowers and their close allies or client-states. This subsystem contained all of the fully industrialized societies and the lion's share of global military capabilities. It was characterized by a bipolar distribution of military power. Under a bipolar system there is but a single way to obtain protection against a threatening superpower. You have to turn to the other one and become its ally, client-state, or protectorate. Most industrialized states recognized this state of affairs and chose one of the superpowers as their protector.

Of course, not all small and middle-sized nations were free to choose for themselves. In the aftermath of World War II the Soviet Union imposed its choice on those Central and East European states that became members of the Warsaw Pact. This imposition persuaded the United States to offer protection to Western Europe, and it persuaded West Europeans to gladly accept the offer. Later this unequal bargain between the United States and its European allies was institutionalized in NATO. A bipolar distribution of military power and a fairly clear-cut alignment of most states with either superpower in the North meant that small wars became unlikely. Major war between East and West remained conceivable, but everybody in the East and West (at least among political and military decisionmakers) seemed to agree that it was dubious whether small or limited wars could be contained. For practical purposes the prospect of war in Europe became indistinguishable from the specter of nuclear war. By ruling out small wars, the firm ties linking European nations and either superpower also reduced the risk of a major war.

Although the United States enjoyed definite nuclear superiority until some time in the 1960s, U.S. officials never came close to confidently believing that they could handle a nuclear exchange (Betts, 1987). The Soviets had little reason for optimism at the beginning of the nuclear age. Once they had become the equal and, according to some analyses, even the superior of the United States in the strategic nuclear relationship, the number and diversity of warheads and delivery vehicles on both sides minimized any hopes for easy or meaningful victory.

Although the military superiority of either side never sufficed to produce credible blueprints for victory, it was nevertheless of crucial importance for political events. Certainly, the U.S. nuclear monopoly in the 1940s and predominance in the 1950s made it easier for U.S. officials to overcome their traditional hesitation over permanent involvement in European affairs.[19] U.S. nuclear superiority held out the prospect of deterring Soviet expansion on-the-cheap. Of course, reliance on U.S. nuclear superiority looked even more attractive to West Europeans because it absolved West European nations from the burden of balancing Soviet conventional capabilities. However, since U.S. nuclear superiority could not be maintained, the credibility of the U.S. promise to resist Soviet aggression in Europe eroded somewhat in the 1970s.

Nevertheless, one may argue that the residual credibility of extended deterrence was all that was needed (Bundy, 1979). Although the United States had ample reason to prefer defeat in conventional war in Europe over nuclear escalation, the Soviets could not rely on it and therefore still had reason to be deterred. For purposes of general deterrence, the risk of escalation to nuclear war may deter even an opponent who is superior in conventional and in nuclear weapons.

For purposes of immediate deterrence, i.e., deterrence in crises, something more than the nuclear threat might be required (Morgan, 1977). In such situations, readily available military forces capable of immediately repelling an invader and preventing the invader from generating undesirable faits accomplis seem to be the most effective deterrents (Huth, 1988a; 1988b; Huth and Russett, 1984; 1988). Unfortunately, the establishment of a favorable short-term balance of forces is not cheap, least of all for a defensive alliance that has to concede the strategic initiative to the invader and that may suffer from all the negative consequences of fighting at a time and place chosen by the opponent (Betts, 1985; Dupuy, 1987; Epstein, 1988). In spite of these factors complicating the military balance between East and West, the perception of a balance of terror did suffice to stabilize the relationship between East and West and to produce "peace through fear" (Aron, 1966; Weede, 1975; 1983c; 1989b; 1994). Given the distribution of military capabilities and the alignment of almost all European nations with one of the superpowers, Europe was the potential conflict area that might most easily trigger nuclear war. Paradoxically, it was therefore the most peaceful part of the globe.

Bipolarity and "peace through fear" in the dominant subsystem of international relations generated two unipolar blocs. Both superpowers were committed to extended deterrence, but both hesitated to commit themselves to the more demanding task of compellence (Schelling, 1966). By and large, the territorial and political status quo established in the aftermath of World War II was respected. This status quo ruled out vigorous and military Soviet interference in Western affairs as well as vigorous and military U.S. interference in Soviet-bloc[20] affairs. Mutual abstention made the Western as well as the Soviet alliance systems into subsystems that were conditionally isolated from each other because of extended deterrence and peace through fear.

As long as neither superpower dared to challenge the other one in its own bloc, the blocs remained unipolar configurations of power. The Soviet Union always had more military power than all of its allies together. Similarly, since the end of World War II the United States has been more powerful than Britain, France, West Germany, Japan, and its lesser allies together. Unipolarity within the Soviet and U.S. blocs made the superpowers into potential substitutes for an order-creating central authority at the subsystemic level. Of course, the entire international system has never benefited from the existence of a single effective central authority.

The Soviet Union experienced no difficulty in assuming this role within its bloc. War within the Soviet bloc was largely inconceivable. For example, Hungarians and Romanians might have occasionally felt like flying at one another's throats, but they knew that the good offices of Soviet "mediation" could always undo whatever might be won on the battlefield. Under these circumstances there was Pax Sovietica. Like other historical brands of imperial peace, Pax Sovietica did not go unchallenged. Uprisings and political instability within allied nations on occasion provoked the Soviet Union to send the Red Army to restore the desired kind of order. In 1953 East Germany suffered from such Soviet "pacification." In 1956 Hungary was the victim. Soviet allies were even allotted subsidiary roles in the provision of "fraternal assistance," i.e., in reestablishing Soviet order in Czechoslovakia in 1968. But independent warfare between Soviet client-states was effectively ruled out.

An evaluation of the U.S. role within the Western bloc is much more complicated. A hegemonic role did not fit as well with U.S. geopolitical traditions and with the democratic system of government as it did with the characteristics of the Soviet Union. In a nutshell, U.S. officials did not ask for the burden of leadership. Sometimes they even resented carrying it. In addition, there was much less demand for imperial pacification in the West than there was in the East. Many U.S. allies, and all of the most important ones, were democracies. Since democracies do not fight each other (Bremer, 1992; Doyle, 1986; Gleditsch, 1992; 1995; Maoz and Russett, 1992; 1993; Rummel, 1983; 1985; Russett, 1993; 1995; Small and Singer, 1976; Weede, 1992b), there was little need for a heavy-handed imposition of peace within large parts of the West.[21]

The lack of need for the imposition of peace within the democratic and industrialized core of the West was underwritten by growing prosperity in the Cold War era.[22] Whereas politicians after World War I "devised ways to impoverish themselves and one another" (Keynes, 1919/1988, p. 99), U.S. economic policy in the Cold War era promoted prosperity by free trade within the West.[23] In a multipolar international system great powers may resist free trade because they fear that free trade might help other states more than themselves and thereby endanger their place in the international pecking order. In the bipolar system of the Cold War era, the United States promoted free trade with and among its allies in order to strengthen them, make them prosperous, and stabilize their democracies.

As Gowa (1994, p. 3) has observed:

> The pursuit of power strongly influenced the pursuit of plenty. During the Cold War, international trade closely paralleled the division of the world into two major political-military blocs. Without exception, member states of the North Atlantic Treaty Organization became signatories of the General Agreement on Tariffs and Trade, and members of the Warsaw Treaty Organization joined the Council for Mutual Economic Assistance. In turn, the Coordinating Committee for Multilateral Export Controls (COCOM), essentially a subset of NATO, controlled trade between East and West.

Of course, free trade was more successful in contributing to the reconstruction of Western Europe and Japan than in much of the U.S.-aligned Third World. As outlined in Sections 2 and 3 of Chapter 5, kleptocracy, rent-seeking, and import substitution instead of export orientation contributed to the poor performance of many LDCs.

In contrast to the East, the Western bloc was not homogeneous. The political systems of Soviet allies were replications of the Soviet system. Some of the replications, such as Poland and Hungary, became somewhat deformed, but the family resemblance remained clearly visible until the late 1980s. By contrast, the political systems of Latin America were definitely not replications either of the U.S. system or of West European regimes (see Gurr, Jaggers, and Moore, 1990). Except for Costa Rica, there were few stable and effective democracies in Latin America. Therefore, inter-American relations were not made peaceful by all of the client-states being democracies. From a Latin American perspective, U.S. leadership looked much more heavy-handed and less benign than it did from a West European perspective.

Since the Monroe Doctrine, the U.S. goal has been to keep hostile foreign powers out of the Western Hemisphere. This aspiration targeted the Soviet Union and its expansive aspirations. But U.S. officials insisted on doing the job without compromising their democratic ideals. U.S. leadership was compatible with those ideals when it was freely accepted, as it usually was in Western Europe.[24] When one's leadership is rejected, one has to face a choice between imposing it or giving it up. In Latin America, the United States occasionally used both policies. Such vacillation generally threatens to undermine the policy of the day, whatever it is.

U.S. vacillation resulted from the free and open character of the U.S. polity as well as from the unstable, authoritarian, and frequently repressive character of Latin American regimes. For democracies like the United States, consistent and persistent policies are always difficult to achieve. Democratic foreign policies are not made by unitary rational actors. Instead they result from bargaining, horse trading, and agreement on "obvious" solutions. Constraining sovereign governments looks illegitimate to democrats even if the economic, democratic, and human rights performance of the target governments leaves much to be desired. Nevertheless, the United States did replace some dangerous, disorderly, or even murderous regimes by force: in 1954 in Guatemala, 1965 in the Dominican Republic, and 1983 in Grenada. Since Western publics and politicians found it difficult to distinguish between military intervention against an elected government and interventions against repressive regimes, even the successful U.S. interventions have attracted much criticism throughout the Western world.

The Bay of Pigs invasion of Cuba in 1961 was the most important case of vacillation and inconsistency: President John F. Kennedy would have liked to get rid of Fidel Castro and to replace him by a more friendly government, but he did not want to send in U.S. troops when Cuban exiles were not up to the task. The Bay of Pigs disaster only reinforced Castro's hostility toward the United States. In Moscow, it must have been read as a signal of Kennedy's lack of decisiveness, if not as an invitation to establish a bridgehead in the Americas—as the Soviets certainly did in 1962. In my view, the Cuban missile crisis would have been inconceivable without the blunders of 1961. Peace through fear between East and West rested on a double basis: first on the balance of terror and second on clear and mutually understood linkages between the superpowers and their protégés. By not bailing out the Cuban exiles at the Bay of Pigs, the United States accepted the snapping of the link to Cuba. Once Cuba teamed up with the Soviets and was on the way to becoming a Soviet missile base, Kennedy attempted to reclaim the U.S. veto over Cuban foreign and military policies that he had unknowingly but effectively given up by inaction during the Bay of Pigs event. This vacillation generated one of the worst and most escalation-prone crises between the superpowers so far.

The military preponderance of the United States in the Western Hemisphere was nearly as overwhelming as Soviet preponderance was in its bloc. But U.S. authority in the Americas was not strong enough to prevent military conflicts and even wars. The football war between El Salvador and Honduras in 1969 and, more recently, the Falklands War between Argentina and Britain, i.e., again between U.S. allies, were among the bloodiest events testifying to the erosion of U.S. authority within the Western bloc.

The core of the Third World has always been Asia and the Middle East. Except for a few neutralized areas, the European extension of the Asian landmass was neatly divided between the Soviet bloc and the Western bloc. North Asia constituted part of the Soviet Union, and Outer Mongolia became a client-state of the Soviet Union as early as the 1920s. Japan and the Philippines were parts of the West and firmly tied to the United States by treaties and, at least as importantly, U.S. bases and troops on their soil. Taiwan was a more complicated case, but it also benefited from U.S. protection, at least until the 1970s. The rest, i.e., most, of Asia suffered from irregular, intermittent, and competitive intervention by both superpowers.

At the end of World War II U.S. forces disarmed the Japanese army in South Korea and invited the Soviets to do the same in North Korea. Thereafter, both superpowers assisted "their" parts of Korea to develop economic and political systems modeled on the liberators who had freed them from Japanese colonial rule. Given the cultural and ethnic homogeneity of Korea, its division was unnatural. Koreans of either ideological persuasion never accepted it as legitimate. So the division of the country set the stage for a fractricidal war.

Having demobilized in a great hurry after the end of World War II, U.S. leaders were not yet psychologically ready for the burden of worldwide leadership that they ultimately and hesitatingly accepted. They couldn't decide whether they would defend South Korea against communist aggression. Worse still, Dean Acheson said that South Korea was outside the U.S. defense perimeter.[25] Of course, one cannot ultimately demonstrate that the North Korean attack was caused by Acheson's unwise remarks. Certainly the remarks could not bolster but only undermine deterrence. The North Koreans attacked, and U.S. officials started thinking and ultimately realized that Korea was important after all. The Korean War got under way.

The first, and ultimately successful, war to contain communism in Asia early demonstrated two rules according to which power politics was to be played in mainland Asia: first, no direct confrontation of superpower troops; second, no use of nuclear weapons.[26] Offending against either of these rules might have produced general war between East and West. Since neither side had a blueprint for victory, global war was avoided and a tacit agreement on these two rules seems to have evolved.[27] Because mainland Asia lacked clear, stable, and mutually respected lines of demarcation, the two rules were necessary in order to reduce the risk of escalation. But the rules transformed the polarity of the Asian international subsystem.[28] The distribution of *usable* military power became quasi-multipolar.[29]

Quasi multipolarity differs from plain multipolarity by referring to perceptions and constraints on the use of military force instead of to capabilities only. In quasi-multipolar mainland Asia the two superpowers did not command superior usable power because inhibitions against the use of nuclear weapons ultimately prevailed and because the second superpower always avoided committing its own troops once the first superpower had done so (and had usually run into quite a bit of trouble).

The two rules of the game made Asia "safe for conventional war." There have been three protracted wars over the line of demarcation between communism on the one hand and local as well as Western defenders on the other hand. First, there was the Korean War. Second, there was the set of Indochinese wars, consisting of a French and a U.S. phase, in Vietnamese, Laotian, and Cambodian (Kampuchean) theaters.[30] Third, there was the Afghanistan War. The common characteristic of all these wars has been an inability or unwillingness of the superpowers to invest sufficient resources to prevail. The United States did not succeed in reunifying Korea, as it intended to do before the Mainland Chinese intervened, but had to settle for the status quo that had existed before the communist aggression. In Indochina, first French and then U.S. forces were beaten or demoralized by local communists who, of course, received a lot of "fraternal aid" from the Soviet Union and Mainland China and who skillfully played on Western public opinion. More recently, the Afghan freedom fighters demonstrated that it has even been possible to demoralize a Soviet politburo leadership and its army of occupation. Of course, both superpowers had the capability to impose their will against local resistance, but they thought it too costly in blood and treasure without nuclear weapons and too costly politically with nuclear weapons.

The Korean, Indochinese, and Afghanistan wars as well as the Indian-Chinese border war and the Taiwan Strait disputes served to define the territorial limits of Asian communism. But communism was never as monolithic in Asia as it was in Europe until the 1980s. Mainland China was always too big to be as subservient to the Soviet Union as East European communist countries have been. The power potential of China always fed great aspirations. Moreover, the Chinese communists always felt that they had fought their way to power themselves, whereas most East European communist leaders knew that they had been put into power by Soviet armies and that Soviet armies were always their most reliable protection against their own peoples.

The size of Mainland China and the independence of its ruling elite undermined the coherence of the Sino-Soviet bloc. Given intellectual and political independence, some ideological disputes had to occur sooner or later. They did. Given the history of Russian expansionism into territories that the Chinese regarded as theirs, or at least as within their traditional sphere of influence, resentment against the Russians had to develop sooner or later. So the stage was set for war between communists in Asia: first between the Soviet Union and China along the Ussuri River border; later between China and Vietnam, which had become a Soviet protégé; and in between these fights one between Vietnam and Cambodia, i.e., between a Soviet protégé and a Chinese protégé.

Except for Outer Mongolia and for a very short period North Korea, communist Asia was never part of the Soviet bloc. The Soviet bloc was ultimately, defined by the closeness of Soviet troops in numbers sufficient to overawe both outsiders and locals. In Asia the Soviet Union had to settle for less, for a mere sphere of influence.[31] But the Soviet sphere of influence in Asia (which in the 1950s and early 1960s even included Mainland China) nevertheless was part of the quasi-multipolar subsystem of international relations. Wars could be fought, whether for local dominance within the communist sphere or for its expansion.

In the noncommunist part of mainland Asia and the Middle East, local actors asserted their sovereignty too. There have been several series of wars between Arabs and Israelis as well as between Indians and Pakistanis. The purposes of these wars were largely unrelated to the East-West conflict. These conflicts concerned local issues and were fought by local contenders against local enemies. Although the superpowers sometimes had quite strong preferences for one party or the other, and although they helped arm the parties to the conflicts, their chief contributions to these protracted conflicts were negative: They (tacitly) permitted local contenders to fight it out. Similar circumstances characterized the Iran-Iraq War of the 1980s. Territorial issues loomed large in all of these wars (see Goertz and Diehl, 1992; Holsti, 1991; Luard, 1968, 1970; Vasquez, 1993; Weede, 1975).

In the 1950s much of sub-Saharan Africa was still under colonial rule, but in the 1960s most African states achieved their independence. As in mainland Asia, the superpowers themselves avoided stable and serious commitments. Since using nuclear weapons or risking direct confrontation between superpower troops was avoided even in Asia, where the stakes were so much higher than in Africa, the two rules could easily be extended to Africa. Given even less direct superpower interference in Africa than in Asia, we again get a quasi-multipolar distribution of power.

So far my treatment of sub-Saharan Africa may look as if it exaggerates the symmetry between the two superpowers. But U.S. leaders avoided military commitment to Africa even more consistently than the Soviets. Before the Vietnam War, the United States regarded Africa as an Anglo-French-Belgian-Portuguese backyard. During and after the Vietnam War, U.S. officials were first distracted and thereafter immobilized by public opinion and by Congress. The French took up the burden of defending Western interests in much of Africa. On the communist side, tiny Cuba acted like a sphere-of-influence-maintaining power in Angola, Mozambique, and Ethiopia. Soviet leaders paid for Cuban services, but they could remain in the background themselves—except in Ethiopia, where they were more visible for a while than elsewhere.

To recapitulate: The bipolar subsystem rested on the extended deterrence that the superpowers provided for their clients. It resulted in Pax Atomica between East and West. The unipolar Soviet bloc was characterized by the subordination of client-states under the Soviet Union, which ruled out war among Soviet clients because the Soviet Union constituted an effective central authority within its bloc. Of course, this subordination did not rule out Soviet campaigns against unruly allies. The unipolarity of the West was not as firm as the East's. Nor was U.S. guidance as regular, predictable, and heavy-handed as was Soviet rule in its own bloc. Being democrats at home, U.S. representatives do not find an imperial role overseas congenial, which is why Pax Americana has sometimes broken down in the West. Fortunately, pluralist Western democracy not only interfered with decisive U.S. leadership but also provided an alternative to imperial peace. Democracies do not need a heavy-handed imperial power to avoid war among themselves. Therefore, the democratic core of the West benefited from Pax Democratica, and the shortcomings of Pax Americana are visible only in what has been the periphery of the West, especially in Latin America.

Extended deterrence in the bipolar subsystem and unipolarity within both blocs were interdependent. Extended deterrence ruled out superpower interference in the other superpower's bloc and thereby established the blocs as unipolar subsystems. Where imperial peace was not efficiently provided in blocs, interference by the other superpower was less and less effectively deterred—even if the interference was dependent on proxies (e.g., Cuban or even Sandinista). The quasi-multipolar subsystem of the Cold War period was residual. In this subsystem neither peace through fear nor imperial peace nor democratic peace prevailed. Because of the tacit agreements between the superpowers to avoid a direct confrontation of their troops, it was the part of the world that was "safe for conventional war." The quasi-multipolar subsystem seems to have expanded over time from mainland Asia and the Middle East to Africa and even to Latin America. Nevertheless, not all parts of the Third World suffered equally from interstate war. By and large, African states tended to be too weak to engage in it. By and large, Latin Americans still benefited from a legacy of Pax Britannica and Pax

Americana and the lack of classical causes to go to war that is the heritage of a long peace.

According to my analysis so far, there have been but two strongly pacifying conditions in Cold War world politics. The risk of war was reduced either by minimizing hopes for victory or by overcoming bellicosity. In principle, it is conceivable to minimize hopes for victory by either conventional or nuclear deterrence. In practice, conventional deterrence is difficult to achieve and unlikely to work. Conventional deterrence is inherently unstable because initiative and surprise are combat power multipliers that generate some pressure toward preemption (see Betts, 1985; Dupuy, 1987; Epstein, 1988; Weede, 1990e). Parity in conventional combat power does *not* overcome this problem. Instead, a surprise attack may look even more attractive under parity than under other circumstances where surprise is either not needed or insufficient to prevail. Conceivably, some defensive restructuring of the armed forces of all medium-sized and major powers might reduce the premium for striking first, but I find it difficult to imagine this occurring. Be that as it may, such extreme defense emphasis has not yet been a characteristic of historical international systems.

By contrast, some crisis stability is inherent in the nuclear deterrence relationship. Mere uncertainty about the effects of large-scale nuclear war suffices to generate worst-case assumptions about war damage that dissuade decisionmakers from exploiting either superiority or the conceivable advantage of striking first. In the 1950–1989 period, nuclear deterrence minimized hopes for victory in some places and thereby contributed to the avoidance of war, in particular to the avoidance of war between the superpowers and their respective allies.

In Section 1 of this chapter I proposed that security dilemmas and territorial issues generate serious and ultimately irreconcilable conflicts of interest that often result in war. These ideas could form the basis of an empirical study. Operationally, the question is: Which states fight each other and why? The first part of the answer must identify which dyads or pairs of nations are most likely to face a security dilemma or territorial conflict of interest. Here, I suggest two *necessary* background conditions of a security dilemma: Nations must either be contiguous to each other or one of them must be very powerful; otherwise they do not threaten each other, and there will be peace by default (for example, between Afghanistan and Mexico). Operationally, proximity is measured by a dummy variable, contiguity by land. During the Cold War period only the two superpowers were strategically interdependent with the rest of the world. Some states are contiguous not by their homeland locations but because of enclaves or exclaves. In some of these cases (as well as in even more physically contiguous cases) there have been forced transfers of territory that are assumed to cause terri-

torial conflicts. Therefore, it is proposed that the subset of dyads characterized either by contiguity, or by at least one of the two states being a superpower, or by forced transfers of territory (or enclaves/exclaves, or a misfit
between linguistic and political borders)[32] contains almost all dyads in
which conflicts of interest may be sufficiently serious for war to become
conceivable.

Serious or irreconcilable conflicts of interest are but one background
condition of war. Other conditions include hopes of prevailing or blueprints
for victory. In the Cold War period there was little hope of prevailing in a
war between East and West. Since any war between a U.S. and a Soviet ally
could easily escalate, both superpowers had an interest in the tight control of
their allies to prevent themselves from being dragged into a war between
minor states for (from a superpower perspective) minor issues. This is the
structure of the mechanism of pacification in the X-Y dyad in which there
might be a conflict of interest and therefore some need for pacification: X is
controlled by (operationally, allied with) the United States. Y is controlled
by the Soviet Union. The superpowers fear mutual (assured) destruction.
Therefore, war between X and Y is not permitted.

The subset of war-prone dyads now contains all dyads in which nations
are contiguous, one is a superpower, or there has been a forced territorial
transfer, minus those dyads covered by extended deterrence because one of
the states was a member of the U.S.-led alliance and the other was a member of the Soviet-led alliance. But this subset still contains too many dyads
in which war is extremely unlikely, for example, Norway and Sweden or the
Netherlands and Belgium, or the United States and Canada. Not coinciden-
tally, all of these dyads consist of two democracies. Thus, the double-
democracy dyads have to be removed from the set of war-prone dyads.
Finally, the Soviet Union (but not the United States) is assumed to have been
the functional equivalent of a blocwide central government. Therefore,
dyads consisting of two Soviet allies are removed from the subset of war-
prone dyads.

For the 1950–1989 period and for 82 nations, or 3,321 dyads, and wars
that meet the Singer and Small (1972; Small and Singer, 1982) criteria, I
(Weede, 1994, p. 72) find that 17 out of 50 war dyads occur where the theory "permits" war and 33 out of 50 where the theory "forbids" war. While
these numbers seem pretty devastating, one gets a *much* more favorable
impression if one looks at the relative frequencies of war. The frequency is
17/203 or about 0.084 where the theory "permits" war but 33/3,118 or 0.011
where the theory "forbids" war; i.e., war is more than seven times as likely
where it is permitted than where it is (theoretically) forbidden.

If one looks at the fourfold table from which these results come, the
relationship is significant at the 0.001 level (chi square = 63.95). Yule's Q or
gamma is 0.79. Although the underlying fourfold table looks like a bivariate

analysis, it actually is a multivariate analysis in which six variables (contiguity, superpower in dyad, territorial transfers, extended deterrence, double democracy, two Soviet allies) are combined in a nonadditive way with theoretically determined (rather than estimated) weights corresponding to either −1 or +1.

The difference in relative frequencies, Yule's Q, or the significance level will not satisfy those critics who focus on the misclassification of 33 out of 50 wars that occurred although war was forbidden by my theory. But 25 out of those 33 cases result from the Korean War. While the theory "permits" war between South and North Korea or between the United States and North Korea or China, it does not account for the auxiliary belligerency of U.S. allies such as Colombia or Turkey against the communist powers. Another unexpected four cases come from the Vietnam War and also arise because of auxiliary belligerency, i.e., the help the United States received from Australia, the Philippines, Thailand, and South Korea against the Vietcong and the North Vietnamese. Another two unexpected cases come from the Arab-Israeli wars, where Iraq and Saudi Arabia became involved in wars with Israel, even though they do not share borders, in 1973. This involvement is also a kind of auxiliary belligerency. If Egypt, Jordan, and Syria had not fought Israel in the Yom Kippur War, it is hard to imagine Iraq and Saudi Arabia warring with Israel. Thus, 31 out of the 33 unexpected cases are due to auxiliary belligerency or lateral escalation. These war dyads do not concern the original or primary war dyads in the wars. The other two odd cases concern the Anglo-French involvement in the 1956 Sinai War. Obviously, one could argue that in the 1950s Britain and France were still great powers and recode accordingly. In my view, however, the loss in simplicity of my coding scheme would outweigh any gains in fit. So I do contend that the theory is quite strongly supported by the test.

While I do not intend to discuss the decline and collapse of the Soviet Union in detail, a few observations have to be made. First, the poor economic performance of state socialism and central planning in the Soviet Union is clearly compatible with the analysis of economic development provided in Chapters 2–6 of this book. In those chapters the importance of limited government and private property rights, of competitive markets and scarcity prices have been elaborated. All these characteristics of wealthy economies were conspicuous in the USSR only by their absence. Second, the deterioration of Soviet economic performance over time since 1950 is compatible with Olson's (1982) general theory about the rise and decline of nations that I endorsed in Chapter 6 (see also Murrell and Olson, 1991). Third, based on geopolitical reasoning and pointing to the Russian loss of marchland advantage, Collins (1986, p. 186) *predicted* at least the general prospect of some future decline of the Russian Empire, as he chose to call the Soviet Union. Fourth, drawing on theories of hegemonic rivalry and power transition, Wohlforth (1994–1995, p. 124) argues that "Soviet decline reaffirmed rather than reversed the existing hierarchy of world politics" and thereby explains the peaceful character of the end of the Cold War. The geopolitical and the hegemonic argument are compatible with the approach to world politics applied here.

Since the Soviet Union, its bloc, and extended deterrence have all gone, what was the quasi-multipolar subsystem of the Cold War era and its zone of insecurity has been substantially expanded and is in the process of being transformed. With the collapse of the Soviet Union, war in the former Soviet bloc has become possible. In effect, the former Soviet bloc has joined what was the quasi-multipolar system or, if one prefers Singer and Wildavsky's (1993) term, the "zone of turmoil." Since there is only a single superpower left, the polarity of this vastly expanded zone of insecurity depends on the United States. The more the United States hesitates to become militarily involved, the more the distribution of usable military power will approach multipolarity. The almost permanent projection of military power and frequently actual use of it—and suffering the casualties—is a costly process. I simply do not see the incentives or the U.S. national interest to be served by attempting to police the entire globe.[33] Moreover, one may question U.S. capabilities, as Moon (1991, p. 24) has done: "The U.S. is neither able nor willing to bear the costs of leadership, resulting in erratic, parochial and imprudent conduct of foreign policy that has undermined its legitimacy as the preeminent global leader."

The starkest effect of the collapse of the Soviet Union and of its economy may be the speeding up of the process of nuclear proliferation (Clancy and Seitz, 1991). The division of the Soviet Union has made four nuclear powers out of the original one. Whether Ukraine and Kazakhstan actually become denuclearized, as they have agreed, remains to be seen. Conceivable Russian threats to their territorial integrity or even independence militate against such disarmament. But the main impetus to proliferation from the troubles of the former USSR is something different: the loss of political control and the economic disaster. Much ex-Soviet knowledge about nuclear weapons might become declassified in practice, if not in law, and available for sale to the highest bidder, both in the forms of components, materials, or weapons and as human capital or expertise. The less comfortable life is for knowledgeable and influential people in the ex-Soviet military-industrial complex, the greater must be the temptation to sell whatever can be turned into hard currency.

If we are destined to live in a world with an expanding number of nuclear powers, some of which are likely to be neither politically stable nor democratic and some of which are involved in hostile and explosive relationships with their neighbors, then the question arises whether nuclear deterrence will work in the vast zone of insecurity beyond the industrialized democracies. It is unlikely that we will see a significant amount of extend-ed deterrence there. Except for Russia's and Mainland China's forces, most nuclear forces are likely to remain comparatively small and vulnerable. This smallness is not what makes extended deterrence credible, so any benefits of nuclear deterrence are likely to be restricted to the relationships between nuclear powers and their antagonists. A nuclear strike by a nuclear power against a nonnuclear power might still be dissuaded by the fear of outside reactions, in particular of punishment inflicted by the United States or a U.S.-led coalition. A nuclear strike of one nuclear power against another seems less likely to attract outside involvement. So, the dyadic balance of terror should carry more weight than outsider-connected scenarios.

Unfortunately, the dyadic nuclear balances in the zone of insecurity are likely to differ from the U.S.-USSR balance in two respects: Because of ini-tial vulnerabilities and the lack of secure second-strike capabilities, there will be incentives to strike first. Moreover, some conceivable nuclear pow-ers may suffer from serious political instability verging on civil war.[34] Therefore, I would expect the pacifying effect of nuclear proliferation to be conditional on the domestic stability of the nations concerned. Nuclear pro-liferation might result sooner or later in some local use of nuclear weapons. Most likely, some poor countries will use them against each other. The rich countries will deplore the breaking of the nuclear taboo and explore strate-gic defenses (see Jastrow and Kampelman, 1992).

In sum, I am closer to Mearsheimer (1990) in my assessment of the destabilizing impact of the end of the Cold War than to Singer and Wildavsky's (1993) optimism. But my scenarios and fears are less Eurocentric than Mearsheimer's. I expect Western Europe, including Germany, to remain part of the OECD island of stability in a global zone of insecurity for a while. I expect an "Islamic" and a (North?) Korean nuclear bomb much earlier than a German one. Whether the OECD island of wealth, democracy, and security can succeed in isolating itself from the wars of the zone of insecurity, or even from possible nuclear strikes, may be doubted. The main advantage of the Cold War order has been that the road to nuclear hell was broad and clearly visible and therefore avoidable. Instead of a high-way we now face a lot of small paths, and nobody knows where they ulti-mately lead.

At the time of this writing (late 1994, early 1995), Russia enjoys friend-ly relations with the West. If Russia were to compete again with the United States and the West—say, after a breakdown of democratic rule—then even the issue of deterrence might resurface. Because Russia's economic and geographic power base are much reduced, Western deterrence of a reassertive Russia might look easier than it was in the Cold War era. Psychologically, however, deterrence of Russia might become more difficult than deterrence of the Soviet Union ever was because Russia is the successor state of the Soviet Union and has lost so much of its previous power, prestige, and territory. Stein (1990, p. 110) has rightly argued: "It is more difficult to deter aggression intended to avoid loss than to deter aggression pursued for gain. Ironically, it takes less to deter adventurous aggressors than it does the fearful and desparate."[35] In Chapter 8 I shall analyze the domestic conditions that impeded deterrence in the past, and will impede deterrence if it is needed again, and that also increase the likelihood that deterrence will be needed again.

Notes

1. Vasquez (1993, p. 219) adds some devastating criticism by pointing out that Bueno de Mesquita's theory cannot adequately deal with the world wars, the Korean War, and the Vietnam War. By and large, the theory seems most successful with simple (dyadic) wars.

2. In my view, social interaction itself tends to generate new desires and thereby to aggravate the problem of scarcity. Moreover, collective decisionmaking often consumes time and other resources, especially where adversaries invest resources in order to frustrate each other's efforts. These resources are then no longer available for productive purposes and the satisfaction of wants.

3. Temporarily, some regions have overcome international anarchy when a civilization only loosely connected with the rest of the world was pacified by some conqueror. Such successes, however, have always been restricted in time and place because they neither lasted nor ever covered the globe.

4. This simplifying assumption is not fully justified because one can no longer account for treason, i.e., for some part of the ruling elite collaborating with the enemy and undermining the defense of the homeland. While such berayal has happened, the focus of this chapter is governmental decisionmaking and the causes of war.

5. Historically there have been periods of offensive as well as defensive advantage. In periods of defensive advantage, the "loss of strength gradient" (Boulding, 1962) tends to make a nation much more powerful at home than abroad, thereby mitigating the security dilemma. If the loss of strength gradient is almost flat, however, or if initiative and surprise are powerful force multipliers, then the security dilemma is made worse.

6. A recent controversy (between Grieco, Powell, and Snidal, 1993) has demonstrated that the impact of relative gains instead of absolute gains depends on the number of states: the larger the number of states, the less the weight of relative gains. For practical purposes, however, "high politics" has always been the preserve of the great powers, i.e., of a fairly small number of states. For small states, relative gains matter little because their viability depends more on what the great powers do or don't do than on their own efforts.

7. I shall (at first) proceed from the assumption that most regime differences do not matter. Almost no regime is so tightly and hierarchically organized that government can reasonably be treated as if all decisions were made by a single person. While some dissenters may point to Hitler or Stalin, I doubt how close even they actually came to their totalitarian ideal. While the number and the identity or back-

ground of decisionmakers varies widely from nation to nation, I assume that national decisionmaking generally is collective decisionmaking and therefore cannot meet the standards of rationality that we apply to individuals. For a similar view, see Singer (1993).

8. I am uncertain whether I should propose the hypothesis that collectives, or corporate actors, are incapable of learning. But I confidently assert the weaker statement: Collectives, or corporate actors not dominated by a single decisionmaker, learn much more slowly than individuals to avoid inefficient means in their attempts to obtain their goals. Concerning the arms race or military-preparation link with war, I carefully chose a formulation that sidesteps the controversy between Wallace (1979; 1982) and his critics (Altfeld, 1983; Diehl, 1983; Houweling and Siccama, 1981; Weede, 1980b).

9. Glaser (1994–1995, p. 54) explicitly endorses this assumption.

10. The work of Goertz and Diehl (1992), Holsti (1991), and Vasquez (1993) promises to remedy this situation.

11. There might be exceptions. After catastrophic defeat such as Germany suffered in World War II, voicing resentment on territorial losses may become taboo. But this situation is exceptional.

12. While there is some disagreement about the definition of polarity in the literature, here it refers only to the distribution of power among states, not to alliance patterns.

13. With Bernholz (1985) or Kaplan (1957), one may also point out that multipolar systems tend to be characterized by fluid alliance patterns in which today's opponent might become tomorrow's ally. The very expectation that one might need a contemporary adversary tomorrow should mitigate and limit conflicts.

14. In a sea power–focused analysis, Thompson (1983) supports the "preponderance reduces the risk of war" proposition for both centuries.

15. Recent treatments of the polarity-and-war relationship include Kegley and Raymond (1992), Mansfield (1994), Russett and Starr (1992, chapter 5), and Vasquez (1993).

16. One may regard insularity as an enhancement of a peripheral location. The advantages of insularity, sea power, and "global reach" play a major role in long-cycle theory (Modelski, 1983; 1987; Thompson, 1983; 1992; Modelski and Thompson, 1993).

17. For the 1648–1815 period, Kim (1992) also reports evidence supporting a positive relationship between equality of dyadic power and dyadic war among great powers. But Kim's list of great powers demonstrates a strong maritime bias, and he adjusts dyadic power balances by contributions of putative allies. Bueno de Mesquita and Lalman (1992, p. 217) also suggest that "the power preponderance theory performs better than the balance-of-power theory." According to Schampel (1993), a faster rate of change in material capabilities contributes to the risk of war.

18. A previous version of this section was presented at a conference in Haifa, Israel, in May 1993 and is likely to be published in a conference volume to be edited by Zeev Maoz. The conference version is intended to stand by itself, whereas this section is linked to previous and later chapters and theories.

19. The potency of this U.S. hesitation to commit itself in European affairs has been demonstrated by the quick demobilization of the U.S. armed forces after the end of World War II. Stalin was in no similar hurry.

20. Although the Soviet bloc is identical to the Warsaw Pact alliance and the U.S.-led bloc to the U.S. alliance systems covering Western Europe, Latin America,

and the Far East, I prefer the word *bloc* over *alliance* in order to downplay the legal aspects of the alliances and the false impression of equality among allies conveyed by an international-law perspective on international affairs.

21. Farber and Gowa (1994) contest the democratic peace proposition. In their empirical analysis, democracies were no less likely than other pairs of states to fight each other before 1913, and democracies were more likely than others to be involved in militarized disputes with each other. But the Farber and Gowa analysis suffers from too loose a definition of democracy. Britain, for example, has been regarded as a democracy since 1837, i.e., even when the overwhelming majority of the adult population was not yet entitled to vote. Since there were few contiguous, full, and stable democracies—which provide the best setting for testing the democratic peace proposition—before 1945, it seems best to focus on the post-1945 period. For this period Farber and Gowa agree that democracies never went to war against each other and that they were less frequently involved in militarized disputes than other pairs of states. Applying process-tracing case studies, Layne (1994) also forcefully contests the democratic peace proposition. Although his cases persuasively reject the idea of democratic peace, all of them refer to the period before 1945, when supporting evidence is weak in any case. Spiro's (1994) criticism of the democratic peace proposition is unpersuasive to me. His approach comes close to guaranteeing insignificant relationships. Had he analyzed the democratic peace proposition among strategically interdependent and therefore comparatively war-prone dyads, the chance of finding significant relationships (after 1945) would have been much better. While Farber and Gowa point to common interests among democracies in the Cold War period, I think that U.S. preponderance among Western democracies was a useful kind of reinsurance against the escalation of conflicts even among Western democracies.

22. We know from the research of Lipset and others (Lipset, 1959; 1994; Lipset, Seong, and Torres, 1993; Bollen and Jackman, 1985; Cutright, 1963; Jackman, 1975; Neubauer, 1967) that prosperity stabilizes democracy.

23. This policy has been a spectacular success. Mueller (1994, p. 365, footnote 7) has made the point well: "Germany and Japan have been converted from violent and intensely destructive enemies into prosperous friends, allies, and peaceful competitors whose perspective on the world is much the same as that of the western victors. As policies go, this may well be among the greatest triumphs of enlightened self-interest in history."

24. Of course, there are exceptions even in Western Europe. By and large, however, anti-Americanism in Europe has infected minorities rather than majorities and opposition parties rather than governments.

25. For the history of the outbreak of the Korean War, see, for example, George and Smoke (1974, chapter 6). The outbreak of the Korean War is also an excellent illustration of the Huth-Russett proposition that the short-term military balance is a crucial determinant of deterrent success (Huth, 1988a; 1988b; Huth and Russett, 1984; 1988). As the history of the early period of the Korean War demonstrates, South Korean and U.S. leaders were insufficiently prepared.

26. Although there were some nuclear threats at the end of Korean War, their effectiveness is dubious. See Betts (1987).

27. In accordance with Schelling (1966), I do regard tacit bargaining as an important ingredient of world politics.

28. Over time, the Asian subsystem and the rules upon which it is based have been extended to Africa and to Latin America.

29. The term *quasi multipolarity* is adapted from Liska (1962, pp. 162, 261).

30. After all of Indochina had become communist, wars did not end. There

have been wars between communist-ruled Vietnam and communist-ruled Cambodia (or Kampuchea) as well as between Vietnam and communist-ruled China. Human suffering from communist rule in South Vietnam, and even worse suffering in Cambodia, also seems to have been at the very least as bad as the suffering from the earlier fight against communism (Rummel, 1994a; 1994b).

31. My distinction between bloc and sphere of influence is a matter of degree. While there are no serious challenges to the leader within a bloc, there are always challenges and contention within a mere sphere of influence.

32. See Weede (1975) for the details of the coding scheme and the data on territorial conflicts.

33. The United States did not persist in its attempt to pacify Somalia in the 1990s, Lebanon in the 1980s, and Vietnam in the 1970s. Why should it attempt the thankless, costly, and occasionally bloody task of pacifying the vast zone of insecurity?

34. Much of this political instability is likely to arise from communal conflict, possibly in interaction with an uncertain and reversible process of democratization. See Gurr (1993).

35. This argument is based on the experimental studies by Kahneman, Tversky, and their associates cited in Chapter 2, Section 1.

8

CONCLUSIONS: DISTRIBUTIONAL COALITIONS AND RENT-SEEKING AS A THREAT TO PROSPERITY AND PEACE

1. A Look Back at Cold War Problems

After Mikhail Gorbachev ended the Cold War and Boris Yeltsin continued Gorbachev's good-neighbor policy toward the West, the West won the Cold War partly by default and partly by U.S. efforts. In my view, the West was seriously challenged by the Soviet Union and its capability to get significant military power out of a poor and deteriorating economic base. According to Luttwak's (1983, p. 115) estimate, the USSR was about five times as effective as the West in transforming economic power into military capabilities. Despite benefit to the West of Gorbachev's redefinition of Soviet national interest as a "search for relief from burdens" (Sestanovich, 1990, p. 14), it is still useful to analyze why a country as economically underdeveloped as the USSR could ever seriously challenge a United States allied with Western Europe and Japan. In essence, I shall argue that distributional coalitions or interest-group politics weakened the West during the Cold War (for a similar view, see Kammler, 1983; 1986). Moreover, the same type of domestic politics that endangered deterrence in the past undermines the "export" of peace and prosperity today.

Western democracy set a ceiling for Western defense efforts that could not easily be overcome and was at best weakly responsive to hostile efforts. If Ronald Reagan or Caspar Weinberger ever dreamed of allocating a percentage of GNP to the military similar to that allocated by the Soviet Union, they did not dare say so. Nobody has ever suggested that the United States should draft as many conscripts as the Soviets and pay them at Soviet levels in order to save money for tanks, missiles, and bombs.

My point is not that either policy was desirable but that democratic government implied limits to U.S. defense efforts that could not be overcome in peacetime and that were almost unrelated to professional assessments of defense needs. The same point could be reiterated for European nations and

Japan with the single qualification that the psychological threshold separating bearable and unbearable defense burdens was significantly lower in most of Europe or Japan than in the United States. Because of democracy the West ran the arms race under some handicaps. If the West did well enough, it was either because the inventiveness of open societies provided it with an advantage that was at least as valuable as the fairly unlimited access of the Soviet military to *available* resources or because of good luck. The former proposition may have been true in the past, but I have challenged its continuing validity concerning conceivable future contenders in Chapter 6. The end of the era of Western economic preponderance is in view. The problem with luck is that we may not have it next time.

Behind the ceiling of Western defense efforts have been interest groups and the problem of collective goods. While one may argue that humankind as a whole would have been better off if both superpowers and the rest of the world had disarmed—and there is nothing wrong with this vision except for the difficulty of getting from here to there—I refer to a less encompassing collective good, i.e., the defense of the United States or the West provided by traditional or military means. Even if every citizen of the United States or of the Western world were convinced of the desirability of military preparation for war and in order to deter war, each citizen would still face strong incentives to freeride. Defense or deterrence are collective goods. Western societies are large groups. In large groups, there are strong incentives to freeride rather than to contribute to the procurement of collective goods (Olson, 1965). Selective incentives (for example, better pay for volunteers) and coercion (for example, in taxation) may mitigate the problem, but they are unlikely to overcome it fully. The provision of the public-goods defense or deterrence is further complicated by the scarcity of another public good, i.e., information about national security matters. Since the overwhelming majority of Western citizens rationally leaves thinking about national security affairs to others, politicians rarely stand to gain votes by promising better defense policies, whatever "better" may mean in a specific strategic context, unless one believes that a reduced defense effort almost always contributes to national security. Since a reduced defense effort frees resources for at least some other projects, whether public spending or private spending made possible by lower taxation, it enjoys a natural constituency even at extremely low levels of information.

I recognize two major objections against this line of thinking. So far, I have neglected interest groups and argued as if there were no intermediate organizations between individual and nation, or even "the West." Moreover, I have neglected vested interests in "defense efforts." Concerning the first objection, I do not see how and why it may affect the conclusion of a serious tendency toward the underprovision of the public goods of deterrence or defense. There are many interest groups in Western societies. Some are small and control only a minor share of national resources. Most of those small interest groups are more urgently concerned with matters other than defense, such as protection for textile or steel industries; subsidies for agriculture; rights for blacks, gays, or women; Spanish-language teaching in U.S. public schools; medical services for the aged; or all kinds of public-welfare benefits. The leaders of these groups have to focus on the provision of goods that are (at best) public for a subnational clientele. They rationally don't care for *national* public goods such as defense unless they or their clientele are asked to share in defense-related burdens. Given the logic of the situation, they must reject such burdens. They know that their cooperation hardly improves defense but that the burden would nonetheless be felt. So freeriding is still an imperative—for democratically accountable leaders even more so than for others because their mandate is to make freeriding possible for their adherents.

While some interest groups are much larger and more powerful than others, most are not large enough to even start thinking about voluntary contributions to the procurement of the *national* public goods of defense or deterrence. "Capitalists" or "big business" (or trade unions for that matter) are too fragmented to be capable of unified action. In essence, the limited size of most interest groups and the fragmentation of a few other interest groups create a situation in which there is a large number of interest groups that control a relatively small part of national income and therefore face an incentive to freeride in terms of deterrence and defense.

There are still those who make their living by producing weapons such as tanks or missiles or by soldiering. They might be candidates for having an interest in a strong national defense or even in the costly overprovision of this public good. At best, the widespread feeling that such interests exist contains a partial truth. There are vigorous special interests in favor of higher defense spending. The public *good,* however, is not spending but defensive and deterrent capabilities. Many types of military spending contribute little to military readiness. Overcharging the Pentagon for spare parts is no contribution to a stronger defense, nor does an aerospace enterprise contribute to any public good by billing overhead and general research and development costs to the Pentagon. Nor do noncommissioned officers who prefer to spend Christmas Eve with their families rather than on some dull, but conceivably essential, guard duty strengthen defense. The jobs and careers of some officers may depend on their withholding recently developed weapons from combat troops in order to keep the weapons on the research and development merry-go-round and themselves "usefully" employed (Luttwak, 1985). Such officers are better paid than many others though they provide no public good such as improving defense or the nation's deterrent posture. Upon closer inspection there are few (if any) special interests in providing a stronger defense and a better deterrent but many civilian and military special interests in diverting as much defense money as they can to private purposes under the pretext of defense. Special interests in misallocating defense resources merely reinforce the tendency toward underprovision of the public good generated by an underallocation of resources.

There are ways to prevent underallocation of resources for defense (or other public goods). If those who are more interested in defense than others, say some ruling class or nomenklatura, can force others to bear the burden, then underallocation of resources for defense becomes rather unlikely. Coercive control from the top may even contain the misallocation of defensive resources for private purposes, but such policies are obviously incompatible with democracy or limited government. Since Western societies did not want to mimic the least attractive traits of their opponents, they had to run the arms race with the handicap of limited resources, a limitation derived from the nature of Western societies rather than from any interpretation of strategic necessities. To further complicate Western defense efforts, freeriding tendencies within Western societies were supplemented by freeriding tendencies within the Western alliance (Olson and Zeckhauser, 1966). The smaller a Western nation was, the less deterrence and defense depended on its own efforts rather than on U.S. efforts. Therefore, the smaller countries spent proportionately less on defense than did the large ones.[1] Finally, the freeriders became welfare states and the model to which others aspire.[2]

I have argued that the United States and the West ran the arms race and the East-West confrontation under the handicap of being unable to respond to defense requests by their strategic merit. Neither the United States nor other Western societies was capable of behaving in national security matters in the same way that a unitary actor would. Conceivably, even the Soviet Union did not come as close to the model of a unitary actor in foreign and defense policies as Soviet leaders would have liked, but the Soviet Union certainly came much closer than the West. However, the peculiar Western mixture of economic strength and comparative lack of military muscle did not end in tragedy. Given past Western performance, it is dubious whether the United States and the West could compete with a more evenly matched challenger than the USSR. Western governments are so busy fulfilling the desires of their special-interest groups—as I have argued in Chapter 6, Section 1—that they simply possess neither the resources nor the time to focus on truly national interests such as deterrence, defense, or survival. Of course, the situation must be at least as bad with respect to cosmopolitan or global interests.[3] Pax Atomica and the effort behind it were U.S. or Western interests. Pax Democratica may be or may become a cosmopolitan interest. If achievable, Pax Democratica would be preferable to Pax Atomica. Is it achievable?

2. Peace by Trade and Democratization?

If democracy, prosperity, and free trade are intimately related, then economic policy may effectively influence international security. Since the future of the world may hinge upon peaceful relations between a rising East Asia and a comparatively declining but still preponderant West, it is appropriate to listen to East Asian voices. Recently, *The Economist* (1993e, p. 24) reminded us of what the former prime minister of Singapore, Lee Kuan Yew, said in a speech to the U.S. Congress in the 1980s: "The most enduring lesson of history is that ambitious growing countries can expand either by grabbing territory, people and resources, or by trading with other countries. The alternative to free trade is not just poverty, it is war."[4] Of course, the pedigree of these views can easily be traced back to nineteenth-century British liberalism and perhaps beyond. But should we accept the proposition that free trade promotes peace?

The older systematic evidence to support the assertion that trade diminishes political conflict (Gasiorowski and Polachek, 1982; Polachek, 1980) is extremely weak. Gasiorowski and Polachek (1982, p. 715) had to admit that their measure of conflict referred "to the character of day-to-day relations between the countries in question, and is by no means limited to military actions." In essence, these two studies did not seriously address the proposed link between international trade and *war* avoidance.[5] More recent research is not afflicted with this shortcoming. Domke (1988, p. 137) analyzed nation-state data and arrived at the conclusion that "governments of nations that are more involved in foreign trade are less likely to make decisions for war." Additional rigorous evidence in favor of the peace-by-trade proposition has been presented by Mansfield (1994, p. 235) who reports an "inverse relationship between the level of global trade and the incidence of all interstate wars." This finding is based on nineteenth- and twentieth-century data, a number of different war data sets, and system-level rather than nation- or dyad-level data. The crucial gap of dyadic evidence is filled by two forthcoming papers. Unfortunately, they arrive at different conclusions. According to Oneal et al. (1996), trade ties reduce the likelihood of conflict involvement. According to Barbieri (1996), trade does not consistently affect war proneness. Whether trade promotes peace directly and instantaneously is still controversial.

The version of the trade-peace link that I analyze now does not assert (nor dispute) that nations avoid war *because* they trade a lot. Instead, I propose a causal chain: Trade within as well as between nations promotes prosperity. Prosperity promotes democracy. There is almost no risk of war among democracies. By promoting prosperity and democracy, free trade does extend the democratic zone of peace. If all major powers were to become democracies, then big wars could be consigned to humankind's barbarian past. Moreover, any democracy that is encircled by other democracies is quite safe from war. The relationship between free trade and prosperity is as close to common and undisputed knowledge among economists as any assertion may ever come (for example, Friedman and Friedman, 1981, pp. 31–46; Bhagwati, 1991, p. 51; or *The Economist,* 1993b, p. 34).[6] Uncoerced trade presupposes that both sides expect some gain. Otherwise, it simply would not happen. By enlarging the size of the market, international trade permits enterprises and nations to specialize according to their comparative advantage, to raise productivity, and to expand gains from trade.

The trade-prosperity link has been investigated by economists who look for cross-national evidence to support the benefits of free trade, open economies, and export orientation. These studies (Balassa, 1981; Dollar, 1992; Greenaway and Nam, 1988; World Bank, 1983;[7] 1987; 1991; 1993b) strongly support the advantages of a free-trade regime for poor countries and of policies to exploit it. A recent study (Dollar, 1992, pp. 535, 538) suggests that Latin American and African countries might have boosted their per capita growth rate by about 2 percent per year if they had avoided exchange-rate distortion and volatility in order to participate more in international trade, as many East Asian economies have done.

A recent challenge to the trade-prosperity link comes from strategic trade theory. It has been demonstrated that national gains from discrimination and protection are feasible—but by no means assured—in oligopolistic markets where there are economies of scale or where learning by doing matters. A leading proponent of strategic trade theory, but not of its misapplication (Krugman, 1987; 1994a, p. 202) summarized the empirical research by two broad conclusions: "First, to identify which industries should receive strategic promotion or the appropriate form and level of promotion is very difficult. Second, the payoffs of even a successful strategic trade policy are likely to be very modest." Moreover, poor and small countries are least likely to succeed in exploiting strategic trade policies. Retaliation by the targets or victims of such policies may generate a negative-sum game (see Borrus et al., 1992). Moreover, Bhagwati (1991, p. 56) has pointed to the specific vulnerabilities of democracies, i.e., to "the fact that trade policy is rarely made in pluralistic democracies by dictators with monolithic objective functions. Instead, it reflects the resolution of sectional interests in the political domain. There is no necessary correspondence, therefore, between the triumphant sectoral interest and the national interest and, most important, the international or cosmopolitan interest that must define the world trading regime." From a global perspective, at least there is no serious reason to challenge the "free trade promotes prosperity" proposition.[8]

There is nearly as much consensus in the comparative politics literature on the prosperity-democracy link as there is in the economics literature on the free trade–prosperity link. In a seminal paper, Lipset (1959) suggested that prosperity reduces class conflict and induces compromise, thereby making democracy viable.[9] Although Lipset's pioneering cross-national test suffers from some technical shortcomings, later quantitative research (Bollen and Jackman, 1985; Burkhart and Lewis-Beck, 1994; Cutright, 1963; Jackman, 1975; Lipset, Seong, and Torres, 1993; Muller, 1985; Neubauer, 1967)[10] avoided these pitfalls and still supported Lipset's early conclusions. Recent synoptic approaches to capitalism or democracy concur (Berger, 1986; Huntington, 1991; Lipset, 1994). In my opinion democracy depends on two prerequisites rather than a single one. Nations have to be prosperous and capitalist at the same time, for only prosperous capitalism can provide losers in democratic elections with attractive alternatives to holding on to political power at all costs. In capitalist societies it happens quite frequently that ousted political leaders earn much more money out of office than they did in office. Under such circumstances, admitting political defeat is less costly than under socialism, where one loses political power and material well-being at the same time. Since being capitalist and being prosperous are highly correlated across nations, however, it will be impossible to distinguish the separate contributions of prosperity and capitalism to democracy.[11]

Of course, the impact of prosperity on democracy is not necessarily direct or due only to the pacifying effects of a bigger pie to be shared. According to Inkeles and Diamond (1980), high incomes promote personal satisfaction, personal efficacy, tolerance, and trust. Such personality traits could make democracy work smoothly. Moreover, high incomes permit a major expansion of secondary schooling[12] that itself promotes a modernization of outlook (Inkeles and Smith, 1974) and may make people feel that they should have a say in choosing their government.

Although there is no general agreement on the following issue, one may argue that free trade directly promotes democracy. Recently, Kasper (1994, p. 32) wrote, "The freedom to trade and to transfer capital between nations circumscribes the sovereignty of the rulers to be beastly to some of their subjects! An open international order therefore biases the evolutionary path of the entire domestic legal and institutional system in favour of individual freedom, entrepreneurial creativity, and hence prosperity." This proposition is very much in agreement with the analysis of the European miracle, or the rise of the West, given in the Chapter 4, Section 1. In that analysis, trade between political units was a determinant of relatively safe property rights, the rule of law, and limited government. It is plausible to posit that these characteristics promote democracy directly as well as indirectly via economic growth and prosperity.

On the final link in my proposed causal chain running from free trade via prosperity and democracy to the avoidance of war, we again find an unusual degree of consensus in the relevant literature. There is much agreement among those who have systematically and quantitatively analyzed the empirical evidence that democracies rarely if ever fight one another (for example: Bueno de Mesquita and Lalman, 1992; Bremer, 1992; Dixon, 1993; Doyle, 1986; Gleditsch, 1992; 1995; Maoz and Russett, 1992; 1993; Ray, 1993; Rummel, 1983; 1985; Russett, 1993; 1995; Small and Singer, 1976; Weede, 1992b).[13] What is still disputed is whether full and stable democracies ever went to war against each other or never did. For my purposes it suffices to stay within the limits of wide agreement, i.e., to note the strong disposition of democracies to avoid fighting each other. This conclusion survives careful attempts to control for other determinants of war such as contiguity, power projection capabilities, alliance ties, wealth, or extended deterrence. What remains under dispute is why democracies don't fight each other. Some point to institutional constraints against war, others to the impact of social norms and a common democratic culture. Under the influence of Dixon, Maoz, and Russett, the adherents of a normative explanation currently constitute the stronger camp.[14] But these details under dispute among specialists need not concern us here.

Although democracies avoid wars among themselves, they tend to be involved in wars about as frequently as other nations (Chan, 1984; Weede, 1984b). Again, there is fairly solid agreement on this point (Bremer and Rummel being the main dissenters). How can we conciliate these two findings with each other? It is plausible to start with Kant's (1795/1963, pp. 94–95) consideration:

> If the consent of the citizens is required in order to decide that war should be declared . . . nothing is more natural than that they would be very cautious in commencing such a poor game, decreeing for themselves all the calamities of war. Among the latter would be: having to fight, having to pay the costs of war from their own resources, having to repair the devastation war leaves behind, and, to fill up the measure of evils, load themselves with a heavy national debt that would embitter peace itself and that can never been liquidated on account of constant wars in the future.

Thus, democracy provides a setting in which the peaceable nature of ordinary men and women counts. Still, the same citizenry that objects to military action may on occasion object to the concessions required for maintaining peace. I have argued earlier (in Chapter 2, Section 3) that corporate actors, including states, may be incapable of consistent and rational decisionmaking. Although this argument may contribute to an explanation of why democracies sometimes get involved in wars, it does not yet explain why they almost never fight each other.

To arrive at the latter explanation, we must look at the interdependence of policies. Peace-loving peoples and democratic governments may try a policy of appeasement of adversaries, thereby projecting an image of weakness and indecision that invites exploitation by more ruthless decisionmakers abroad. Therefore, such a policy may increase the risk of war. Moreover, under such a policy it may be difficult to maintain a costly deterrent posture, and domestic policy disputes within democracies may undermine the credibility of declaratory policies that aim to resist challenges. If the other side is peaceable too, then "appeasement" does no harm and does not deserve a bad name. Deterrence failures matter only when there is a need for deterrence in the first place. A complementary explanation has been suggested by Doyle (1993, p. 33): "Because nonliberal governments are in a state of aggression with their own people, their foreign relations become for liberal governments deeply suspect. In short, fellow liberals benefit from a presumption of amity; nonliberals suffer from a presumption of enmity. Both presumptions may be accurate. Each, however, may also be self-fulfilling."

Putting the separate pieces together, we find rather strong support for the proposition that free trade promotes peace via prosperity and democracy. Admittedly, the evidence is partial, link by link, rather than a test of the entire causal chain. Moreover, the peace promoted by free trade in the long run is confined to stable and prosperous democracies.[15] But even this support suffices to point to the national and cosmopolitan interest of each nation in having prosperous, democratic, and peaceable neighbors and in seeing democracy established among all great powers.[16] By implication, each nation has a *security* interest in free trade with its neighbors and with all great powers. This security interest is *not harmed* even if free trade improves the welfare of one's partners more than one's own. Absolute gains for oneself make free trade economically worthwhile, irrespective of the partner's gains. From a security perspective, large absolute gains for the other side are welcome if they tend to promote democratic stability.[17]

The relationship between free trade and democratic peace is not as simple as I have suggested so far. Some causal influences seem to run the other way. Gowa and Mansfield (1993) did recently demonstrate that trade tends to be freer within alliances than between nonaligned nations. Although the general expectation that allies do not fight each other may be misplaced (Bueno de Mesquita, 1981a; Siverson and Emmons, 1991; Weede, 1975), decisionmakers may still believe in it.[18] Moreover, most of the evidence demonstrating a link between trade and alliances comes from the juxtaposition of the interwar period and the Cold War era; i.e., the U.S.-centered alliance system of the Cold War period or U.S. hegemony have contributed to a liberal trade regime. Although hegemonic stability theory[19] is hotly disputed (Gowa, 1989; Keohane, 1984b; Kindleberger, 1973; Krasner, 1985), much of the controversy concerns the question of whether hegemony is absolutely necessary in order to maintain a liberal trading regime. From the perspective of the logic of collective action (Olson, 1965) on which hegemonic stability theory rests,[20] there can be little doubt that hegemony significantly improves the prospects of international cooperation and free trade.

The core of the free-trade regime in the Cold War era has been the industrialized democracies, or the North America–Western Europe–Japan triangle. Alliances between the United States and Western Europe as well as Japan have underwritten this economic cooperation. Allies are less worried about relative gains (in contrast to absolute gains) than are other states. For this reason alone, the maintenance of the U.S.-led alliance system inherited from the Cold War period is desirable. We still want prosperity, democracy, and peace. There is no contrast between the classical proposition that free trade promotes peace and the proposition that free trade rests on political foundations, conceivably even on occasional order-establishing wars such as the one recently waged against Saddam Hussein. Since World War II, the political foundation of free trade, prosperity, and democracy has been Pax Americana or U.S. hegemony. By underwriting free trade with security guarantees to many countries and thereby promoting prosperity and democracy, Pax Americana has always stabilized Pax Democratica.

The collapse of the Soviet Union and the Warsaw Pact and the democratization of Eastern Europe provide us with a unique opportunity of extending the democratic zone of peace. However, the collapse of the Soviet Union was also the collapse of Pax Sovietica in Eastern Europe. Structural obstacles to war in this area have been removed without any replacement. Pax Sovietica may be replaced by another "zone of turmoil" (Singer and Wildavsky, 1993). Moreover, the economic catastrophes in many ex-communist societies provide some incentives for nuclear proliferation (Clancy and Seitz, 1991). Thus, there is new danger and new opportunity. The danger is an expanded zone of turmoil, including most of the Third World as well as most ex-communist societies, in which some unstable governments control nuclear weapons and others have a chance to acquire them. The opportunity is to provide a helping hand to nascent democracies in Eastern Europe, in Russia, everywhere. Then the democratic zone of peace may expand.[21]

How can the West help Eastern Europe and other new and yet unstable democracies? In my view, the prescription is clear: Democracy needs prosperity, prosperity needs free trade. Thus, the order of the day is to open Western markets to East European and other poor-country products for *security* reasons. Of course, aid may help too: food aid in order to avoid mass starvation where necessary, assistance in agriculture and oil exploration or recovery, advice in building a banking system, expertise and even payment for the destruction of nuclear warheads. The bottom line, however, is that the impact of most of these measures is likely to remain marginal. The record of Western aid to the Third World doesn't justify much optimism about the effectiveness of such aid (Bauer, 1981; Bornschier, Chase-Dunn, and Rubinson, 1978; Krauss, 1983; Mosley, 1987, pp. 33, 135, 165). By contrast, open U.S. markets in the immediate post–World War II period did a lot to promote economic recovery in Western Europe, Japan, and later the "four tigers" of East Asia.[22] By now the economic situation of the world is different: Less depends on the United States alone, more on the West in general (including Japan).[23] But open Western markets, though helping to stabilize democracy in the East only in the long run, provide our best chance of expanding the zone of democratic peace.

A policy for democracy and peace by free trade may either be global or it may be targeted on specific countries whose transition to stable and peaceable democracy appears most urgent. At first it may seem as if a targeted policy of opening Western markets is most desirable from an international-security (rather than purely economic) perspective. After all, targeting market access to specific beneficiaries is likely to help them more than throwing the door wide open to all comers. But one should also consider that such selective grants of market access tend to promote conflicts within and between Western democracies. From a security perspective, each Western democracy should be most interested in the stability and democratization of its own neighbors and therefore may be tempted to give them special market access. If the United States gives privileged access to Latin America, Japan to Asia, and Western Europe to Eastern Europe, then we might build trading blocs and generate tensions between them. This result could exact a security price on top of the certain economic cost of trading blocs compared to globally free trade. Granting market access to specific countries for security reasons also requires that one know where the prospects of democracy are better or worse. Do we really know, for example, that the prospects of democracy in Poland are much better than in Russia, or that the size of this difference justifies better treatment of Poles than Russians in regard to market access? Do we know whether the prospect of democracy is better in Russia than in Ukraine? Thus, the information requirements of a security-driven policy of granting privileged market access to some but denying it to others are high.

Moreover, targeting market access is likely to generate domestic conflicts, most of all in multiethnic immigrant societies such as the United States. Americans of East European descent might favor privileged market access for East Europeans in order to stabilize democracy there. Americans of Jewish and Arab descent might find themselves on the same side arguing in favor of targeting trading privileges to the Middle East in order to stabilize the peace process between Israelis and Arabs. Americans of African descent might focus their sympathies on African countries, which need a stimulus for growth more than most countries, and they might point to the need for racial reconciliation in postapartheid South Africa. All of these demands are sensible and conceivably driven by humane concerns. Still, they may conflict with each other.

Those who do not want to generate or reinforce conflicts within or among Western societies and who distrust the prognostic capabilities of politicians or humans in general should endorse a global policy of free trade. A targeted policy in favor of ex-communist countries would have two additional deficiencies. In the South, from Latin America via Africa to Asia, it would probably be perceived as racist, a manifestation of white solidarity against nonwhites. Moreover, targeting trade privileges to ex-communist nuclear-weapons states may seem to be a Realist prescription but simultaneously would appear to be a reward for the possession of nuclear weapons. Such perceptions could only undermine the nonproliferation regime.

The cosmopolitan or global interest in free trade rests on two solid foundations: First, free trade is in the welfare interest of humankind. Second, because of the trade-prosperity, prosperity-democracy, and double democracy-peace links as well as the less numerous studies establishing direct links between trade or prosperity and war avoidance, free trade is also in the security or survival interest of humankind. If one defines the (economic) national interest by something related to the greatest good for the greatest number, or by high and growing average incomes, there can be little doubt about the compatibility of free trade and national interests. Moreover, benefits from free trade do not depend on reciprocity. The advantages of reciprocity are purely political. According to Bhagwati (1991, p. 51), "the mutuality of concessions on a reciprocal basis offers some definite, practical advantages even though it builds on the notion, not consonant with good economic sense, that trade liberalization is a cost rather than a source of gain." Or, as *The Economist* (1993d, p. 11) recently observed, "true self-interest lies in stimulating and invigorating your own economy, not 'getting away with' maintaining protection for one industry or another."

For about two centuries, most economists have advocated free trade, but a considerable and sometimes overwhelming number of governments have not been persuaded. Why? Free trade reinforces competition. As Schumpeter (1942) pointed out, capitalist competition is a process of "creative destruction," that is, an endless replacement of ailing enterprises, industries, and even regions by upstarts. Thus, structural change and the need to adapt are inevitable under capitalism. Such competition is the secret behind capitalism's success in overcoming mass poverty in OECD nations but is also an inevitable source of anticapitalist, anticompetitive, anti–free trade resentment.

It is impossible to have competition and free trade without having losers too.[24] While the benefits of free trade are either spread thinly over large numbers of consumers or concentrated on those who cannot know the benefits in advance, i.e., those who get well-paid jobs in new export-oriented enterprises, the costs of free trade tend to be narrowly focused on those who can know the cost in advance, i.e., employers and employees in noncompetitive industries who are destined to lose their enterprises and their jobs under free trade. While consumers and other conceivable beneficiaries of free trade are likely to be distracted, disorganized, and rationally ignorant, narrow special-interest groups are likely to be attentive, well informed, and organized for collective action. The purpose of special-interest groups or distributional coalitions, of course, is rent-seeking. Since rents presuppose barriers to competition, government support or acquiescence is crucial in rent-seeking.

Governments could abolish most monopolies, cartels, and restrictive practices; they could serve their societies and the cosmopolitan interest simultaneously if they removed all tariffs as well as nontariff barriers to international trade. Restrictive practices established in protected national or regional markets generally would not survive such a policy. Similarly, governments in industrialized societies could easily smash rent-seeking by unskilled and semiskilled Western workers if they were ready to tap the Third World's labor surplus (Krauss, 1983). Indeed, open borders and reduced government regulation of skilled work and of the professions—as well as free trade in services—would almost certainly reduce rent-seeking by the more privileged strata of Western society as well. Thus, open economies and free trade constitute the most powerful weapons against the transformation of dynamic capitalist societies into sluggish rent-seeking societies.

It is difficult or impossible to predict whether the proponents of the general national and cosmopolitan interest in free trade or the special-interest groups clamoring for protection will prevail. On the one hand, tariffs have been heading downward for some decades (*The Economist,* 1993e). On the other hand, the replacement of tariffs by nontariff barriers or even so-called voluntary export restraint may be a move from bad to worse. The U.S. predilection for unilateralism in opening foreign markets as well as the attempt to distinguish between free trade and fair trade are signs of the difficulty that Western democracies face in pursuing national and cosmopolitan interests (Bhagwati, 1991).

The Western inclination to buy domestic peace by appeasing distributional coalitions is worst if it affects the largest economies, especially that of the United States. Ten years ago Keohane (1984b, p. 179) had already offered the following diagnosis:

> Thus the United States contracted a disease of the strong: refusal to adjust to change. Small states do not have the luxury of deciding whether or how fast to adjust to external change. They do not seek adjustment. The stronger

they are, and the less responsive they have to be to other countries, the longer it can be postponed. For Spain in the sixteenth century, discoveries of bullion in America had disastrous effects; for Britain in the nineteenth century the existence of Empire, into which it could retreat, fatally delayed an effective national reaction to industrial decline.

One might add that at least some West European politicians want a European Union so that they may become capable of refusing to adjust to change too. Those who no longer tolerate "creative destruction," including the creative destruction of jobs, and who refuse to adjust effectively pursue a policy of decline.

Under the Ming and Manchu (or Ching and Qing) dynasties, China could afford not to adjust. A similar statement may be made about Tokugawa Japan. Thus, the West could overtake those economies. Ultimately East Asia had to adjust, and it did. Now China, Japan, and other Asian economies challenge the Western capability to adjust as well as the Western capability to "export" prosperity and peace by providing open access to Western markets.

Democracies don't fight each other because they are normatively and/or institutionally constrained against making war. Although trade promotes prosperity, and although prosperity promotes democracy, democracies are still constrained against pursuing a peace-by-trade policy.[25] Most special-interest groups are concerned not with international security issues but with domestic advantage and redistribution, i.e., with rent-seeking. Nevertheless, they may effectively undermine international security.

In order to pacify the rest of the world, the West and its hegemonic power, the United States, must keep rent-seeking at home under control and must overcome an interest in economic superiority. The consequences of free trade include enrichment of the United States and the West, but they also entail the leveling world-order effects described by Stein (1990, p. 139): "A hegemonic power's decision to enrich itself is also a decision to enrich others more than itself. Over time, such policies will come at the expense of the hegemon's relative standing and will bring forth challengers. Yet choosing to sustain its relative standing . . . is a choice to keep others impoverished at the cost of increasing its own absolute wealth"—and, I want to underline, at the cost of preventing the spread of Pax Democratica.

Although free trade promotes prosperity and, in the long run, the democratic peace, it may in the short run exacerbate rather than mitigate security dilemmas. Not only interest groups in declining sectors of the economy demand protection. Some protectionism is generated by national security considerations (Brezis, 1995). In previous centuries, mercantilists aimed at a surplus of exports over imports in order to hoard bullion that was needed to hire mercenaries in case of war. Currently armaments industries and, more generally, high-technology industries receive protection or subsidies primarily for national security rather than welfare reasons. Despite some negative impact on living standards, such policies are not irrational or self-defeating if the purpose is to achieve security by military deterrence and defense. In the short run, peace by trade via prosperity and democracy may be simply unattainable. So the long-run policy of promoting peace by trade, prosperity, and democracy and the short-run policy of surviving by military strength may point in opposite directions.

Unfortunately, I cannot claim that my preferred policy option, i.e., the attempt to secure peace by trade, is risk free. For example, one may imagine that such a policy helps build a richer and stronger but still autocratic China capable of massively challenging the West. Betts (1993–1994, pp. 53–54) rightly worries: "With only a bit of bad luck in the evolution of political conflict between China and the West, such high economic development would make the old Soviet threat and the more recent trade frictions with Japan seem comparatively modest challenges." Therefore, we might have to buy some insurance against rising and hostile powers that combine capitalist efficiency and authoritarian expansionism. In my view, the West should not buy insurance by protectionism—except perhaps in narrowly defined military industries—but instead by maintaining its unity and upgrading organizations such as NATO. A united West could afford the confidence to promote peace by trade, prosperity, and democracy. While this policy is not risk free, security-inspired protectionism carries its own risks, i.e., missing the chance to overcome the threats to human existence implied by the risk of major-power war in the nuclear age. Free trade, or the principle of nondiscrimination, is a kind of cosmopolitan morality (Giersch, 1995, pp. 23–24). The principle of nondiscrimination between peoples or races, between domestic and foreign producers, is the one type of social capital upon which a prosperous and truly peaceable global order can be built.

Small and poor countries need an open economic order most. Helleiner (1993, p. 404) neatly explains why:

> While it is true that all countries benefit from a stable, transparent and non-discriminatory system of trading rules—and that all should therefore cooperate in its pursuit—it is *not* true that all benefit from it equally. The importance of a strong multilateral system is much greater for smaller, weaker countries than it is for the strong. The strong, after all, will broadly be able to have their own way in a lawless environment.

Although the strong often demonstrate sovereign disregard of the needs of the poor, the spread of Pax Democratica by means of a globally open economy requires that the United States and the West perceive a long-run commonality of interest with still-poor countries in the East and in the South.

If states were unitary actors, even if democratic states such as the

United States were unitary actors, then the United States and the West could choose between a policy of U.S. or Western superiority on the one hand and the promotion of Pax Democratica by free trade on the other hand. Relative rather than absolute gains matter in both policies. If you want to base security on superiority, then maintaining superiority over others is even more important than absolute benefits.[26] If you want to export Pax Democratica via the free-trade route, then relatively greater gains for poorer and yet unstable and nondemocratic countries should be welcomed. However, since states are *not* unitary actors, and democracies are even less so than some others, choosing either policy is beyond Western capabilities. Some influential groups in the West will advocate the need to maintain U.S. or Western economic superiority over Japan, or China, or Russia because of the ultimately military implications of economic advantage. Others will advocate free trade and Pax Democratica. Because they are not states-as-unitary-actors, neither the United States nor the West will attempt to maximize superiority or to maximize the chances of Pax Democratica. Nor will any balance of these mutually incompatible policies with which we may end up reflect strategic reasoning instead of interest-group politics and political infighting.

Notes

1. While the United States carried a disproportionate burden in safeguarding the free world, it has found ways to shift some of the burden to its allies, particularly West Germany and Japan. By accepting overvalued (and soon to be devalued) dollars in the late 1960s and early 1970s, U.S. allies paid the functional equivalent of a hegemonic tax and contributed to financing the defense of the free world (Mayer 1991, pp. 89–100). Even after the end of the Cold War, the United States succeeded in shifting part of the burden to its allies. While the United States (and Britain and France) risked the lives of its soldiers in the war to liberate Kuwait, Germany and Japan had to pay.

2. European and Japanese freeriding at the expense of the United States goes beyond defense. The United States has not only provided a nuclear umbrella to its allies but has also largely shaped the contemporary economic order. Therefore, Keohane (1984a, p. 22) claims: "The European welfare state was built on foundations provided by American hegemony." Unfortunately, the international repercussions of recent U.S. economic policies—I think of the deficit—seem less benign. Moreover, the openness of the international trading system might overburden the adaptive capabilities of governments and societies (see Krasner, 1976; Keohane, 1984a; Strange, 1985; 1986; and later in this chapter).

3. An obvious example of a cosmopolitan interest is sustainable development or protection of the environment. This issue is not dealt with in this book because natural scientists do not agree with each other about the severity of ecological threats and what will happen if present trends continue and because I do not feel competent to take sides in these debates. Conceivably, some environmental issues such as global warming affect the interests of nations in different ways. For an overview of these issues, some warnings about premature global planning, and further literature, see Lal (1989).

4. As well as quoting an Asian politician I might also have quoted a contemporary U.S. scholar (Rosecrance, 1986, p. 31): "The greater the restraints on trade and the fewer its likely benefits, the more willing nations have to seek to improve their positions through military force. The higher the cost of war and the more uncertain its benefits, the more nations have sought trade as a livelihood."

5. The papers by Gasiorowski and Polachek primarily concern verbal and diplomatic conflict behavior rather than war.

6. Some dependency theorists disagree. For my criticism of this approach, see Chapter 5, Section 1. Some economic historians and economists point out that some countries grew fast for long periods under protectionist trade regimes (Bairoch, 1993, on the United States before 1945; Samuels, 1994, on Japan; Wade, 1990, on Taiwan). The East Asian cases have been dealt with in Chapter 6, Section 2. So far as the United States is concerned, it has been pointed out that the United States itself "has been a very large area of free trade" (Corden, 1993, p. 57), which greatly mitigates the negative impact of protectionism. Others, such as Tonelson (1994, p. 133), generalize the infant-industry argument and make it a catch-all justification for protection because "fundamentally new technologies and manufacturing processes now emerge so rapidly and product cycles are so short (even in long-established sectors such as steel and textiles) that the functional equivalents of infant industries may be springing up in developed and developing countries alike." This argument would convince me if a persuasive case could be made for (democratic) governments being immune to special-interest groups and rent-seeking or if I knew of quantitative studies simultaneously recording the successes and failures of protection and demonstrating that successes significantly outweigh failures.

7. Here, I refer to the World Bank's (1983, pp. 57–63) work on the negative effects of price distortion on economic growth rates. One of the components of the price distortion index refers to exchange rates, which of course directly affect international trade. On the negative effect of price distortions, see also Barro (1991).

8. It may be argued, however, that international trade theory needs to answer new questions if the clamor for fair trade is to be confronted. As a starting point Bhagwati (1993b, p. 41) suggested this insight: "There is simply no way that we can pretend that there is a (wholly) market determined comparative advantage. Comparative advantage is inevitably 'distorted,' 'created,' in fact 'shaped' by myriad governmental policies, wittingly or unwittingly." This observation does not necessarily imply a need for harmonization in order to generate a level playing field. Imagine, for example, that some nation has a uniquely efficient educational system. This possession would affect comparative advantage. Should it justify trade barriers against the nation with an efficient educational system? More generally, the call for harmonization may be a cover for ulterior motives. Bhagwati (1993c, p. 47) suggested that "by asking for harmonization that is impossible to get, one can then get the protection that is otherwise beyond reach."

9. Actually, Lipset referred not only to prosperity but to a broad set of development indicators. Some later research (for example, Feierabend and Feierabend, 1966; Huntington, 1968) attempted to distinguish between stability-promoting and destabilizing components of economic development. By and large, these efforts did not lead to replicable and robust results. One reason for this lack of success is multicolinearity. The other one is substantial: Some candidates for measuring the destabilizing impact of development, such as school enrollment ratios or literacy, actually contribute to economic growth (World Bank, 1993b, pp. 51, 61) and equality (Ahluwalia, 1976). Be that as it may, there is no strong theory or evidence to call the proposed link between prosperity (or wealth or per capita incomes) and democratic performance into question. The relationship does not seem to be strictly monotonic.

In the 1970s and 1980s some richer LDCs were less democratic than a poorer group of LDCs. Beyond a threshold close to 5,000 U.S. dollars per capita income, however, democracy became secure in the 1980s (Lipset, Seong, and Torres, 1993).

10. In some respects, Muller (1985) is a dissenting voice. He points to the fact that many Latin American societies exceeded the per capita income of European democracies at the turn of the century in the 1960s but were nevertheless lagging in democratic performance. While this objection is true, its meaning is not obvious. Conceivably, democracy depends not on absolute but on relative prosperity. In order to stabilize democracy, nations may need to belong to the richest societies. If this were true, then democratic peace would always remain limited to a privileged set of nations.

11. Moreover, capitalism probably has some direct effect on democracy as well as some indirect effect that is mediated by prosperity. Excellent treatments of how and why capitalism promotes democracy are Berger (1993), Kim (1993), and Lipset (1994, especially pp. 2, 4). The dangers of promoting democracy before sufficient economic development has been achieved are analyzed by Mahbubani (1992) with special reference to Asia. Jones (1994, p. 28) offers a critical response but still rejects "authoritarianism unmodified by successful growth" as "the least probable prospect" for China. Despite their other disagreements, Mahbubani and Jones seem to agree that prosperity promotes democracy.

12. It is also true that schooling promotes economic growth.

13. There are some dissenters (Farber and Gowa, 1994; Layne, 1994; Spiro, 1994) whose work has been discussed in note 21 of Chapter 7.

14. The case for a normative rather than an institutional explanation of war avoidance among democracies is not fully persuasive for two reasons. First, even Russett (1993, p. 92) admits that institutional constraints matter in preventing war rather than low-level conflict involvement. Second, lack of domestic violence is used as one measure of the strength of democratic norms or a democratic political culture. Maybe it is an acceptable measure. But we also know from previous research (Gurr and Duvall, 1973; Pearson, 1974; Weede, 1975; 1978) that domestic conflict attracts military intervention from the outside, whereas domestic tranquillity provides little opportunity for external intervention. A persuasive test of the normative explanation of why democracies do not fight each other should either avoid using the lack of domestic violence as a measure of normative strength or should somehow take the link between domestic conflict and becoming the target of external intervention into account. Moreover, Owen (1994) has recently argued that democratic peace requires normative and institutional support.

15. Although there has been less research on the direct effects of wealth or economic growth on war avoidance, there is some evidence (Bremer, 1992; Maoz and Russett, 1993; Russett, 1993) that wealthy and growing countries are less likely to fight each other than other nations.

16. These restrictions of national interest apply because most wars are fought either among contiguous countries or with great-power participation (Bremer, 1992; Maoz and Russett, 1993; Russett, 1993; Weede, 1975). Mongolia and Bolivia need not be democracies in order to avoid war between them.

17. From the perspective of structural Realism, there has been some debate whether a focus on relative instead of absolute gains impedes international cooperation (see the controversy between Grieco, Powell, and Snidal [1993] and the literature quoted there). If one accepts the view that democracies do not fight each other—and this view is not a Realist one—then nations may even have an interest in other nations scoring greater relative gains than themselves. For example, the rich Western

societies should have a security interest in ex-communist countries scoring greater absolute and relative gains from international trade than themselves in order to underwrite those countries' nascent democracies.

18. For the post-1945 period, Maoz and Russett (1993) and Russett (1993, p. 85) find some pacifying impact of alliance bonds. In my view, this finding depends on the hegemonic leadership of alliances in the Cold War era. For alliances among equals I would not expect a similar relationship.

19. In my view, Keohane's (1984b, p. 35) criticism is most devastating. If the theory is refined in order to distinguish between economic capabilities and the actual exercise of global leadership, it is no longer falsifiable. Then hegemons by definition stabilize the global economy. The cruder version of the theory is falsifiable but runs into empirical problems.

20. Since free trade is not a genuinely collective good, however, the foundation of hegemonic stability theory in the logic of collective action may be disputed. See Gowa (1989) and Keohane (1984b, p. 38).

21. However, one should not exaggerate the usefulness of a helping hand. According to the World Bank (1991, p. 157), domestic policies are about twice as important as the international environment for the growth prospects of nations. Although this statement refers to LDCs rather than ex-communist economies, it might give us a feel for the order of magnitude of domestic and external factors in promoting growth.

22. Of course, Western Europe also benefited from the Marshall Plan. Although the Marshall Plan did help, I contend that U.S. troops and security guarantees as well as comparatively open markets for European products were even more important. In the Japanese case, the Korean War and U.S. military demand provided an important stimulus for reconstruction (Tsuru, 1993, p. 58). Similarly, the Vietnam War benefited South Korea and other "tiger" economies.

23. Recently a prominent Japanese economist (Tsuru, 1993, pp. 233–234) has argued in favor of Japan opening its markets to Third World exports in order to assist these countries in their efforts to overcome poverty.

24. According to Rogowski (1987) or Wood (1994, pp. 28–30, 41), protection benefits and free trade harm the owners of factors in which the society under consideration is poorly endowed compared to the rest of the world. This idea applies, for example, to unskilled labor in OECD countries because so much unskilled labor is available in the Third World. Recently the French Nobel laureate Allais (1994) has argued that Western democracies must either practice protectionism or accept increasing income inequality and growing levels of unemployment. So there might be a trade-off between the "international peace by trade" strategy advocated here and the promotion of domestic stability by protectionism advocated by Allais. While Allais analyzes the negative impact of free trade on some workers and their conditions of employment and pay, he neglects the positive and job-creating impact of free trade on others in industrialized as well as developing countries.

25. Western Europe's lack of readiness to open its agricultural, coal, steel, and textile markets to Czech, Hungarian, and Polish producers (see *The Economist,* 1993a) in order to stabilize these nascent democracies provides a good example. By contrast, the United States has accepted the North American Free Trade Association (NAFTA), which only marginally affects the U.S. economy but does effectively assist Mexico (Krugman, 1993a).

26. This is Grieco's (1990) argument. In his view, negotiations about nontariff barriers to trade actually have been significantly affected by concerns about relative gains. This view is probably true. But, in contrast to Grieco, I am convinced that gov-

ernments typically respond not to a serious evaluation of "national interests" in trade negotiations but to narrow special interests. I have never been persuaded that either the German government or the EC ever defended German or European interests in negotiations about agriculture. Instead, they took exceptional care of the interests of a tiny and dwindling minority. Moreover, governments respond to different interest groups with sometimes incompatible goals on different occasions. They are not unitary rational actors.

BIBLIOGRAPHY

Abramovitz, Moses. 1986. "Catching Up, Forging Ahead, and Falling Behind." *Journal of Economic History* 46(2): 386–405.

Ahluwalia, Montek S. 1976. "Income Distribution and Development: Some Stylized Facts." *American Economic Review* 66: 128–135.

Ahluwalia, Montek S., Nicholas G. Carter, and Hollis B. Chenery. 1979. "Growth and Poverty in Developing Countries." *Journal of Development Economics* 6: 299–341.

Ahmed, Akbar S. 1988. *Discovering Islam.* London: Routledge & Kegan Paul.

Albert, Hans. 1986. *Freiheit und Ordnung.* Tübingen: Mohr.

Alchian, Armen A. 1950. "Uncertainty, Evolution, and Economic Theory." *Journal of Political Economy* 58: 211–221.

Alchian, Armen A., and Harold Demsetz. 1972. "Production, Information Costs, and Economic Organization." *American Economic Review* 62: 777–795.

Allais, Maurice. 1994. *Combats pour L'Europe 1992–1994.* Paris: Clément Juglar.

Alschuler, Lawrence R. 1976. "Satellization and Stagnation in Latin America." *International Studies Quarterly* 20(1): 39–82.

Altfeld, Michael F. 1983. "Arms Races?—and Escalation? A Comment on Wallace." *International Studies Quarterly* 27(2): 225–231.

Amsden, Alice H. 1985. "The State and Taiwan's Economic Development." In Peter B. Evans, Dietrich Rueschemeyer, and Theda Skocpol (eds.), *Bringing the State Back In,* pp. 78–106. Cambridge: Cambridge University Press.

Andreski, Stanislav. 1964. *The Uses of Comparative Sociology.* Berkeley: University of California Press.

———. 1968a. *Military Organization and Society.* 2d ed. Stanford: Stanford University Press.

———. 1968b. *The African Predicament.* New York: Atherton.

———. 1969. *Parasitism and Subversion: The Case of Latin America.* New York: Schocken.

———. 1984. *Max Weber's Insights and Errors.* London: Routledge & Kegan Paul.

Arjomand, Said Amir. 1992. "Constitutions and the Struggle for Political Order." *Archives Européenes de Sociologie* 33(1): 39–82.

Aron, Raymond. 1966. "The Anarchical Order of Power." *Daedalus* 95: 479–502.

Arrow, Kenneth J. 1951. *Social Choice and Individual Values.* New York: Wiley.

Axelrod, Robert. 1984. *The Evolution of Cooperation.* New York: Basic Books.

Bairoch, Paul. 1993. *Economics and World History.* Chicago: The University of Chicago Press.

Balassa, Bela. 1981. *The Newly Industrialized Countries in the World Economy.* New York: Pergamon.

Baldwin, Robert E. 1993. "Changes in the Global Trading System: A Response to Shifts in National Economic Power." In Dominick Salvatore (ed.), *Protectionism and World Welfare,* pp. 80–98. Cambridge: Cambridge University Press.

Barbieri, Katherine. 1996 (forthcoming). "Economic Interdependence and Militarized Interstate Conflict, 1870–1985." *Journal of Peace Research* 33.

Barro, Robert J. 1991. "Economic Growth in a Cross-Section of Countries." *Quarterly Journal of Economics* 106: 407–443.

Barry, Norman. 1994. "Making Sense of Hayek: The Theory of Spontaneous Order." Paper delivered at the Mont Pèlerin Society General Meeting, Cannes, September 25–30.

Bates, Robert H. 1983. *Essays on the Political Economy of Rural Africa.* Berkeley: University of California Press.

———. 1988a. "Lessons from History, or the Perfidy of English Exceptionalism and the Significance of Historical France." *World Politics* 40(4): 498–516.

———. 1988b. *Toward a Political Economy of Development.* Berkeley: University of California Press.

Bauer, Peter T. 1981. *Equality, the Third World and Economic Delusion.* London: Weidenfeld and Nicholson.

Baumol, William J. 1986. "Productivity Growth, Convergence, and Welfare: What the Long-Run Data Show." *American Economic Review* 76: 1072–1084.

Becker, Gary S. 1971. *The Economics of Discrimination.* 2d ed. Chicago: The University of Chicago Press.

Bell, Daniel, and Irving Kristol (eds.). 1981. *The Crisis in Economic Theory.* New York: Basic Books.

Berger, Peter L. 1986. *The Capitalist Revolution.* New York: Basic Books.

———. 1993. "The Uncertain Triumph of Democratic Capitalism." In Larry Diamond and Marc F. Plattner (eds.), *Capitalism, Socialism, and Democracy Revisited,* pp. 1–10. Baltimore: The Johns Hopkins University Press.

Berman, Harold J. 1983. *Law and Revolution: The Formation of the Western Legal Tradition.* Cambridge, MA: Harvard University Press.

Bernholz, Peter. 1977. "Dominant Interest Groups and Powerless Parties." *Kyklos* 30: 411–420.

———. 1982. "Expanding Welfare State, Democracy and Free Market Economy: Are They Compatible?" *Zeitschrift für die gesamte Staatswissenschaft* 138: 583–598.

———. 1985. *The International Game of Power.* Amsterdam, Berlin, and New York: Mouton.

———. 1986. "Growth of Government, Economic Growth and Individual Freedom." *Journal of Institutional and Theoretical Economics* 142: 661–683.

Bernholz, Peter, and Friedrich Breyer. 1994. *Grundlagen der Politischen Ökonomie. Bd. 2. Ökonomische Theorie der Politik.* Tübingen: Mohr.

Betts, Richard K. 1985. "Conventional Deterrence: Predictive Uncertainty and Policy Confidence." *World Politics* 37: 153–179.

———. 1987. *Nuclear Blackmail and Nuclear Balance.* Washington, DC: Brookings.

———. 1993–1994. "Wealth, Power, and Instability: East Asia and the United States After the Cold War." *International Security* 18(3): 34–77.

Bhagwati, Jagdish N. 1991. *The World Trading System at Risk.* London: Harvester and Wheatsheaf.

———. 1993a. "Democracy and Development." In Larry Diamond and Marc F.

Plattner (eds.), *Capitalism, Socialism and Democracy Revisited*, pp. 31–38. Baltimore: The Johns Hopkins University Press.

———. 1993b. *India in Transition: Freeing the Economy*. Oxford: Clarendon.

———. 1993c. "Fair Trade, Reciprocity, and Harmonization: The Novel Challenge to the Theory and Policy of Free Trade." In Dominick Salvatore (ed.), *Protectionism and World Welfare*, pp. 17–53. Cambridge: Cambridge University Press.

Blainey, Geoffrey. 1973. *The Causes of War.* London: Macmillan.

Blau, Peter M. 1964. *Exchange and Power in Social Life.* New York: Wiley.

Blecher, Marc. 1991. "Sounds of Silence and Distant Thunder: The Crisis of Economic and Political Administration." In David S. G. Goodman and Gerald Segal (eds.), *China in the Nineties*, pp. 35–63. Oxford: Clarendon.

Bollen, Kenneth A., and Robert Jackman. 1985. "Economic and Non-Economic Determinants of Political Democracy in the 1960s." *Research in Political Sociology* 1: 27–48.

Borcherding, Thomas E. 1985. "The Causes of Government Expenditure Growth: A Survey of the U.S. Evidence." *Journal of Public Economics* 28: 359–382.

Bornschier, Volker. 1980a. *Multinationale Konzerne, Wirtschaftspolitik und nationale Entwicklung im Weltsystem.* Frankfurt/Main: Campus.

———. 1980b. "Multinational Corporations and Economic Growth." *Journal of Development Economics* 7: 191–210.

———. 1981a. "Dependent Industrialization in the World Economy." *Journal of Conflict Resolution* 25(3): 371–400.

———. 1981b. "Comment" (on Weede and Tiefenbach, 1981a). *International Studies Quarterly* 25: 283–288.

———. 1982. "Dependence on Foreign Capital and Economic Growth." *European Journal of Political Research* 10(4): 445–450.

———. 1985. "World Social Structure in the Long Economic Wave." Paper delivered at the 26th Annual Meeting of the International Studies Association, Washington, DC, March 5–9.

———. 1989. "Legitimacy and Comparative Economic Success in the Core of the World System." *European Sociological Review* 5(3): 215–229.

Bornschier, Volker, and Thanh-Huyen Ballmer-Cao. 1979. "Income Inequality: A Cross National Study of the Relationships Between MNC-Penetration, Dimensions of the Power Structure and Income Distribution." *American Sociological Review* 44: 487–506.

Bornschier, Volker, and Christopher Chase-Dunn. 1985. *Transnational Corporations and Underdevelopment.* New York: Praeger.

Bornschier, Volker, Christopher Chase-Dunn, and Richard Rubinson. 1978. "Cross-National Evidence of the Effects of Foreign Investment and Aid on Economic Growth and Inequality: A Survey of Findings and a Reanalysis." *American Journal of Sociology* 84: 651–683.

Borrus, Michael, Steve Weber, and John Zysman with Joseph Willihnganz. 1992. "Mercantilism and Global Security." *The National Interest* 29: 21–29.

Boulding, Kenneth E. 1962. *Conflict and Defense.* New York: Harper and Row.

Bradshaw, York W. 1985a. "Dependent Development in Black Africa." *American Sociological Review* 50: 195–207.

———. 1985b. "Overurbanization and Underdevelopment in Sub-Saharan Africa." *Studies in Comparative International Development* 20(3): 74–101.

———. 1987. "Urbanization and Underdevelopment." *American Sociological Review* 52(2): 224–239.

Bremer, Stuart A. 1992. "Dangerous Dyads: Interstate War, 1816–1965." *Journal of Conflict Resolution* 36: 309–341.

Brennan, Geoffrey. 1990. "What Might Rationality Fail to Do?" In Karen Schweers Cook and Margaret Levi (eds.), *The Limits of Rationality,* pp. 51–59. Chicago: The University of Chicago Press.

Brezis, Elise S. 1995. "Competitiveness, Mercantilism and the Power of Nations." Paper delivered at the European Public Choice Annual Meeting, Saarbrücken, April 19.

Brunner, Karl. 1978. "Reflections on the Political Economy of Government: The Persistent Growth of Government." *Schweizerische Zeitschrift für Volkswirtschaft und Statistik* 114: 649–680.

———. 1985. "The Poverty of Nations." *Cato Journal* 5(1): 37–49.

Buchanan, James M. 1980. "Rent-Seeking and Profit Seeking." In James M. Buchanan, Robert D. Tollison, and Gordon Tullock (eds.), *Toward a Theory of the Rent-Seeking Society,* pp. 3–15. College Station: Texas A&M University Press.

———. 1988. "Economists and Gains from Trade." *Managerial and Decision Economics,* special issue (Essays in Honour of W. H. Hutt): 5–12.

Buchanan, James M., Robert D. Tollison, and Gordon Tullock. 1980. *Toward a Theory of the Rent-Seeking Society.* College Station: Texas A&M University Press.

Buchanan, James M., and Gordon Tullock. 1962. *The Calculus of Consent.* Ann Arbor: University of Michigan Press.

Bueno de Mesquita, Bruce. 1981a. *The War Trap.* New Haven: Yale University Press.

———. 1981b. "Risk, Power Distributions, and the Likelihood of War." *International Studies Quarterly* 25(4): 541–568.

Bueno de Mesquita, Bruce, and David Lalman. 1992. *War and Reason.* New Haven: Yale University Press.

Bueno de Mesquita, Bruce, Randolph M. Siverson, and Gary Woller. 1992. "War and the Fate of Regimes: A Comparative Analysis." *American Political Science Review* 86: 638–646.

Bundy, McGeorge. 1979. "The Future of Strategic Deterrence." *Survival* 21: 268–272.

Burkhart, Ross E., and Michael S. Lewis-Beck. 1994. "Comparative Democracy: The Economic Development Thesis." *American Political Science Review* 88(4): 903–910.

Cameron, David. 1985. "Public Expenditure and Economic Performance in International Perspective." In R. Klein and M. O'Higgins (eds.), *The Future of Welfare,* pp. 8–21. Oxford: Basil Blackwell.

Castles, Francis G., and Steve Dowrick. 1990. "The Impact of Government Spending Levels in Medium-Term Economic Growth in the OECD, 1960–85." *Journal of Theoretical Politics* 2: 173–204.

Chan, Anita. 1991. "The Social Origins and Consequences of the Tiananmen Crisis." In David S. G. Goodman and Gerald Segal (eds.), *China in the Nineties,* pp. 105–130. Oxford: Clarendon.

Chan, Steve. 1984. "Are Freer Countries More Pacific?" *Journal of Conflict Resolution* 28(4): 617–648.

———. 1987a. "Comparative Performance of East Asian and Latin American NICs." *Pacific Focus* 2: 35–56.

———. 1987b. "Growth with Equity: A Test of Olson's Theory for the Asian-Pacific-Rim Countries." *Journal of Peace Research* 24: 135–149.

————. 1989. "Income Inequality Among LCDs: A Comparative Analysis of Alternative Perspectives." *International Studies Quarterly* 33: 45–65.

————. 1993. *East Asian Dynamism: Growth, Order, and Security in the Pacific Region.* 2d ed. Boulder, CO: Westview Press.

Chan, Steve, and Alex Mintz (eds.). 1992. *Defense, Welfare, and Growth.* London: Routledge.

Chase-Dunn, Christopher. 1975. "The Effects of International Economic Dependence on Development and Inequality." *American Sociological Review* 40: 720–738.

Chirot, Daniel. 1986. *Social Change in the Modern Era.* San Diego: Harcourt Brace Jovanovich.

Choi, Kwang. 1983a. "A Statistical Test of Olson's Model." In Dennis C. Mueller (ed.), *The Political Economy of Growth,* pp. 57–78. New Haven: Yale University Press.

————. 1983b. *Theories of Comparative Economic Growth.* Ames: Iowa State University Press.

Clancy, Tom, and Russell Seitz. 1991. "Five Minutes Past Midnight and Welcome to the Age of Proliferation." *The National Interest* 26: 3–12.

Claude, Inis L. 1962. *Power and International Relations.* New York: Random House.

Coase, Ronald H. 1937. "The Nature of the Firm." *Economica* 4: 386–405.

Coleman, James S. 1978. "A Theory of Revolt Within an Authority Structure." *Peace Science Society (International) Papers* 28: 15–25.

————. 1987. "Norms as Social Capital." In Gerard Radnitzky and Peter Bernholz (eds.), *Economic Imperialism,* pp. 133–155. New York: Paragon.

————. 1988. "Social Capital in the Creation of Human Capital." *American Journal of Sociology* 94 (supplement): 95–120.

————. 1990. *Foundations of Social Theory.* Cambridge, MA: Harvard University Press (Belknap).

Collins, Randall. 1980. "Weber's Last Theory of Capitalism: A Systematization." *American Sociological Review* 45: 925–942.

————. 1986. *Weberian Sociological Theory.* Cambridge: Cambridge University Press.

Cooper, Richard N. 1993. "US Response to Foreign Industrial Policies." In Dominick Salvatore (ed.), *Protectionism and World Welfare,* pp. 131–159. Cambridge: Cambridge University Press.

Corden, W. Max. 1993. "The Revival of Protectionism in Developed Countries." In Dominick Salvatore (ed.), *Protectionism and World Welfare,* pp. 54–79. Cambridge: Cambridge University Press.

Crozier, Michel. 1975. "Western Europe." In Michel Crozier, Samuel P. Huntington, and Joji Watanuki (eds.), *The Crisis of Democracy,* pp. 11–57. New York: New York University Press.

Cutright, Philips. 1963. "National Political Development." *American Sociological Review* 28: 253–264.

Dahl, Robert A. 1993. "Why Free Markets Are Not Enough." In Larry Diamond and Marc F. Plattner (eds.), *Capitalism, Socialism and Democracy Revisited,* pp. 76–83. Baltimore: The Johns Hopkins University Press.

Dahrendorf, Ralf. 1965. *Gesellschaft und Demokratie in Deutschland.* München: Piper.

Deger, Saadet. 1986. *Military Expenditure in Third World Countries.* London: Routledge & Kegan Paul.

Delacroix, Jacques. 1977. "Export of Raw Materials and Economic Growth." *American Sociological Review* 42: 795–808.

Delacroix, Jacques, and Charles C. Ragin. 1978. "Modernizing Institutions, Mobilization, and Third World Development: A Cross-National Study." *American Journal of Sociology* 84: 123–150.

———. 1981. "Structural Blockage: A Cross-National Study of Economic Dependency, State Efficiency, and Underdevelopment." *American Journal of Sociology* 86: 1311–1347.

De Long, J. Bradford. 1986. "Productivity Growth, Convergence, and Welfare: Comment (on Baumol)." *American Economic Review* 78(5): 1038–1048.

De Long, J. Bradford, and Lawrence H. Summers. 1991. "Equipment Investment and Economic Growth." *Quarterly Journal of Economics* 106: 445–502.

Demsetz, Harold. 1982. *Economic, Legal and Political Dimensions of Competition.* Amsterdam: North-Holland.

Deutsch, Karl W. 1968. *The Analysis of International Relations.* Englewood Cliffs, NJ: Prentice-Hall.

Deutsch, Karl W., and J. David Singer. 1964. "Multipolar Power Systems and International Security." *World Politics* 16: 390–406.

Diehl, Paul F. 1983. "Arms Races and Escalation: A Closer Look." *Journal of Peace Research* 20(2): 205–212.

Dixon, William J. 1993. "Democracy and the Management of International Conflict." *Journal of Conflict Resolution* 37(1): 42–68.

Dixon, William J., and Bruce E. Moon. 1986. "The Military Burden and Basic Human Needs." *Journal of Conflict Resolution* 30: 660–684.

d'Lugo, David, and Ronald Rogowski. 1993. "The Anglo-German Naval Race and Comparative Constitutional Fitness." In Richard Rosecrance and Arthur A. Stein (eds.), *The Domestic Bases of Grand Strategy,* pp. 65–95. Ithaca, NY: Cornell University Press.

Dollar, David. 1992. "Outward-Oriented Developing Economies Really Do Grow More Rapidly: Evidence from 95 LDCs." *Economic Development and Cultural Change* 40(3): 523–544.

Domes, Jürgen. 1985. *The Government and Politics of the PRC.* Boulder, CO: Westview Press.

Domes, Jürgen, and Marie-Luise Näth. 1992. *Geschichte der Volksrepublik China.* Mannheim: B.I.-Taschenbuch.

Domke, William K. 1988. *War and the Changing Global System.* New Haven: Yale University Press.

Dornbusch, Rudiger W. 1993. "The Case for Bilateralism." In Dominick Salvatore (ed.), *Protectionism and World Welfare,* pp. 180–199. Cambridge: Cambridge University Press.

Downing, Brian M. 1992. *The Military Revolution and Political Change.* Princeton: Princeton University Press.

Downs, Anthony. 1957. *An Economic Theory of Democracy.* New York: Harper and Row.

Dowrick, Steve, and Duc-Tho Nguyen. 1989. "OECD Comparative Economic Growth 1950–85: Catch-Up and Convergence." *American Economic Review* 79(5): 1010–1030.

Doyle, Michael W. 1986. "Liberalism and World Politics." *American Political Science Review* 80: 1151–1169.

———. 1993. "Politics and Grand Strategy." In Richard Rosecrance and Arthur A. Stein (eds.), *The Domestic Bases of Grand Strategy,* pp. 22–47. Ithaca, NY: Cornell University Press.

Dudley, Leonard, and Claude Montmarquette. 1992. "Government Size and Economic Convergence." Paper presented at the Meeting of the European Public Choice Society, Torino, April 22–25.

Dupuy, Trevor N. 1987. *Understanding War: History and Theory of Combat.* New York: Paragon.

Durkheim, Emile. 1895/1930. *De la division du travail social.* Paris: Presses Universitaires de France.

Economist, The. 1992. "Survey: When China Wakes." *The Economist,* vol. 325, no. 7787, November 28.

————. 1993a. "Asia's Arms Race: Gearing Up." *The Economist,* vol. 326, no. 7799, February 20: 21–24.

————. 1993b. "Survey: The European Community." *The Economist,* vol. 328, no. 7818, July 3.

————. 1993c. "Economic Giants." *The Economist,* vol. 328, no. 7819, July 10: 63.

————. 1993d. "China's Perpetual Revolution." *The Economist,* vol. 328, no. 7824, August 14: 53–54.

————. 1993e. "Survey: Asia. A Billion Consumers." *The Economist,* vol. 329, no. 7835, October 30.

————. 1993f. "Nirvana by Numbers." *The Economist,* vol. 329, no. 7843, December 25: 75.

————. 1994a. "Economic Focus: China." *The Economist,* vol. 331, no. 7861, April 30: 77.

————. 1994b. "The Left's New Start." *The Economist,* vol. 331, no. 7867, June 11: 11–12.

————. 1994c. "Survey: The Global Economy." *The Economist,* vol. 333, no. 7883, October 1.

Ekelund, Robert B., and Robert D. Tollison. 1981. *Mercantilism as a Rent-Seeking Society.* College Station: Texas A&M University Press.

Elster, Jon. 1989. *The Cement of Society.* Cambridge: Cambridge University Press.

————. 1990. "When Rationality Fails." In Karen Schweers Cook and Margaret Levi (eds.), *The Limits of Rationality,* pp. 19–51. Chicago: The University of Chicago Press.

————. 1994. "The Impact of Constitutions on Economic Performance." Paper prepared for the World Bank's Annual Conference on Development Economics, Washington, DC, April 28–29.

Emmanuel, Arghiri. 1972. *Unequal Exchange: A Study of the Imperialism of Trade.* New York: Monthly Review Press.

Epstein, Joshua M. 1988. "Dynamic Analysis of the Conventional Balance in Europe." *International Security* 12(4): 154–165.

Faith, Roger L., and Nancy C. Short. 1995. "Bureaucratic Tenure and Economic Performance in Centrally Planned Economies." *Public Choice* 83(1–2): 139–157.

Farber, Henry S., and Joanne Gowa. 1994. "Polities and Peace." Paper delivered at the 90th Annual Meeting of the American Political Science Association, New York, September 4.

Feierabend, Ivo K., and Rosalind L. Feierabend. 1966. "Aggressive Behavior Within Polities, 1948–1962." *Journal of Conflict Resolution* 10: 249–271.

Fingleton, Eamonn. 1995. "Japan's Invisible Leviathan." *Foreign Affairs* 74(2): 69–85.

Firebaugh, Glenn. 1992. "Growth Effects of Foreign and Domestic Investment." *American Journal of Sociology* 98: 105–130.

Firebaugh, Glenn, and Frank D. Beck. 1994. "Does Economic Growth Benefit the

Masses? Growth, Dependence, and Welfare in the Third World." *American Sociological Review* 59(5): 631–653.

Frank, Robert H. 1985. *Choosing the Right Pond: Human Behavior and the Quest for Status.* Oxford and New York: Oxford University Press.

Frey, Bruno S. 1986. "Economists Favor the Price System—Who Else Does?" *Kyklos* 39(4): 537–563.

Frey, Bruno S., and Richard Eichenberger. 1991. "Anomalies in Political Economy." *Public Choice* 68: 71–89.

Frey, Bruno S., Werner W. Pommerehne, and Beat Gygi. 1993. "Economics Indoctrination or Selection?" *Journal of Economic Education* 24(3): 271–281.

Friedman, Milton. 1962. *Capitalism and Freedom.* Chicago: The University of Chicago Press.

Friedman, Milton, and Rose Friedman. 1981. *Free to Choose.* New York: Avon.

Frohlich, Norman, and Joe A. Oppenheimer. 1978. *Modern Political Economy.* Englewood Cliffs, NJ: Prentice-Hall.

Frohlich, Norman, Joe A. Oppenheimer, and Oran R. Young. 1971. *Political Leadership and Collective Goods.* Princeton: Princeton University Press.

Frum, David. 1994. "It's Big Government, Stupid." *Commentary* 97(6): 27–31.

Fu, Zhengyuan. 1993. *Autocratic Tradition and Chinese Politics.* Cambridge: Cambridge University Press.

Fukuyama, Francis. 1993. "Capitalism and Democracy: The Missing Link." In Larry Diamond and Marc F. Plattner (eds.), *Capitalism, Socialism, and Democracy Revisited,* pp. 94–104. Baltimore: The Johns Hopkins University Press.

Galtung, Johan. 1971. "A Structural Theory of Imperialism." *Journal of Peace Research* 8: 81–117.

Garnier, Maurice A., and Lawrence E. Hazelrigg. 1977. "Military Organization and Distributional Inequality." *Journal of Political and Military Sociology* 5: 17–33.

Gasiorowski, Mark, and Solomon Polachek. 1982. "Conflict and Interdependence: East-West Trade and Linkages in the Era of Détente." *Journal of Conflict Resolution* 26(4): 709–729.

Geller, Dan S. 1992. "Capability Concentration, Power Transition, and War." *International Interactions* 17: 269–284.

Gellner, Ernest. 1981. *Muslim Society.* Cambridge: Cambridge University Press.

George, Alexander, and Richard Smoke. 1974. *Deterrence in American Foreign Policy: Theory and Practice.* New York: Columbia University Press.

Gerschenkron, Alexander. 1962. *Economic Backwardness in Historical Perspective.* Cambridge, MA: Belknap (Harvard University Press).

Giersch, Herbert. 1995. "Wirtschaftsmoral als Standortfaktor." *Lectiones Jenenses.* Heft 2. Jena: Max Planck Institute for Research into Economic Systems.

Gilpin, Robert. 1981. *War and Change in World Politics.* Cambridge: Cambridge University Press.

Glaser, Charles G. 1994–1995. "Realists as Optimists." *International Security* 19(3): 50–90.

Gleditsch, Nils Petter. 1992. "Democracy and Peace." *Journal of Peace Research* 29(4): 369–376.

———. 1995. "Geography, Democracy, and Peace." *International Interactions* 20(4): 297–323.

Gobalet, Jeanne G., and Larry J. Diamond. 1979. "Effects of Investment Dependence on Economic Growth: The Role of Internal Structural Characteristics and Periods in the World Economy." *International Studies Quarterly* 23: 412–444.

Goertz, Gary, and Paul F. Diehl. 1992. *Territorial Changes and International Conflict.* London: Routledge.

Goldstone, Jack A. 1991. *Revolution and Rebellion in the Early Modern World.* Berkeley: University of California Press.

Goodman, David S. G. 1991. "Introduction: The Authoritarian Outlook." In David S. G. Goodman and Gerald Segal (eds.), *China in the Nineties,* pp. 1–18. Oxford: Clarendon.

Gowa, Joanne. 1989. "Rational Hegemony, Excludable Goods, and Small Groups: An Epitaph for Hegemonic Stability Theory." *World Politics* 41(3): 307–324.

———. 1994. *Allies, Adversaries, and International Trade.* Princeton: Princeton University Press.

Gowa, Joanne, and Edward D. Mansfield. 1993. "Power Politics and International Trade." *American Political Science Review* 87(2): 408–420.

Gray, Virginia, and David Lowery. 1988. "Interest Group Politics and Economic Growth in the US States." *American Political Science Review* 52(1): 109–132.

Green, Donald P., and Ian Shapiro. 1994. *Pathologies of Rational Choice Theory: A Critique of Applications in Political Science.* New Haven: Yale University Press.

Greenaway, David, and Chong Hyun Nam. 1988. "Industrialization and Macroeconomic Performance in Developing Countries Under Alternative Trade Strategies." *Kyklos* 41(3): 419–435.

Grieco, Joseph M. 1990. *Cooperation Among Nations.* Ithaca, NY: Cornell University Press.

Grieco, Joseph M., Robert Powell, and Duncan Snidal. 1993. "Controversy: The Relative Gains Problem for International Cooperation." *American Political Science Review* 87(3): 729–743.

Grobar, Lisa M., and Richard C. Porter. 1989. "Benoit Revisited: Defense Spending and Economic Growth in LDCs." *Journal of Conflict Resolution* 33: 318–345.

Gurr, Ted Robert. 1968. "A Causal Model of Civil Strife." *American Political Science Review* 62(4): 1104–1124.

———. 1993. "Why Minorities Rebel: A Global Analysis of Communal Mobilization and Conflict Since 1945." *International Political Science Review* 14(2): 157–197.

Gurr, Ted Robert, and Raymond Duvall. 1973. "Civil Conflict in the 1960s." *Comparative Political Studies* 6: 135–169.

Gurr, Ted Robert, Keith Jaggers, and Will H. Moore. 1990. "The Transformation of the Western State: The Growth of Democracy, Autocracy, and State Power Since 1800." *Studies in Comparative International Development* 25(1): 73–108.

Hall, John A. 1985. *Powers and Liberties: The Causes and Consequences of the Rise of the West.* Berkeley: University of California Press.

Hall, John W. 1964. "The Nature of Traditional Society: Japan." In Robert E. Ward and Dankwart A. Rustow (eds.), *Political Modernization in Japan and Turkey,* pp. 14–41. Princeton: Princeton University Press.

Hansson, Pär, and Magnus Henrekson. 1994. "A New Framework for Testing the Effect of Government Spending on Growth and Productivity." *Public Choice* 81: 381–401.

Hayek, Friedrich August von. 1960. *The Constitution of Liberty.* Chicago: The University of Chicago Press.

———. 1973–1976–1979. *Law, Legislation and Liberty.* 3 vols. London: Routledge & Kegan Paul.

———. 1988. *The Fatal Conceit: The Errors of Socialism.* London: Routledge.

Hechter, Michael. 1987. *Principles of Group Solidarity.* Berkeley: University of California Press.

Hechter, Michael, and Satoshi Kanazawa. 1993. "Group Solidarity and Social Order in Japan." *Journal of Theoretical Politics* 5(4): 455–493.

Helleiner, G. K. 1993. "Protectionism and the Developing Countries." In Dominick Salvatore (ed.), *Protectionism and World Welfare*, pp. 396–418. Cambridge: Cambridge University Press.

Herz, John H. 1950. "Idealist Internationalism and the Security Dilemma." *World Politics* 2: 157–180.

Hintze, Otto. 1941. *Staat und Verfassung*, ed. Fritz Hartung. Leipzig: Koehler und Amelang.

Hirsch, Fred. 1976. *Social Limits to Growth.* Cambridge, MA: Harvard University Press.

Hirschman, Albert O. 1970. *Exit, Voice and Loyalty.* Cambridge, MA: Harvard University Press.

Hofstätter, Peter R. 1957. *Gruppendynamik.* Reinbek bei Hamburg: Rowohlt.

Holsti, Kalevi J. 1991. *Peace and War: Armed Conflicts and International Order 1648–1989.* Cambridge: Cambridge University Press.

Homann, Karl, and Andreas Suchanek. 1992. "Grenzen der Anwendbarkeit einer Logik des kollektiven Handelns." In Klaus Schubert (ed.), *Leistungen und Grenzen Politisch-Ökonomischer Theorie*, pp. 13–27. Darmstadt: Wissenschaftliche Buchgesellschaft.

Homans, George Caspar. 1950. *The Human Group.* New York: Harcourt, Brace and Co.

———. 1961. *Social Behavior: Its Elementary Forms.* New York: Harcourt, Brace and World.

Houweling, Henk W., and Jan G. Siccama. 1981. "The Arms Race–War Relationship: Why Serious Disputes Matter." *Arms Control* 2 (September): 157–197.

Huntington, Samuel P. 1968. *Political Order in Changing Societies.* New Haven: Yale University Press.

———. 1975. "The United States." In Michel Crozier, Samuel P. Huntington, and Joji Watanuki (eds.), *The Crisis of Democracy*, pp. 59–118. New York: New York University Press.

———. 1988–1989. "The U.S.—Decline or Renewal?" *Foreign Affairs* 67(2): 76–96.

———. 1991. *The Third Wave: Democratization in the Late Twentieth Century.* Norman: University of Oklahoma Press.

———. 1993. "The Clash of Civilizations?" *Foreign Affairs* 72(3): 22–49.

Huntington, Samuel P., and Joan M. Nelson. 1976. *No Easy Choice: Political Participation in Developing Countries.* Cambridge, MA: Harvard University Press.

Huth, Paul. 1988a. "Extended Deterrence and the Outbreak of War." *American Political Science Review* 82(2): 423–443.

———. 1988b. *Extended Deterrence and the Prevention of War.* New Haven: Yale University Press.

Huth, Paul, and Bruce M. Russett. 1984. "What Makes Deterrence Work?" *World Politics* 36: 496–526.

———. 1988. "Deterrence Failure and Crisis Escalation." *International Studies Quarterly* 32: 29–45.

Ibn Khaldun. ca. 1377/1958. *The Muqaddimah: An Introduction to History*, trans. Franz Rosenthal. New York: Pantheon.

Inkeles, Alex, and Larry J. Diamond. 1980. "Personal Development and National Development: A Cross-National Perspective." In Alexander Szalay and Frank M. Andrews (eds.), *The Quality of Life*, pp. 73–109. London: Sage.

Inkeles, Alex, and David H. Smith. 1974. *Becoming Modern: Individual Change in Six Developing Countries.* Cambridge, MA: Harvard University Press.

Isaac, R. Marc, James M. Walker, and Susan H. Thomas. 1984. "Divergent Evidence on Free Riding." *Public Choice* 43: 113–149.

Jackman, Robert W. 1975. *Politics and Social Equality.* New York: Wiley.

————. 1982. "Dependence on Foreign Investment and Economic Growth in the Third World." *World Politics* 34: 175–196.

Janis, Irving L. 1972. *Victims of Groupthink.* Boston: Houghton Mifflin.

Jasay, Anthony de. 1985. *The State.* Oxford: Basil Blackwell.

Jastrow, Robert, and Max M. Kampelman. 1992. "Why We Still Need SDI." *Commentary* 94(5): 23–29.

Jencks, Harlan W. 1991. "China's Army, China's Future." In David S. G. Goodman and Gerald Segal (eds.), *China in the Nineties,* pp. 131–159. Oxford: Clarendon.

Johnson, Chalmers. 1982. *MITI and the Japanese Miracle: The Growth of Industrial Policy, 1925–1975.* Stanford: Stanford University Press.

Jones, Eric L. 1981. *The European Miracle.* Cambridge: Cambridge University Press.

————. 1988. *Growth Recurring.* Oxford: Clarendon.

————. 1994. "Asia's Fate." *The National Interest* 35: 18–28.

Kahn, Herman. 1979. *World Economic Development.* London: Croom Helm.

Kahneman, Daniel, and Amos Tversky. 1979. "Prospect Theory: An Analysis of Decisions Under Risk." *Econometrica* 47: 263–291.

————. 1984. "Choices, Values and Frames." *American Psychologist* 39: 341–350.

Kammler, Hans. 1983. "Ordnungsspezifische Probleme der westlichen Sicherheitspolitik." *Zeitschrift für Politik* 30: 349–365.

————. 1986. "Versagen der Demokratien? Sicherheit und andere öffentliche Güter." *Zeitschrift für Politik* 33: 235–253.

————. 1990. "Interdependenz der Ordnungen: Zur Erklärung der osteuropäischen Revolutionen von 1989." *Ordo* 41: 45–59.

Kant, Immanuel. 1795/1963. *Zum ewigen Frieden.* Translation in Lewis White Beck (ed.), *Kant on History.* New York: Macmillan.

Kaplan, Morton A. 1957. *System and Process in International Politics.* New York: Wiley.

Kasper, Wolfgang. 1994. "The East Asian Challenge: What Can Australians Offer Their East Asian Neighbours?" In Helen Hughes, Wolfgang Kasper, and John Macleod (eds.), *Australia's Asian Challenge,* pp. 19–34. St. Leonards, NSW: The Center for Independent Studies.

Kaufmann, Robert R., Harry I. Chernotsky, and Daniel S. Geller. 1975. "A Preliminary Test of the Theory of Dependency." *Comparative Politics* 7: 303–330.

Kegley, Charles W., and Gregory A. Raymond. 1992. "Must We Fear a Post–Cold War Multipolar System?" *Journal of Conflict Resolution* 36: 573–585.

Kennedy, Paul. 1987. *The Rise and Fall of the Great Powers.* New York: Random House.

Keohane, Robert O. 1984a. "The World Political Economy and the Crisis of Embedded Liberalism." In John H. Goldthorpe (ed.), *Order and Conflict in Contemporary Capitalism,* pp. 16–37. Oxford: Clarendon.

————. 1984b. *After Hegemony.* Princeton: Princeton University Press.

Keynes, John Maynard. 1919/1988. *The Economic Consequences of the Peace.* New York: Penguin USA.

Kim, Dae Jung. 1994. "Is Culture Destiny? The Myth of Asia's Anti-Democratic Values." *Foreign Affairs* 73(6): 189–194.

Kim, Jeong-Hyun, and Chi Huang. 1991. "Dynamics of State Strength and Policy Choices: A Case Study of South Korea and Taiwan." *Pacific Focus* 6(2): 83–108.

Kim, Kyung-won. 1993. "Marx, Schumpeter, and the East Asian Experience." In Larry Diamond and Marc F. Plattner (eds.), *Capitalism, Socialism, and Democracy Revisited,* pp. 11–25. Baltimore: The Johns Hopkins University Press.

Kim, Oliver, and Mark Walker. 1984. "The Free Rider Problem: Experimental Evidence." *Public Choice* 43: 3–24.

Kim, Woosang. 1992. "Power Transitions and Great Power War from Westphalia to Waterloo." *World Politics* 45: 153–172.

Kindleberger, Charles P. 1973. *The World in Depression, 1929–1939.* Berkeley: University of California Press.

Kirchgässner, Gebhard. 1992. "Towards a Theory of Low-Cost Decisions." *European Journal of Political Economy* 8: 305–320.

Korpi, Walter. 1983. *The Democratic Class Struggle.* London: Routledge & Kegan Paul.

———. 1985. "Economic Growth and the Welfare State: Leaky Bucket or Irrigation System?" *European Sociological Review* 1: 97–118.

Krasner, Stephen D. 1976. "State Power and the Structure of International Trade." *World Politics* 28: 317–347.

———. 1985. *Structural Conflict: The Third World Against Global Liberalism.* Berkeley: University of California Press.

Krauss, Melvyn B. 1983. *Development Without Aid: Growth, Poverty and Government.* New York: New Press (McGraw-Hill).

Kristof, Nicholas D. 1993. "The Rise of China." *Foreign Affairs* 72(5): 59–74.

Krueger, Anne O. 1992. *The Political Economy of Agricultural Pricing.* Baltimore: The Johns Hopkins University Press.

Krueger, Anne O., Maurice Schiff, and Alberto Valdés in collaboration with Jorge Quiroz. 1992. *The Political Economy of Agricultural Price Intervention in Latin America.* San Francisco: ICS Press.

Krugman, Paul. 1987. "Is Free Trade Passé?" *Journal of Economic Perspectives* 1(2): 131–144.

———. 1993a. "The Uncomfortable Truth About NAFTA." *Foreign Affairs* 72(5): 13–19.

———. 1993b. "The Current Case for Industrial Policy." In Dominick Salvatore (ed.), *Protectionism and World Welfare,* pp. 160–179. Cambridge: Cambridge University Press.

———. 1994a. "Proving My Point." *Foreign Affairs* 73(4): 198–203.

———. 1994b. "The Myth of Asia's Miracle." *Foreign Affairs* 73(6): 62–78.

Kugler, Jacek, and A. F. K. Organski. 1993. "The Power Transition: A Retrospective and Prospective Evaluation." In Manus I. Midlarsky (ed.), *Handbook of War Studies,* 2d ed., pp. 142–194. Ann Arbor: University of Michigan Press.

Kuhn, Thomas S. 1962. *The Structure of Scientific Revolutions.* Chicago: The University of Chicago Press.

Kuznets, Simon. 1966. *Modern Economic Growth.* New Haven: Yale University Press.

Lakatos, Imre. 1968–1969. "Criticism and the Methodology of Scientific Research Programmes." *Proceedings of the Aristotelian Society* 69: 149–186.

Lal, Deepak. 1989. *The Limits of International Co-operation.* Occasional Paper 83. London: The Institute of Economic Affairs.

Landau, Daniel. 1983. "Government Expenditure and Economic Growth." *Southern Economic Journal* 49: 783–792.

Lane, Jan-Erik, and Svante Errson. 1986. "Political Institutions, Public Policy and Economic Growth." *Scandinavian Political Studies* 9: 19–34.

Layne, Christopher. 1994. "Kant or Cant: The Myth of Democratic Peace." *International Security* 19(2): 5–49.

Ledic, Michèle. 1991. "Hongkong and China." In David S. G. Goodman and Gerald Segal (eds.), *China in the Nineties,* pp. 199–218. Oxford: Clarendon.

Lee, Tai To. 1991. "Taiwan and the Reunification Question." In David S. G. Goodman and Gerald Segal (eds.), *China in the Nineties,* pp. 183–198. Oxford: Clarendon.

Lenski, Gerhard. 1966. Power and Privilege. New York: McGraw-Hill.

Lenski, Gerhard, and Jean Lenski. 1982. *Human Societies.* 4th ed. New York: McGraw-Hill.

Levine, Ross, and David Renelt. 1992. "A Sensitivity Analysis of Cross-Country Growth Regressions." *American Economic Review* 82: 942–963.

Levy, Marion J. 1953–1954. "Contrasting Factors in the Modernization of China and Japan." *Economic Development and Cultural Change* 2: 161–197.

Lieber, Robert J. 1993. "Existential Realism After the Cold War." *Washington Quarterly* 16: 155–168.

———. 1995. *No Common Power: Understanding International Relations.* 3d ed. New York: HarperCollins.

Lindenberg, Siegwart. 1985. "Rational Choice and Sociological Theory." *Journal of Institutional and Theoretical Economics* 141: 244–255.

———. 1989. "Social Production Functions, Deficits, and Social Revolutions." *Rationality and Society* 1: 51–77.

———. 1990. "Homo Socio-Oeconomicus: The Emergence of a General Model of Man in the Social Sciences." *Journal of Institutional and Theoretical Economics* 146: 727–746.

Lipset, Seymour M. 1959. "Some Social Requisites of Democracy." *American Political Science Review* 53: 69–105.

———. 1993. "Some Concluding Reflections." In Larry Diamond and Marc F. Plattner (eds.), *Capitalism, Socialism, and Democracy Revisited,* pp. 119–131. Baltimore: The Johns Hopkins University Press.

———. 1994. "The Social Requisites of Democracy Revisited." *American Sociological Review* 59(1): 1–22.

Lipset, Seymour M., Kyoung-Ryung Seong, and John Charles Torres. 1993. "A Comparative Analysis of the Social Requisites of Democracy." *International Social Science Journal* 136: 155–175.

Lipton, Michael. 1977. *Why Poor People Stay Poor.* London: Temple Smith.

———. 1984. "Urban Bias Revisited." *Journal of Development Studies* 20(3): 139–166.

Liska, George. 1962. *Nations in Alliance: The Limits of Interdependence.* Baltimore: The Johns Hopkins University Press.

Lockwood, William W. 1964. "Economic and Political Modernization: Japan." In Robert E. Ward and Dankwart A. Rustow (eds.), *Political Modernization in Japan and Turkey,* pp. 117–145. Princeton: Princeton University Press.

London, Bruce, and David A. Smith. 1988. "Urban Bias, Dependence, and Economic Stagnation." *American Sociological Review* 53(3): 454–463.

Luard, Evan. 1968. *Conflict and Peace in the Modern International System.* Boston: Little, Brown.

———. 1970. *The International Regulation of Frontier Disputes.* London: Thames and Hudson.

Luttwak, Edward N. 1983. *The Grand Strategy of the Soviet Union.* New York: St. Martin's Press.

———. 1985. *The Pentagon and the Art of War.* New York: Simon and Schuster.

MacKinnon, Malcolm H. 1988a. "Calvinism and the Infallible Assurance of Grace: The Weber Thesis Reconsidered." *British Journal of Sociology* 39: 143–177.

———. 1988b. "Weber's Exploration of Calvinism: The Undiscovered Provenance of Capitalism." *British Journal of Sociology* 39: 178–210.

Maddison, Angus. 1969. *Economic Growth in Japan and the USSR.* London: George Allen and Unwin.

———. 1982. *Phases of Capitalist Development.* Oxford: Oxford University Press.

Mahbubani, Kishore. 1992. "The West and the Rest." *The National Interest* 28: 3–12.

Mann, Michael. 1986. *The Sources of Social Power.* Vol. 1. Cambridge: Cambridge University Press.

———. 1993. *The Sources of Social Power.* Vol. 2. *The Rise of Classes and Nation-States, 1760–1914.* Cambridge: Cambridge University Press.

Mansfield, Edward D. 1994. *Power, Trade, and War.* Princeton: Princeton University Press.

Maoz, Zeev, and Bruce M. Russett. 1992. "Alliance, Contiguity, Wealth, and Political Stability: Is the Lack of Conflict Among Democracies a Statistical Artifact?" *International Interactions* 17: 245–267.

———. 1993. "Normative and Structural Causes of Democratic Peace, 1946–1986." *American Political Science Review* 87(3): 624–638.

Marsden, Keith. 1983. "Steuern und Wachstum," *Finanzierung und Entwicklung* (HWWA-Institut für Wirtschaftsforschung, Hamburg) 20(3): 40–43.

Marwell, Gerald, and Ruth E. Ames. 1979. "Experiments in the Provision of Public Goods: I. Resources, Interest, Group Size, and the Free Rider Problem." *American Journal of Sociology* 84: 1335–1360.

———. 1980. "Experiments in the Provision of Public Goods: II. Provision Points, Stakes, Experience, and the Free Rider Problem." *American Journal of Sociology* 85: 926–937.

Marx, Karl. 1852/1966. "Der achtzehnte Brumaire des Louis Bonaparte." *Marx-Engels-Studienausgabe.* Vol. 4, pp. 34–121. Frankfurt/Main: Fischer.

Mayer, Klaus. 1991. *Die Evolution der transatlantischen Welt 1945–1990.* Frankfurt/Main: Lang.

Mayer, Thomas. 1993. *Truth Versus Precision in Economics.* Aldershot, England: Edgar Elgar.

McCallum, John, and André Blais. 1987. "Government, Special Interest Groups, and Economic Growth." *Public Choice* 54: 3–18.

McKenzie, Richard B., and Gordon Tullock. 1978a. *The New World of Economics.* 2d ed. Homewood, IL: Irwin.

———. 1978b. *Modern Political Economy.* Tokyo: McGraw-Hill Kogakusha.

McNeill, William H. 1963. *The Rise of the West: A History of the Human Community.* Chicago: The University of Chicago Press.

———. 1982. *The Pursuit of Power: Technology, Armed Force, and Society Since A.D. 1000.* Chicago: The University of Chicago Press.

Mearsheimer, John J. 1990. "Back to the Future: Instability in Europe After the Cold War." *International Security* 15(1): 5–56.

————. 1994–1995. "The False Promise of International Institutions." *International Security* 19(3): 5–49.

Meyer, John W., and Michael T. Hannan (eds.). 1979. *National Development and the World System: Educational, Economic and Political Change*. Chicago: The University of Chicago Press.

Michels, Robert. 1910/1970. *Zur Soziologie des Parteiwesens in der modernen Demokratie*. Stuttgart: Kröner.

Modelski, George. 1983. "Long Cycles of World Leadership." In William R. Thompson (ed.), *Contending Approaches to World System Analysis*, pp. 115–139. Beverly Hills, CA: Sage.

————. 1987. "The Study of Long Cycles." In George Modelski (ed.), *Exploring Long Cycles*, pp. 1–15. Boulder, CO: Lynne Rienner Publishers.

Modelski, George, and William R. Thompson. 1993. In Manus I. Midlarsky (ed.), *Handbook of War Studies*. 2d ed., pp. 23–54. Ann Arbor: University of Michigan Press.

Moon, Bruce E. 1991. *The Political Economy of Basic Human Needs*. Ithaca, NY: Cornell University Press.

Moon, Chung-in. 1991. "Managing Regional Challenges: Japan, the East Asian NICs and New Patterns of Economic Rivalry." *Pacific Focus* 6(2): 23–47.

Moore, Barrington. 1966. *Social Origins of Democracy and Dictatorship*. Harmondsworth: Penguin.

Morgan, Patrick M. 1977. *Deterrence: A Conceptual Analysis*. Beverly Hills, CA: Sage.

Morris, M. David. 1979. *Measuring the Condition of the World's Poor: The Physical Quality of Life Index*. New York: Pergamon.

Mosley, Paul. 1987. *Overseas Aid: Its Defence and Reform*. Brighton: Wheatsheaf.

Moul, William Brian. 1992. "Polarity, Balances of Power and War: Explaining Some Puzzling Correlates of War Project Results." *International Interactions* 18(2): 165–193.

Mueller, John. 1994. "The Catastrophe Quota: Trouble After the Cold War." *Journal of Conflict Resolution* 38(3): 355–375.

Muller, Edward N. 1984. "Financial Dependence in the Capitalist World Economy and Distribution of Income Within Nations." In Mitchell A. Seligson (ed.), *The Gap Between Rich and Poor*, pp. 256–282. Boulder, CO: Westview Press.

————. 1985. "Income Inequality, Regime Repressiveness, and Political Violence." *American Sociological Review* 50: 47–61.

————. 1988. "Democracy, Economic Development, and Income Inequality." *American Sociological Review* 53: 50–68.

————. 1994. "Egalitarian and Inegalitarian Consequences of Development and Democracy." Paper presented at the 90th Annual Meeting of the American Political Science Association, New York, September 2.

Murray, Charles. 1984. *Losing Ground: American Social Policy 1950–1980*. New York: Basic Books.

Murrell, Peter, and Mancur Olson. 1991. "The Devolution of Centrally Planned Economies." *Journal of Comparative Economics* 15: 239–265.

Nardinelli, Clark, Miles S. Wallace, and John T. Warner. 1986. "Explaining Differences in State Growth: Catching-up Versus Olson." *Public Choice* 52: 210–213.

Neubauer, Deane E. 1967. "Some Conditions of Democracy." *American Political Science Review* 61(4): 1002–1009.

Nicholson, Michael. 1992. *Rationality and the Analysis of International Conflict.* Cambridge: Cambridge University Press.

Nie, Norman H., and Sidney Verba. 1975. "Political Participation." In Fred I. Greenstein and Nelson W. Polsby (eds.), *Handbook of Political Science, Vol. 4: Nongovernmental Politics,* pp. 1–74. Reading, MA: Addison-Wesley.

Nielson, François. 1994. "Income Inequality and Industrial Development." *American Sociological Review* 59(5): 654–677.

North, Douglass C. 1981. *Structure and Change in Economic History.* New York: Norton.

———. 1985. "The Growth of Government in the United States." *Journal of Public Economics* 28: 383–399.

———. 1990. *Institutions, Institutional Change and Economic Performance.* Cambridge: Cambridge University Press.

North, Douglass C., and Robert Paul Thomas. 1973. *The Rise of the Western World: A New Economic History.* Cambridge: Cambridge University Press.

Oberschall, Anthony. 1973. *Social Conflict and Social Movements.* Englewood Cliffs, NJ: Prentice Hall.

OECD. 1993. *Employment Outlook.* Paris: Organization for Economic Co-operation and Development.

Oliver, Pamela E., and Gerald Marwell. 1988. "The Paradox of Group Size in Collective Action." *American Sociological Review* 53(1): 1–8.

Olson, Mancur. 1965. *The Logic of Collective Action.* Cambridge, MA: Harvard University Press.

———. 1982. *The Rise and Decline of Nations: Economic Growth, Stagflation and Social Rigidities.* New Haven: Yale University Press.

———. 1985. "Space, Agriculture, and Organization." *American Journal of Agricultural Economics* 67(5): 928–937.

———. 1987. "Diseconomies of Scale and Development." *Cato Journal* 7(1): 77–97.

———. 1993. "Dictatorship, Democracy, and Development." *American Political Science Review* 87(3): 567–576.

Olson, Mancur, and Richard Zeckhauser. 1966. "An Economic Theory of Alliances." *Review of Economics and Statistics* 48: 266–279.

Oneal, John R., Frances H. Oneal, Zeev Maoz, and Bruce M. Russett. 1996 (forthcoming). "The Liberal Peace: Interdependence, Democracy, and International Conflict, 1950–1986." *Journal of Peace Research* 33.

Opp, Karl-Dieter. 1979. "Das ökonomische Programm in der Soziologie." In H. Albert and K. H. Stapf (eds.), *Theorie und Erfahrung,* pp. 313–350. Stuttgart: Klett-Cotta.

———. 1991. "Das Modell rationalen Verhaltens: Seine Struktur und das Problem der weichen Anreize." In H. Bouillon and G. Andersson (eds.), *Wissenschaftstheorie und Wissenschaften,* pp. 105–124. Berlin: Duncker und Humblot.

Organski, A. F. K. 1958. *World Politics.* New York: A. A. Knopf.

Organski, A. F. K., and Jacek Kugler. 1980. *The War Ledger.* Chicago: The University of Chicago Press.

Ostrom, Elinor. 1990. *Governing the Commons: The Evolution of Institutions for Collective Action.* Cambridge: Cambridge University Press.

Ostrom, Vincent. 1991. *The Meaning of American Federalism: Constituting a Self-Governing Society.* San Francisco: Institute for Contemporary Studies Press.

Overholt, William H. 1993. *The Rise of China.* New York: Norton.

Owen, John M. 1994. "How Liberalism Produces Democratic Peace." *International Security* 19(2): 87–125.

Pampel, Fred C., and John B. Williamson. 1989. *Age, Class, Politics, and the Welfare State.* Cambridge: Cambridge University Press.

Payne, James L. 1989. *Why Nations Arm.* Oxford: Basil Blackwell.

Pearson, Frederic S. 1974. "Foreign Military Interventions and Domestic Disputes." *International Studies Quarterly* 18: 259–290.

Pejovich, Svetozar. 1990. "Quo Vadis Eastern Europe? A Review of Institutional Alternatives." In Otto Molden (ed.), *Freiheit, Ordnung, Verantwortung: Europäisches Forum Alpbach,* pp. 366–378. Wien: Österreichisches College.

———. 1995. *Economic Analysis of Institutions and Systems.* Dordrecht: Kluwer.

Pipes, Richard. 1974. *Russia Under the Old Regime.* London: Weidenfeld and Nicolson.

———. 1990. *The Russian Revolution.* New York: A. A. Knopf.

Plott, Charles R. 1990. "Rational Choice in Experimental Markets." In Karen Schweers Cook and Margaret Levi (eds.), *The Limits of Rationality,* pp. 146–175. Chicago: The University of Chicago Press.

Polachek, Solomon. 1980. "Conflict and Trade." *Journal of Conflict Resolution* 24(1): 55–78.

Popper, Karl R. 1959. *The Logic of Scientific Discovery.* London: Hutchinson.

Porter, Bruce D. 1994. *War and the Rise of the State.* New York: Free Press.

Porter, Michael E. 1990. *The Competitive Advantage of Nations.* New York: Free Press.

Pryor, Frederic L. 1984. "Rent-Seeking and the Growth and Fluctuation of Nations." In D. C. Colander (ed.), *Neoclassical Political Economy: The Analysis of Rent-Seeking and DUP Activities,* pp. 155–175. Cambridge, MA: Ballinger.

Przeworski, Adam. 1993. "The Neoliberal Fallacy." In Larry Diamond and Marc F. Plattner (eds.), *Capitalism, Socialism and Democracy Revisited,* pp. 39–53. Baltimore: The Johns Hopkins University Press.

Pye, Lucian W. 1985. *Asian Power and Politics.* Cambridge, MA: Harvard University Press (Belknap).

Radnitzky, Gerard. 1987a. "The Constitutional Protection of Liberty." In Eamon Butler and Madsen Pirie (eds.), *Hayek on the Fabric of Human Society,* pp. 17–46. London: Adam Smith Institute.

———. 1987b. "An Economic Theory of the Rise of Civilization and Its Policy Implications." *Ordo* 38: 47–90.

Ray, James Lee. 1993. "Wars Between Democracies: Rare or Non-Existent?" *International Interactions* 18(3): 251–276.

Ray, James Lee, and Thomas Webster. 1978. "Dependency and Economic Growth in Latin America." *International Studies Quarterly* 22: 409–434.

Riker, William H. 1965. *Democracy in the United States.* New York: Macmillan.

Rodinson, Maxime. 1966. *Islam et capitalisme.* Paris: Éditions du Seuil.

Rogowski, Ronald. 1987. "Political Cleavages and Changing Exposure to Trade." *American Political Science Review* 81(4): 1121–1137.

Rosecrance, Richard. 1986. *The Rise of the Trading State.* New York: Basic Books.

Rosecrance, Richard, and Zara Steiner. 1993. "British Grand Strategy and the Origins of World War II." In Richard Rosecrance and Arthur A. Stein (eds.), *The Domestic Bases of Grand Strategy,* pp. 124–153. Ithaca, NY: Cornell University Press.

Rosenberg, Nathan, and L. E. Birdzell. 1986. *How the West Grew Rich.* New York: Basic Books.

Rossabi, Morris (ed.). 1983. *China Among Equals: The Middle Kingdom and Its Neighbors, 10th–14th Centuries.* Berkeley: University of California Press.

Rubinson, Richard. 1976. "The World Economy and the Distribution of Income Within States." *American Sociological Review* 41: 638–659.

————. 1977. "Dependence, Government Revenue, and Economic Growth, 1955–1970." *Studies in Comparative International Development* 12: 3–28.

Rubinson, Richard, and Dan Quinlan. 1977. "Democracy and Social Inequality." *American Sociological Review* 42: 611–623.

Rueschemeyer, Dietrich, Evelyne Huber Stephens, and John D. Stephens. 1992. *Capitalist Development and Democracy.* Chicago: The University of Chicago Press.

Ruestow, Alexander. 1950–1957. *Ortsbestimmung der Gegenwart.* 3 vols. Zürich: Rentsch.

Rummel, Rudolph J. 1983. "Libertarianism and International Violence." *Journal of Conflict Resolution* 27(1): 21–71.

————. 1985. "Libertarian Propositions on Violence Within and Between Nations." *Journal of Conflict Resolution* 29(3): 419–455.

————. 1994a. "Power, Genocide and Mass Murder." *Journal of Peace Research* 31(1): 1–10.

————. 1994b. *Death by Government.* New Brunswick, NJ: Transaction.

Russett, Bruce M. 1985. "The Mysterious Case of Vanishing Hegemony." *International Organization* 39(2): 207–231.

————. 1993. *Grasping the Democratic Peace.* Princeton: Princeton University Press.

————. 1995. "The Democratic Peace: And Yet It Moves." *International Security* 19(4): 164–175.

Russett, Bruce M., and Harvey Starr. 1992. *World Politics.* 4th ed. San Francisco: Freeman.

Samuels, Richard J. 1994. *Rich Nation, Strong Army.* Ithaca, NY: Cornell University Press.

Sandholtz, Wayne, Michael Borrus, John Zysman, Ken Conca, Jay Stowsky, Steven Vogel, and Steve Weber. 1992. *The Highest Stakes.* New York: Oxford University Press.

Scalapino, Robert A. 1964. "Environmental and Foreign Contributions: Japan." In Robert E. Ward and Dankwart A. Rustow (eds.), *Political Modernization in Japan and Turkey,* pp. 64–90. Princeton: Princeton University Press.

Schampel, James H. 1993. "Change in Material Capabilities and the Onset of War." *International Studies Quarterly* 37: 395–408.

Scharping, Rudolf. 1994. "Rule-Based Competition." *Foreign Affairs* 73(4): 192–194.

Schelling, Thomas C. 1960. *The Strategy of Conflict.* Cambridge, MA: Harvard University Press.

————. 1966. *Arms and Influence.* New Haven: Yale University Press.

Schumpeter, Joseph A. 1942. *Capitalism, Socialism and Democracy.* New York: Harper and Brothers.

Scully, Gerald W. 1992. *Constitutional Environments and Economic Growth.* Princeton: Princeton University Press.

Seldon, Arthur. 1990. *Capitalism.* Oxford: Basil Blackwell.

Sestanovich, Stephen. 1990. "Inventing the Soviet National Interest." *National Interest* 20: 3–16.

Shin, Doh Chull. 1994. "On the Third Wave of Democratization: A Synthesis and

Evaluation of Recent Theory and Research." *World Politics* 47(1): 135–170.

Simon, Herbert A. 1982. *Models of Bounded Rationality.* 2 vols. Cambridge, MA: MIT Press.

———. 1985. "Human Nature and Politics." *American Political Science Review* 79(2): 293–304.

Singer, J. David. 1993. "System Structure, Decision Processes, and the Incidence of International War." In Manus I. Midlarsky (ed.), *Handbook of War Studies,* 2d ed., pp. 1–31. Ann Arbor: University of Michigan Press.

Singer, J. David, Stuart Bremer, and John Stuckey. 1972. "Capability Distribution, Uncertainty and Major Power War, 1820–1965." In Bruce M. Russett (ed.), *Peace, War, and Numbers,* pp. 19–48. Beverly Hills, CA: Sage.

Singer, J. David, and Melvin Small. 1968. "Alliance Aggregation and the Onset of War, 1815–1945." In J. David Singer (ed.), *Quantitative International Politics,* pp. 247–286. New York: Free Press.

———. 1972. *The Wages of War: A Statistical Handbook.* New York: Wiley.

Singer, Max, and Aaron Wildavsky. 1993. *The Real World Order: Zones of Peace, Zones of Turmoil.* Chatham, NJ: Chatham House.

Singh, Ram D. 1985. "State Intervention, Foreign Economic Aid, Savings and Growth in LDCs." *Kyklos* 38(2): 216–232.

Sirowy, Larry, and Alex Inkeles. 1990. "The Effects of Democracy on Economic Growth and Income Inequality: A Review." *Studies in Comparative International Development* 25(1): 126–157.

Siverson, Randolph, and Juliann Emmons. 1991. "Birds of a Feather: Democratic Political Systems and Alliance Choices in the Twentieth Century." *Journal of Conflict Resolution* 35: 285–306.

Small, Melvin, and J. David Singer. 1976. "The War-Proneness of Democratic Regimes." *Jerusalem Journal of International Relations* 1(2): 50–69.

———. 1982. *Resort to Arms: International and Civil Wars, 1816–1980.* Beverly Hills, CA: Sage.

Smith, Adam. 1776/1976. *An Inquiry into the Nature and Causes of the Wealth of Nations.* Oxford: Oxford University Press.

Snyder, Jack. 1991. *Myths of Empire: Domestic Politics and International Ambition.* Ithaca, NY: Cornell University Press.

Sombart, Werner. 1916/1969. *Der moderne Kapitalismus. 1. Band: Die vorkapitalistische Wirtschaft.* Berlin: Duncker und Humblot.

———. 1917/1969. *Der moderne Kapitalismus. 2. Band: Das europäische Wirtschaftsleben im Zeitalter des Frühkapitalismus.* Berlin: Duncker und Humblot.

Soto, Hernando de. 1989. *The Other Path.* New York: Harper and Row.

Spiro, David E. 1994. "The Insignificance of the Liberal Peace." *International Security* 19(2): 50–86.

Stein, Arthur A. 1990. *Why Nations Cooperate.* Ithaca, NY: Cornell University Press.

———. 1993. "Domestic Constraints, Extended Deterrence, and the Incoherence of Grand Strategy: The United States, 1938–1950." In Richard Rosecrance and Arthur A. Stein (eds.), *The Domestic Bases of Grand Strategy,* pp. 96–123. Ithaca, NY: Cornell University Press.

Stokes, Randall, and David Jaffee. 1982. "The Export of Raw Materials and Economic Growth." *American Sociological Review* 47(3): 402–407.

Strange, Susan. 1985. "Protectionism and World Politics." *International Organization* 39(1): 233–259.

————. 1986. "The Bondage of Liberal Economics." *SAIS Review* 6(1): 25–38.
Sullivan, Lawrence R. 1991. "The Chinese Communist Party and the Beijing Massacre: The Crisis in Authority." In David S. G. Goodman and Gerald Segal (eds.), *China in the Nineties,* pp. 87–104. Oxford: Clarendon.
Sumner, William Graham. 1906/1940. *Folkways: A Study of the Sociological Importance of Usages, Manners, Custom, Mores, and Morals.* Boston: Ginn.
Talavera, Arturo Fontaine. 1993. "The Future of an Illusion." In Larry Diamond and Marc F. Plattner (eds.), *Capitalism, Socialism, and Democracy Revisited,* pp. 105–111. Baltimore: The Johns Hopkins University Press.
Tamas, G. M. 1993. "Socialism, Capitalism, and Modernity." In Larry Diamond and Marc F. Plattner (eds.), *Capitalism, Socialism, and Democracy Revisited,* pp. 54–68. Baltimore: The Johns Hopkins University Press.
Thompson, William R. 1983. "Cycles, Capabilities, and War." In William R. Thompson (ed.), *Contending Approaches to World System Analysis,* pp. 141–163. Boulder, CO: Lynne Rienner Publishers.
————. 1992. "Dehio, Long Cycles, and the Geohistorical Context of Structural Transition." *World Politics* 45(1): 127–152.
Tilly, Charles. 1978. *From Mobilization to Revolution.* Reading, MA: Addison-Wesley.
————. 1985. "War Making and State Making as Organized Crime." In Peter B. Evans, Dietrich Rueschemeyer, and Theda Skocpol (eds.), *Bringing the State Back In,* pp. 169–191. Cambridge: Cambridge University Press.
————. 1990. *Coercion, Capital, and European States.* Oxford: Basil Blackwell.
Tollison, Robert D. 1982. "Rent-Seeking: A Survey." *Kyklos* 35(4): 575–602.
Tollison, Robert D., and Richard E. Wagner. 1993. *Who Benefits from WHO? The Decline of the World Health Organization.* London: The Social Affairs Unit.
Tominaga, Ken'ichi. 1989. "Some Comparative Observations on Modernization of Social Structure Between China and Japan." In W. Klenner (ed.), *Trends of Economic Development in East Asia,* pp. 171–186. Heidelberg: Springer.
————. 1990. "Modernisierung und Wandel der Werte in Japan." In Brunhilde Scheuringer (ed.), *Wertorientierung und Zweckrationalität,* pp. 39–56. Opladen: Leske und Budrich.
Tonelson, Alan. 1994. "Beating Back Predatory Trade." *Foreign Affairs* 73(4): 123–135.
Torstensson, Johan. 1994. "Property Rights and Economic Growth." *Kyklos* 47(2): 231–247.
Tsuru, Shigeto. 1993. *Japan's Capitalism: Creative Defeat and Beyond.* Cambridge: Cambridge University Press.
Tullock, Gordon. 1974. *The Social Dilemma: The Economics of War and Revolution.* Blacksburg, VA: University Publications.
————. 1980a. "Rent-Seeking as a Negative-Sum Game." In James B. Buchanan, Robert D. Tollison, and Gordon Tullock (eds.), *Toward a Theory of the Rent-Seeking Society,* pp. 16–36. College Station: Texas A&M University Press.
————. 1980b. "The Transitional Gains Trap." In James B. Buchanan, Robert D. Tollison, and Gordon Tullock, (eds.), *Toward a Theory of the Rent-Seeking Society.* College Station: Texas A&M University Press.
————. 1983. *Economics of Income Redistribution.* Boston, The Hague, and London: Kluwer-Nijhoff.
————. 1993. *Rent Seeking.* Aldershot, England: Edgar Elgar.
Tversky, Amos, and Daniel Kahneman. 1986. "Rational Choice and the Framing of Decisions." *Journal of Business* 59: 251–278.

Tversky, Amos, Paul Slovic, and Daniel Kahneman. 1990. "The Causes of Preference Reversal." *American Economic Review* 80: 204–217.

Usher, Dan. 1981. *The Economic Prerequisite to Democracy.* Oxford: Basil Blackwell.

Vanberg, Viktor. 1994. "Hayek's Legacy and the Future of Liberal Thought: Rational Liberalism vs. Evolutionary Agnosticism." Paper delivered at the Mont Pèlerin Society General Meeting, Cannes, September 25–30.

Vasquez, John A. 1993. *The War Puzzle.* Cambridge: Cambridge University Press.

Vaubel, Roland. 1994. "The Political Economy of Centralization and the European Community." *Public Choice* 81(1–2): 151–190.

———. 1995. "Social Regulation and Market Integration: A Critique and Public Choice Analysis of the Social Chapter." Paper delivered at the European Public Choice Society Meeting, Saarbrücken, April 22.

Vedder, Richard, and Lowell Gallaway. 1988. "Rent-Seeking, Distributional Coalitions, Taxes, Relative Prices and Economic Growth." *Public Choice* 51: 93–100.

Wade, Robert. 1990. *Governing the Market.* Princeton: Princeton University Press.

———. 1992. "East Asia's Economic Success." *World Politics* 44: 270–320.

Wallace, Michael D. 1979. "Arms Races and Escalation." *Journal of Conflict Resolution* 23(1): 3–16.

———. 1982. "Armaments and Escalation." *International Studies Quarterly* 26(1): 37–51.

Walleri, R. Dan. 1978a. "The Political Economy Literature on North-South Relations: Alternative Approaches and Empirical Evidence." *International Studies Quarterly* 22: 587–624.

———. 1978b. "Trade Dependence and Underdevelopment." *Comparative Political Studies* 11: 94–127.

Wallerstein, Immanuel. 1974. *The Modern World System: Capitalist Agriculture and the Origins of the European World Economy in the Sixteenth Century.* New York: Academic Press.

———. 1979. *The Capitalist World-Economy (Essays).* Cambridge: Cambridge University Press.

———. 1980. *The Modern World System II: Mercantilism and the Consolidation of the European World-Economy, 1600–1750.* New York: Academic Press.

Wallis, John J., and Wallace E. Oates. 1988. "Does Economic Sclerosis Set In with Age?" *Kyklos* 41(3): 397–417.

Waltz, Kenneth N. 1964. "The Stability of a Bipolar World." *Daedalus* 93: 881–909.

———. 1979. *Theory of International Politics.* Reading, MA: Addison-Wesley.

Wang, Kevin, and James Lee Ray. 1994. "Beginners and Winners: The Fate of Initiators of Interstate Wars Involving Great Powers Since 1495." *International Studies Quarterly* 38: 139–154.

Weber, Max. 1920/1972. *Gesammelte Aufsätze zur Religionssoziologie.* 1. Band. Tübingen: Mohr.

———. 1921/1978. *Gesammelte Aufsätze zur Religionssoziologie.* 2. Band. Tübingen: Mohr.

———. 1922/1964. *Wirtschaft und Gesellschaft.* Köln: Kiepenheuer und Witsch.

———. 1923/1981. *Wirtschaftsgeschichte.* Tübingen: Mohr.

Weede, Erich. 1975. *Weltpolitik und Kriegsursachen im 20. Jahrhundert.* München: Oldenbourg.

———. 1978. "US Support for Foreign Governments or Domestic Disorder and Imperial Intervention." *Comparative Political Studies* 10(4): 497–527.

————. 1980a. "Beyond Misspecification in Sociological Analyses of Income Inequality." *American Sociological Review* 45: 497–501.

————. 1980b. "Arms Races and Escalation: Some Persisting Doubts." *Journal of Conflict Resolution* 24(2): 285–288.

————. 1983a. "The Impact of Democracy on Economic Growth." *Kyklos* 36(1): 21–39.

————. 1983b. "Military Participation Ratios, Human Capital Formation, and Economic Growth." *Journal of Political and Military Sociology* 11: 11–19.

————. 1983c. "Extended Deterrence by Superpower Alliance." *Journal of Conflict Resolution* 27: 231–253 and 739 (where misprints are corrected).

————. 1984a. "Democracy, Creeping Socialism, and Ideological Socialism in Rent-Seeking Societies." *Public Choice* 44(2): 349–366.

————. 1984b. "Democracy and War Involvement." *Journal of Conflict Resolution* 28(4): 649–664.

————. 1986a. "Rent-Seeking, Military Participation and Economic Performance in LDCs." *Journal of Conflict Resolution* 30(2): 291–324.

————. 1986b. "Catch-up, Distributional Coalitions and Government as Determinants of Economic Growth or Decline in Industrialized Democracies." *British Journal of Sociology* 37: 194–220.

————. 1986c. "Sectoral Reallocation, Distributional Coalitions and the Welfare State as Determinants of Economic Growth Rates in Industrial Democracies." *European Journal of Political Research* 14: 501–519.

————. 1986d. "Rent-Seeking or Dependency as Explanations of Why Poor People Stay Poor." *International Sociology* 1(4): 421–441.

————. 1987a. "A Note on Pryor's Criticism of Olson's Rise and Decline of Nations." *Public Choice* 52: 215–222.

————. 1987b. "Urban Bias and Economic Growth in Cross-National Perspective." *International Journal of Comparative Sociology* 28(1–2): 30–42.

————. 1989a. "Democracy and Income Inequality Reconsidered." *American Sociological Review* 54: 865–868.

————. 1989b. "Extended Deterrence, Superpower Control, and Militarized Interstate Disputes, 1962–76." *Journal of Peace Research* 26(1): 7–17.

————. 1990a. *Wirtschaft, Staat und Gesellschaft.* Tübingen: Mohr.

————. 1990b. "Ideas, Institutions and Political Culture in Western Development." *Journal of Theoretical Politics* 2: 369–389.

————. 1990c. "Redistribution and Income Inequality in Industrial Democracies." *Research in Social Movements, Conflicts and Change* (ed. L. Kriesberg) 12: 301–326.

————. 1990d. "Democracy, Party Government and Rent-Seeking as Determinants of Distributional Inequality in Industrial Societies." *European Journal of Political Research* 18: 515–533.

————. 1990e. "Beyond Pax Atomica: Is Conventional Stability Conceivable? Does Tension-Reduction Matter?" In Rainer K. Huber (ed.), *Military Stability.* Baden-Baden: Nomos.

————. 1991. "The Impact of State Power on Economic Growth Rates in OECD Countries." *Quality and Quantity* 25: 421–438.

————. 1992a. *Mensch und Gesellschaft.* Tübingen: Mohr.

————. 1992b. "Some Simple Calculations on Democracy and War Involvement." *Journal of Peace Research* 29: 377–383.

————. 1992c. "Military Participation, Economic Growth and Income Inequality." In Steve Chan and Alex Mintz (eds.), *Defense, Welfare and Growth,* pp. 211–230. London: Routledge, 1992.

————. 1993a. "The Impact of Democracy or Repressiveness on the Quality of Life, Income Distribution and Economic Growth Rates." *International Sociology* 8(2): 177–195.

————. 1993b. "The Impact of Military Participation on Economic Growth and Income Inequality." *Journal of Political and Military Sociology* 21(2): 241–258.

————. 1994. "Determinanten der Kriegsverhütung während des Kalten Krieges und danach: Nukleare Abschreckung, Demokratie und Freihandel." *Politische Viertejahresschrift* 35(1): 62–84.

————. 1995 (forthcoming). "Economic Policy and International Security: Rent-Seeking, Free Trade and Democratic Peace." *European Journal of International Relations* 1.

Weede, Erich, and Wolfgang Jagodzinski. 1981/1987. "National Security, Income Inequality and Economic Growth." *Social Science and Policy Research* (Seoul, S. Korea) 3: 91–107. Reprinted in J. H. P. Paelinck and P. H. Vossen (eds.), *Axiomatics and Pragmatics of Conflict Analysis,* pp. 269–288. London: Gower, 1987.

Weede, Erich, and Horst Tiefenbach. 1981a. "Some Recent Explanations of Income Inequality." *International Studies Quarterly* 25: 255–282, 289–293.

————. 1981b. "Three Dependency Explanations of Economic Growth." *European Journal of Political Research* 9(4): 391–406.

————. 1982. "A Reply to Volker Bornschier." *European Journal of Political Research* 10(4): 451–454.

Wesson, Robert G. 1978. *State Systems.* New York: Free Press.

Wilensky, Harold L. 1975. *The Welfare State and Equality.* Berkeley: University of California Press.

Williamson, Oliver E. 1981. "The Economics of Organization: The Transaction Cost Approach." *American Journal of Sociology* 87(3): 548–577.

————. 1987. *The Economic Institutions of Capitalism.* New York: Free Press (Macmillan).

Wimberley, Dale W., and Rosario Bello. 1992. "Effects of Foreign Investment, Exports, and Economic Growth on Third World Food Consumption." *Social Forces* 70: 895–921.

Wippler, Reinhard. 1982. "The Generation of Oligarchic Structures in Constitutionally Democratic Organizations." In Werner Raub (ed.), *Theoretical Models and Empirical Analyses,* pp. 43–62. Utrecht: E and S Publications.

Wohlforth, William C. 1994–1995. "Realism and the End of the Cold War." *International Security* 19(3): 91–129.

Wood, Adrian. 1994. *North-South Trade, Employment and Inequality.* Oxford: Oxford University Press (Clarendon).

World Bank. 1981. *World Development Report 1981.* New York: Oxford University Press.

————. 1983. *World Development Report 1983.* New York: Oxford University Press.

————. 1987. *World Development Report 1987.* New York: Oxford University Press.

————. 1991. *World Development Report 1991.* New York: Oxford University Press.

————. 1993a. *World Development Report 1993.* New York: Oxford University Press.

————. 1993b. *The East Asian Miracle.* New York: Oxford University Press.

————. 1994. *World Development Report 1994.* New York: Oxford University Press.

Yang, Tai-Shuenn. 1987. *Property Rights and Constitutional Order in Imperial China.* Ph.D. dissertation, Indiana University, Bloomington.

Young, Alwyn. 1994. "Lessons from the East Asian NICs: A Contrarian View." *European Economic Review Papers and Proceedings.*

Zartman, I. William. 1992. "Democracy and Islam: The Cultural Dialectic." *The Annals of the American Academy of Political and Social Science* 524: 181–191.

INDEX

Name Index

ABOUT THE BOOK

Based on methodological individualism and a public choice approach to social theory—and sure to stimulate considerable debate—this book analyzes the interdependence of economic development, social order, and interstate conflict.

Weede contrasts the rise of the West over the past five hundred years with the stagnation in the great Asian civilizations, arguing that political constraints on Western rulers allowed the conditions of prosperity, i.e., law and liberty, to develop. Now, however, the West suffers a slow erosion of individual liberty and enterprise caused by an expansion of collective decisionmaking, rent-seeking, and the welfare state, while the dynamic, growing East Asian societies increasingly hold individuals responsible for the consequences of their actions.

Capitalism, Weede avows, is a prerequisite of democracy; and free trade promotes the global diffusion of capitalism and, ultimately, of democracy and democratic peace. Nevertheless, special-interest groups within Western society enforce misguided policies—policies that simultaneously undermine democracy, Western economic primacy, and a "peace by trade" strategy that would be promising if only the West were capable of executing it.

ERICH WEEDE is professor of sociology at the University of Cologne. He has served as president of the Peace Science Society (International), vice president of the International Studies Association, and is European editor of *International Interactions*. He has published seven books and contributed more than one hundred papers to a variety of U.S., European, and Asian publications.